our perfect wild

Brimming with rollicking wilderness adventure and priceless lessons on the Old Ways, all woven tight as a reed basket with the courage, humility and tenacity it takes to stand and fight for what you know and love, this story is vital to understanding modern-day Alaska.

—Marybeth Holleman, author of
The Heart of the Sound *and co-author of* Among Wolves

Read and be inspired ... They (Banes) became one with the landscape and culture of the wild North and committed their lives to protecting Alaska's wilderness. Even in their sunset years, the Banes continue to advocate for the "perfect wild" they hold so dear.

—Cindy Shogun, Executive Director,
Alaska Wilderness League

Full of insights about life in the Alaskan bush, the politics of park protection, Our Perfect Wild will have you turning the pages long into the night.

—George Wuerthner, author, photographer and
Ecological Projects Director for the Foundation for Deep Ecology

our
perfect
wild

Ray and Barbara Bane's Journeys
and the Fate of the Far North

by Kaylene Johnson-Sullivan with Ray Bane

University of Alaska Press
Fairbanks

Library of Congress Cataloging-in-Publication Data

Johnson-Sullivan, Kaylene, 1961–
  Our perfect wild : Ray and Barbara Bane's journeys and the fate of the Far North / by
Kaylene Johnson-Sullivan with Ray Bane.
    pages cm
  Includes bibliographical references and index.
  ISBN 978-1-60223-278-5 (paperback : acid-free paper)—ISBN 879-1-60223-
279-2 (e-book)
  1. Bane, G. Ray. 2. Bane, Barbara, 1937– 3. Alaska—Biography. 4. Alaska—
Description and travel. 5. Wilderness areas—Alaska. 6. Conservationists—Alaska—
Biography. 7. Iñupiat—Social life and customs. 8. Anthropologists—Alaska—Biography.
9. Teachers—Alaska—Biography. 10. Alaska—Environmental conditions. I. Bane, G.
Ray. II. Title.
  F910.7.B36J64 2016
  979.8—dc23
                        2015016327

Mapmaker: Marge Mueller, Graymouse Graphics
Photo editing: Nanette Stevenson
Website design: Erik Johnson, Northern Vista Enterprises
Text design and layout: Paula Elmes

Note to Readers: The use of the word "Eskimo" has fallen out of favor since the 1960s
when Ray and Barbara Bane were school teachers in Alaska. However, at the time, it was
commonly used by Native Iñupiaq and Yup'ik peoples. In quotes and Ray Bane's journal
excerpts, the author has left the term "Eskimo" as it was originally used. In other references
within the text, the author will endeavor to use currently accepted Native cultural
terms. That being said, many northern Alaska Iñupiat still proudly refer to themselves as
. . . Eskimos.

Website: www.ourperfectwild.com

Donny Club's name in Chapter 1 was changed to protect the privacy of Ray Bane's
childhood friend.

Printed in China

Here is your country. Cherish these natural wonders, cherish the natural resources, cherish the history and romance as a sacred heritage, for your children and your children's children. Do not let selfish men or greedy interests skin your country of its beauty, its riches or its romance.

—Theodore Roosevelt

— ❖❖ —

Having loved the north and its people, having heard for the first time the sound of trucks in the wilderness, (the Banes) had joined the fight for what (they) believed in.

—John Kauffmann author of
Alaska's Brooks Range: The Ultimate Mountains

Contents

Bob Waldrop

ARCTIC OCEAN

BEAUFORT SEA

POINT BARROW
■ Barrow

• Wainwright
• Atkasuk
Point Lay •

Prudhoe Bay

CHUKCHI SEA

Point Hope •

Cape Thompson

• Kivilina

BROOKS RANGE
Colville River

⑩

Noatak River

⑪ • Noatak

Anaktuvuk Pass •

Kotzebue
■ • Kiana

⑨

⑧

N Fork Koyukuk River

Wiseman •

Noorvik •
Selewik •

Ambler •
• Shungnak
Kobuk •

Coldfoot •

⑫

Deering •

ARCTIC CIRCLE

Alatna • Bettles
Allakaket •

Teller •

Koyukuk River

• Hughes
■

Fort Yukon

Upper Yukon River

AREA OF DET.

Nome •

■ Huslia

Circle •

NORTON SOUND

AREA OF DETAIL A

Circle Hot Springs ⑦ Ea

Fairbanks •

A L A S K A

Eagle Villa

Yukon River

⑥

Kuskokwim River

▲ DENALI

Glennallen •

②

Anchorage ●
Bligh Reef
Valdez •

③

COOK INLET

AREA OF DETAIL C

Seward •

Cordova •

Igiugig •
Naknek •
■ King Salmon

PRINCE WILLIAM SOUND

BRISTOL BAY

④

Homer •

Coastline impacted by Exxon Valdez oil spill

BERING SEA

Port Heiden •

SHELIKOF STRAITS

KODIAK ISLAND

GULF OF ALASKA

⑤

• Kodiak

PACIFIC OCEAN

Coastline impacted by Exxon Valdez oil spill

SCALE FOR OVERALL MAP
MILES
0   50   100   150

0   50   100   150
KILOMETERS

• Communities where Ray Bane traveled for work
■ Communities where the Banes lived
▲ Mountain peak
— Roads
--- Water travel
---- Foot travel
-·-·- Winter dog team travel

N

NATIONAL PARKS & PRESERVES
1. Glacier Bay National Park & Preserve
2. Wrangell-St. Elias National Park & Preserve
3. Lake Clark National Park & Preserve
4. Katmai National Park & Preserve
5. Aniakchak National Monument & Preserve
6. Denali National Park & Preserve
7. Yukon-Charley Rivers National Preserve
8. Gates of the Arctic National Park & Preserve
9. Kobuk Valley National Park
10. Noatak National Preserve
11. Cape Krusenstern National Monument
12. Bering Land Bridge National Preserve
This is a partial list of the parks and preserves in Alaska.
Noted here are those where the Banes worked and travele

Ray and Barbara Bane's Travels 1960–1997

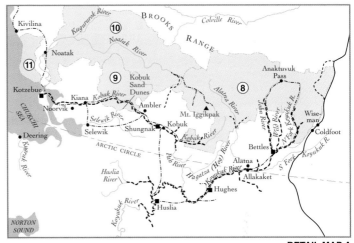

DETAIL MAP A

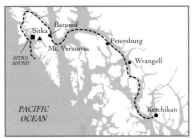

DETAIL MAP B

AREA OF DETAIL B

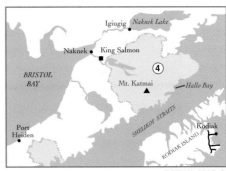

DETAIL MAP C

DETAIL MAP D

SCALE FOR DETAIL MAPS

MILES
0   50   100   150

0   50   100   150
KILOMETERS

Winter camping by dog team in the upper Noatak Valley. (Bane Collection)

---··✧··---

introduction

The granite spires of the Arrigetch Peaks in the central Brooks Range of northern Alaska surge from the ground like a new world being born—wild, raw, and unruly. Angular walls of rock jut upward to 6,000 feet while in their valleys lie lakes so clear they appear to be portals to the sky. It is a place at once fearsome and achingly beautiful. The lives of Ray and Barbara Bane were molded by peaks like these, whose striking spires command a certain acknowledgement of one's place in the universe, by landscapes whose revelations come as a gift and at times at a cost.

Ray and Barbara helped to shape the future of these mountains and other places just as remote and sacred. Their journeys deep into the land convinced them to join a cause that wasn't—and sometimes still isn't—popular. Without conviction like theirs, however, the wilderness in Alaska might look very different today. These places might have been developed and drilled and ultimately diluted of their raw, unspoiled power. We need the stories of people like Ray and Barbara Bane to truly understand the history of these lands and what was at stake during a pivotal time in Alaska's history. And while their contribution to the state might easily have been overlooked, their story demonstrates how ordinary people are capable of extraordinary courage when defending the things they love. From the gritty coal mines and factories of West Virginia, to their adventures across the pristine Arctic plains, Ray and Barbara grew from naïve young school teachers to champions of the places they came to revere.

The name Arrigetch means "fingers of the outstretched hand" in Iñupiat, the language spoken by the Native people who Ray and Barbara worked closely with during their early careers teaching school in Barrow and Wainwright. Like other mountains in Gates of the Arctic National Park, the Arrigetch's remoteness and their fickle, sometimes severe weather are not to be trifled with. This is the wild north, a place austere and at times dangerous, a place where the echoes of Native elders' voices still ring from the past.

I was first approached by Ray and Barbara's friend, Janice Tower, who showed me a scrapbook with newspaper clippings and photos that offered a glimpse into the couple's adventuresome lives. When I later agreed to read Ray's journals, it didn't take long to become absorbed by the Banes' story. Their commitment to each other along with their rich and colorful adventures in the Arctic reminded me of Olaus and Mardy Murie's classic autobiography, *Two in the Far North*. Only later did I learn that the Banes were in fact friends with Mardy—they sent her cards and letters from villages along the route of their 1,200-mile dog team trip in 1974. Mardy encouraged their conservation work in Alaska, and they eventually visited her at her home in Moose, Wyoming.

Ray had been working on his journals and memoirs for decades. They were thoughtfully written—and some 800 pages long. He wrote with the detail of a trained anthropologist and added social, political and, at times, philosophical analysis of his observations. He kept reams of records and data to document his commentary. For all its factual detail, Ray's volume of work also revealed that he was a man passionate about the places and people of Alaska's far north. The Banes' careers spanned four decades and during the turbulent times when the future of Alaska's lands would be decided, they leaned on and were guided by the ancient wisdom of their Native elder friends. I found myself laughing and sometimes misty-eyed at what I increasingly saw as a most remarkable story.

When I finally met Ray and Barbara in person, Ray's energy and optimism was infectious. At age 79, he rode his bicycle twenty miles each day, keeping his body as fit as his mind. He answered even the most tedious of questions with patience, detail, and invariably added a good story.

After more than fifty-three years of marriage, Barbara was still amused at her husband's enthusiasm. Her demeanor was one of enduring kindness; her quiet smile offered a calm river to Ray's white-water intensity. She helped Ray tell stories, interjecting whenever a name or detail eluded him. Their memories were astonishing. When I interrupted Ray to ask Barbara her version of a story, she usually referred me back to Ray. As he told the tale, she would then continue to add any necessary detail. It quickly became apparent that this was not a his-versus-her account. They were clearly a team and the story they shared was one they had crafted together.

The question was how to compile their story into a reasonably sized book. While the journals were encyclopedic in length, simply editing them into a shorter format would have left out much of the context in which they were written. Yet leaving out the journals completely seemed a travesty, given the erudition and elegance of Ray's prose. We decided the best approach would be to use liberal excerpts from the journals alongside a narrative that moved the story forward. This approach would offer readers the opportunity to enjoy excerpts of Ray's writing but also included the larger framework and context of the times. Throughout this book, excerpts from Ray's journals are shown in italics. In two chapters, "A Hungry Country" and "Hog River Gary," Ray tells the story almost entirely in his own words.

Ray and I spent many hours interviewing, discussing, and corresponding over the course of the year that we collaborated on the book. His comments during our interviews were often eloquent and articulate. I included many of these remarks, which are quoted in the narrative text.

It is a strange process to dissect a life and then re-assemble it into a story with chapters and quotes and excerpts and photos. As always, the hard part is what to leave out. When I asked Ray to choose a few photos for each chapter, the task was daunting. The best we could do was to choose a few representative photos that might illustrate, beyond the text, additional nuances of their experience.

Mark Twain wrote, "Biographies are but the clothes and buttons of a man. The biography of the man himself cannot be written."

The pages of a single book cannot fully encompass the richness of a life well lived. My goal was to tell a story worthy of the couple whose lives have become an inspiration. The hope is that readers of *Our Perfect Wild* will come away not only with an adventure story about the Banes' call to conservation, but also a sense of possibility and even resolve—that future generations may always experience the thrill of discovering mountains like the Arrigetch, rivers like the Noatak, and valleys like Katmai's Ten Thousand Smokes.

─ �֍ ─

prologue

Ray Bane sat quietly on the bank of the Koyukuk River, a winding ribbon of blue so clear that the slant of sun on its pebble-strewn floor bounced back a million shards of light. The river meandered down and along the south flank of the Arctic's continental divide through the heart of Alaska's central Brooks Range. Hidden in a grove of willows, Ray breathed in the scent of Alaska's slender summer. The river murmured in endless, fluid conversation as it tumbled over rocks along the narrow gravel bar.

Ray had not been sitting long—when he saw movement along the edge of the willows about thirty yards away. A female gray wolf stepped into sight. As she ambled toward the river, a pup rushed out behind her. Four more pups bounded out of the willows, trouncing each other as they followed their mother.

Ray wrote later in his journal

> The female reached a broken tree trunk that had been left on the bar by the spring flood. She lowered herself in its scant shade where the breeze flowing down the river could still hold off the stinging attention of mosquitos.

The year was 1971, and Ray and his wife, Barbara, had come to Alaska a decade earlier as schoolteachers to the Native villages of the far north. They were learning about the Old Ways from the Native people who lived closest to the land. While they taught math and science inside the village school, outside the classroom they had become the apprentices of their friends and neighbors. They wanted to learn the ways of the elders, the ones who had been subsisting on this spare and hungry land for centuries.

Eventually the Banes would move from teaching to living out their beliefs through advocacy for wilderness. The Banes did not intend to become activists. They just followed their passions and let the wilderness itself guide their decisions and their careers. What began as a one-year experiment of teaching in the North grew into a vocation in service to a place they revered. Over time they would live and work in eight rural Alaska villages and visit dozens more in their travels, mostly across the northern tier of the state.

Many saw Alaska's hinterlands as a place to exploit for its rich mineral and oil resources, but others, like the Banes, saw wild places as an increasingly rare and fragile treasure.

Shortly after their arrival in Alaska, Ray and Barbara went "Bushy," according to their colleagues. Many non-Native educators spent winters holed up in small quarters trying to cope with the astringent cold and endless dark. Instead, the Banes borrowed sled dogs and bought others until they had assembled enough huskies to call a team. And while other teachers played interminable hours of bridge Ray went out hunting seal and caribou with the locals.

The principal at the school in the village of Barrow threatened to cancel the Banes' leave when he learned that Ray was planning to make a 200-mile round trip trek to the neighboring village of Wainwright by dog team.

"He considered my activities running around by dog team and going out hunting and socializing with the Eskimos to be foolhardy and setting a poor example," Ray said. "He was particularly critical of my attempts to learn the Eskimo language and use it in the classroom."

Ray made his trip anyway and the couple transferred to Wainwright the following year. It was a smaller, more remote community of Iñupiat Eskimos. The Banes always tried to migrate toward living a little closer to the heart of wilderness.

On the day of the wolf encounter, Ray had been told by villagers that a group of wolves had been sighted on a gravel bar about ten miles upstream. His earlier sightings of wolves as he traveled across the snow-clad landscape with his dog team had kindled his interest in these elusive animals.

Now as he watched, hidden and kneeling behind a thicket, the wolf pups played tag, ambushed each other, and tumbled in mock battle. One pup tried to run away with a willow stalk that was still rooted to the ground. Running in circles, the fearsome fellow was at times swung off his feet by centrifugal force. Bane observed through his binoculars, rapt. Then he heard a sound behind him, a twig breaking or a dry leaf being crushed underfoot. The hair on his neck prickled. He slowly lowered his binoculars and turned.

On a slight rise just behind him, only an arm's length away, a male wolf gazed at him with yellow-rimmed eyes.

"Time seemed to momentarily freeze. The wolf met my eyes," Ray remembered. "I felt no sense of threat, although I realized that I was not in control of my immediate future."

The wolf lowered his head and quietly melted back into the willows. As Ray watched, he saw several more shapes moving back and forth in the surrounding brush.

He decided not to push his luck. He folded up the camera tripod and stepped out of the willows onto the open bar.

The female wolf leapt to her feet. With lowered head she angled away from Ray as he walked quietly toward his floatplane. Paying no attention to Ray's movements, the pups continued their romp on the bar. In the willow thicket, at least two gray shapes kept pace, escorting him around the bend to where his airplane was tied. Without starting the engine, Ray untied the mooring line and pushed off into the river current. Standing on the float of the plane, Ray used his paddle to steer the aircraft as it quietly drifted back toward the gravel bar. As the plane floated within sight of the pups, Ray tipped his head back and let out his approximation of a wolf howl.

"The entire willow grove seemed to explode into a wild chorus of howls that washed across the sky, filling the land and me with an indescribable sense of wildness. Even the pups lifted their muzzles and cried out a youthful version of their ancestors' primordial call," Ray recalled.

These were the kinds of experiences that sustained Ray when he found himself, years later, a human lightning rod in the middle of a gathering storm—when a neighbor speaking for others in the community would stand up in a crowd and shout to his face, "*I hate your guts!*"

The discovery of oil on the North Slope of Alaska in 1968 set off a fevered land rush as stakeholders vied for the possibility of cashing in. Oil companies wanted to build a pipeline; the State of Alaska had legal claim to a percentage of federally managed lands; and the federal government had yet to settle aboriginal claims to the public lands of the state. Millions of acres of Alaska's untouched wilderness were about to change forever. What that change might look like became the flashpoint of heated economic, political, and environmental debate.

When the Alaska Native Claims Settlement Act (ANCSA) was signed into law by President Richard Nixon on December 18, 1971, it became the largest land claims settlement in U.S. history. One provision of the law— Section 17 (d) (2)—directed the Secretary of the Interior to withdraw 80 million acres of federal lands from development. These lands, referred to as "d-2" lands, were to be held for possible Congressional designation as national parks, wildlife refuges, wild and scenic rivers, or national forests. This "d-2" provision of ANCSA set a deadline for Congress to respond; if it did not act to designate these lands for special protections by 1978, the withdrawal would expire and the lands would be reopened to development.

While these lands were being considered, the National Park Service (NPS) learned about a couple in rural Alaska who had plans to take a 1,200-mile dog team expedition across the northern tier of Alaska. The Banes' trip offered the NPS an opportunity to gather research about the subsistence lifestyle of local residents. Ray and Barbara were happy to help by passing along their notes and observations.

Following the trip, Ray was invited to go to work on contract for the NPS as a cultural anthropologist, a perfect fit, since Ray had recently received graduate training in anthropology. The Banes were intrigued by the notion of setting aside large tracts of wilderness to preserve ancient ways of life. They sensed, even then, that they were setting sail into currents that would steer the course of Alaska's history.

In 1978, with Congress dragging its feet on the "d-2" lands issue, President Jimmy Carter proclaimed seventeen national monuments including the eight-million-acre Gates of the Arctic. The eventual passage of the Alaska National Interest Lands Conservation Act (ANILCA) in 1980 declared 104 million acres as national parks, wildlife refuges, and wilderness. ANILCA more than doubled the acreage of the national park system and tripled the amount to public land closed to development, and was considered by some, the greatest act of conservation in United States history.

"Predictably, all hell broke loose in the hinterlands," wrote author William E. Brown in his book, *History of the Central Brooks Range: Gaunt Beauty,*

Tenuous Life. "Ray and Barbara Bane, still the only resident field representatives near the proposed northern parklands, received the full brunt of
resentment in their community."

The village store owner refused to serve them. Children threw stones.
Their year's supply of firewood to heat their home was stolen. Banes' airplane
was vandalized, its steering cables cut and tires slashed. The NPS urged the
Banes to move away to the safer offices of Fairbanks or Anchorage.

Instead, in a place considered a land of ice and snow, the Banes stepped
into the fire.

1

—⸰✦⸰—

"when are we going?"

Barbara Bane walked toward the tiny apartment in Huntington, West Virginia. She was tired after a day of teaching, but couldn't wait to tell Ray about the day's antics of her students. It was 1960, and she was just growing accustomed to being called Mrs. Bane. As a new bride and teacher, there was much to share at the end of each day. Ray was training to become a teacher too, with just a few months left of college to finish his degree.

When she walked in the door, she knew something was up. Their one-room apartment held only a twin-size bed and small table for eating. The kitchen was no bigger than a closet. Smaller yet was the bathroom. They could hear the murmur of other couples through the paper-thin walls of the married student housing.

Small as it was, they cherished their space precisely because it was theirs alone. Just starting a life together, they could not have been more enthusiastic about the prospects that lay ahead. Barbara had known Ray now since junior high school and as she walked in the door of the apartment, Ray had that look, an expression of earnest excitement. He sat on the bed and gazed at her with his intent blue eyes. He didn't say a word. Pinned on the wall was a giant map of Alaska.

She knew this was not one of Ray's college homework assignments. And she knew the heart of her husband. He was nothing if not adventuresome; that was partly why she had married the man. Their plans for Cleveland were a lovely thought for the future, but she saw, pinned to the wall, a detour in the making. She felt a shivery little thrill. Matrimony was going to be a bigger adventure than she'd anticipated.

Ray and Barbara were an unlikely couple from the start.

Barbara Ann Cox, born May 20, 1937, in Wheeling, West Virginia, was the only child of a gentle man and his stern wife. Barbara's father, Arch Cox, had quit school in the third grade to go to work and help support the family. Later, he made a living driving a truck delivering coal. Barbara's mother, Zana, had immigrated as a child from Czechoslovakia. Zana was fiercely religious and devoted to her daughter. Barbara inherited the easy-going personality of her father and found friendship in her father's company as she grew up. From her mother she inherited a great capacity for commitment, which she applied in all that she set out to do over the years.

Barbara was only five years old when a woman at church offered to give away a piano. With surprising determination little Barbara said she *wanted* it. So her father loaded it up in the coal truck and brought it home. That began her love affair with music. She immediately began taking lessons and soon became a skilled pianist. Her days were spent immersed in church, school, and music. She excelled at school.

Ray on the other hand, lived a Huck Finn kind of childhood where he was often left to fend for himself. Born July 14, 1936, in Wellsburg, West Virginia, he was the third surviving child to Bill Bane and Ester Zornes.

Ray's father was a short, fireplug of a man and impressively strong. Bill Bane had been born and raised on a hilltop farm in the northern panhandle of West Virginia. For a brief time in his early years, he was a prize fighter and fought under the name of "Battling Bill Bane." Handsome, with a zest for life, he was known as a "rounder."

"When they heard his jalopy coming, fathers 'rounded' up their daughters," Ray explained. Ray's father loved people, enjoyed joking, and people were drawn to him, including the ladies. Bill fathered one son outside Ray's immediate family.

"He was very good to me but strict. My dad was brought up with 'spare the rod, spoil the child' and he did not spare the rod. But when I got it, I knew I deserved it and the best thing to do was mend my ways," Ray remembered. Ray loved his father's cheerful good humor.

Ray's mother, on the other hand, seemed bowed by the difficulties of her life. Ester Zorne's parents had divorced when she was an infant. Her mother remarried and had a second child. Ester's early life was trying and she married Bill in her early teens. Among her four children, she gave birth to a stillborn daughter. Their second daughter was severely burned in a house fire. Caring for their disabled daughter consumed Ray's parents, which left Ray and his brother Pete mostly on their own. When Ray was in junior high, his mother lost part of her right hand while operating a press on a factory assembly line. She could no longer operate machinery, so she was given a broom and cleaned the factory floors until she was able to collect Social Security.

By the time Ray was in the fourth grade, he spent his summers camping alone along a bass stream, and working odd jobs for owners of fishing camps. He lived in a pup tent in the woods along the river. This became a haven of quiet predictability, where the rhythms of the river shaped his days. If he needed something, he rode his bike five miles to the country store at Elm Grove. He enjoyed reading books about the Western frontier, and summers became the time to forge his own adventures. While he was still in grade school, he was given a 20-gauge shotgun and a .22 rifle, which meant he could hunt small game and "live off the land" just like the early pioneers. His father occasionally joined him on the weekends and they camped together.

"My father loved to fish and hunt from the time I remember, I followed him around like a puppy. He taught me that we hunted and fished for food for the table, not for the fun of killing. That was significant. I stood in line for day-old bread at the local bakery. That was for poor people and we qualified," Ray said. "My father made me aware that animals have feelings, and that they were to be treated respectfully. You hunt to feed your family."

Summers on the bass stream were happy days when notions about wilderness began to take root in Ray's consciousness. He saw how nature provided sustenance. And while he could not yet put it to words exactly, he also felt a sense of possibility and connectedness, and a freedom that he found nowhere else. To him, the natural world was a place of solace and a welcome reprieve from the tumult of his home life.

He hated returning to school in the fall. The family always seemed to be on the move, following better jobs or less expensive rentals. Their unsettled lifestyle took its toll. Ray and his brother, Pete, missed many days of school during the transitions from one neighborhood to the next. Both of them were held back in their classes. Pete gave up and quit school by the time he was sixteen.

In 1949, Ray's family landed in Warwood, a working class suburb of Wheeling, West Virginia, the suburb where Barbara and her family lived. Ray was thirteen and Barbara was twelve when they met in junior high school. Although they attended the same school, they moved in distinctly different social circles.

Ray failed the seventh grade—the second time he'd been held back for a year. He and his buddy, Donny Club, worked at a job collecting money from pinball and other gambling machines. Their work took them to some seamy neighborhoods including the red-light district. Ray learned early on that getting by on the streets meant being tougher or faster than the next guy. Fighting and drinking were commonplace. After all, Ray was the son of "Battling Bill Bane." By the age of fifteen, he was known as "Boozer Bane" by his friends.

Barbara sailed through her classes with top grades, played piano at church, and enjoyed the attention of many young beaus.

Ray's wayward ways came to a head in the tenth grade when a police officer showed up at the school principal's office. A gang fight was rumored to take place on the coming weekend and Ray had been implicated. For once, in this particular case, he was innocent. Regardless, the principal, Mr. Phipps had finally reached his limit with the young delinquent.

"Bane, you're finished here," Phipps said. "You're never going to make anything of yourself. Do you realize what your IQ is? You should be one of the highest academic achievers here. You're lazy. Why don't you just quit? "

This caught Ray up short.

"No, sir," he said. He had friends who had quit and others who had spent time in jail or were working at dead-end jobs.

It was a defining moment in the principal's office, one in which he decided that he wanted more out of life. No one in his family had finished high school.

"I wanted to be the first," he remembered.

Ray managed to convince Mr. Phipps that he was not involved in the upcoming fight. The principal reluctantly agreed to give him another chance. That one chance was all Ray needed. He earnestly began focusing on earning his high school diploma.

Barbara had noticed how young men in certain circles often seemed to disappear into the same patterns and problems they learned and lived as youngsters. Everyone knew these hoodlums often came to no good end. But Ray seemed different. Ever since junior high school, he'd had a streak of independence—even fierceness—and it appeared that once he set his mind to something, his resolve was unwavering. Although he was a year older—she had passed him a grade level in junior high—Barbara noted that Ray was funny, kind, and smarter than people knew.

It was a warm spring evening in 1956, when the song of the phoebe and meadowlark had returned. Virginia bluebells had just begun to bloom and a young Elvis was crooning his way to the top of the charts with songs like "Love Me Tender." That night, Barbara and Ray arrived separately at the Saturday dance, with other friends. Ray couldn't help noticing Barbara's quick smile. Barbara was a popular girl with any choice of suitors. He doubted that this smart young woman would give him the time of day. She was a freshman in college while he, at age nineteen, was still working to finish his senior year of high school. He gathered his courage anyway and—amazingly—she agreed to a dance.

At the end of the evening, Barbara allowed Ray to take her home. Their attraction was immediate. Ray enjoyed her sparkling sense of humor. Barbara was captivated by his sense of adventure. Ray ventured a kiss and they agreed to see each other again.

The only one more surprised than Barbara's friends—or astonished than her mother—at Barbara's interest in the once wayward Bane, was Ray himself. The first time Ray and Barbara arrived as a couple at a high school football game, a number of people in the bleachers stood up to stare in disbelief.

While Ray finished high school, Barbara lived at home and attended the local college. Ray planned to continue his education beyond high school, an endeavor no one in his family could fathom.

"What for?" they asked. Wasn't it time to buckle down and get to work in the factories or coal mines like everyone else they knew?

During his senior year, an acquaintance from the old red-light district sought him out at one of the high school football games, showed him a revolver, and asked if he wanted to help with a "job." Ray emphatically declined. His old pal, Donny, would eventually serve time for murder. Ray wanted to leave that world behind. He enrolled in Marshall College 200 miles away to put distance between himself and his ruffian past.

The one connection he nurtured was his blossoming relationship with Barbara. She gave him one more reason to succeed.

"I wanted to be worthy of her," Ray said. And at age 79, he said, "I still do."

College opened up the world to him. He had to work hard to compensate for all he'd missed academically over the years. But the biggest challenge

Barbara graduated second in her class with a scholarship to a local college. (Bane Collection)

Ray (far left) was elected to the student senate and served as vice president of the student body during his senior year in college. (Bane Collection)

was paying for school. That summer he labored in the same foundry where his father worked. The blistering heat created by the foundry furnaces, the pound of pneumatic hammers, and noxious fumes were a preview to hell. Ray watched as day-after-day, men who had worked there for twenty years shoveled sand into molds from the same pile that had been there the day before. The spit in his mouth turned black from inhaling the suspended dust. The job erased any doubts he may have had about going to college.

At school he took work wherever he could, cleaning rooms, washing dishes, and digging ditches. He joined Pi Kappa Alpha fraternity, in part because they offered work to pay for his room and board. The fraternity encouraged involvement in student government and civic service so he ran for a seat in the student senate. He won and near the end of his junior year was elected student body vice president. All of this was new and invigorating. The world was so much bigger than the coal mines, foundries, and factories of northern West Virginia.

Much to the dismay of Barbara's mother, Barbara and Ray were engaged in 1958 and married in 1960. More than fifty years later, with laughing eyes and a serene smile Barbara would say, "I was after his body. Simple as that."

Through their four-year courtship, they had lots of time to think and talk about how they would order their lives. After they graduated, they planned to move to Cleveland, Ohio. Barbara had relatives there. They would get teaching jobs, buy a home in the suburbs, and eventually have children. Theirs was the classic American dream of the 1950s.

Then, a few weeks before their wedding, Ray and Barbara went to see a movie called "White Wilderness," a documentary about the Arctic. Settling into their theater seats, the big screen in front of them was suddenly filled by an expansive landscape unlike any they had ever seen. Caribou migrated in massive herds across a land unbroken by human constructs. Bears and wolves roamed free. White mountain sheep climbed nimbly over breath-taking terrain. Rivers shimmered bank to bank with migrating salmon. It reminded Ray of the frontier he had read about as a child, when buffalo lay claim to the plains of the American West. It fueled every dream Ray had ever harbored as a boy when he'd fished and camped along that pretty bass stream.

Barbara and Ray talked about what an adventure it would be to visit Alaska someday. Meanwhile they settled into Huntington, West Virginia,

Ray and Barbara Bane, 1959. (Bane Collection)

where Ray continued his final year at Marshall College and Barbara taught at a rural elementary school.

Barbara loved married life, loved being called "Mrs. Bane." She had a gift for connecting with people. She found ways to draw others into conversation, always reflecting back to people their unique value and place in the world.

"Tell me about yourself," she would ask, and then settled in to listen with genuine interest. She had an uncanny memory for the details of other people's stories and decades later she could recall the names of people she had met only in casual conversation. She enjoyed teaching in the rural setting and her gift for music brought people together for song and fellowship.

Ray could not get the images of the Arctic out of his mind. They haunted his dreams. They pestered his daytime thoughts. He just couldn't get over those vast tracts of wilderness, free of human alterations. No highways, bridges, or dams. No power lines or radio towers. Nothing but untouched landscape, from one horizon to the other.

Just for kicks, he decided to inquire about possible teaching positions in Alaska. Having just gained statehood in 1959, surely some resources were going toward education. Ray learned that Alaska had a shortage of qualified teachers, especially in rural areas. Getting a job would not be a problem.

When Barbara walked into their small apartment that afternoon, she saw the large map of Alaska hanging on the wall. She looked at the map and then at Ray.

"When are we going?" she asked. It would be a question she would ask many times in the years to come.

Ray and Barbara made a pact that day. They would find teaching jobs in Alaska and spend one year before returning and settling down in Cleveland. One year in Alaska would give them the honeymoon of a lifetime and a year of adventure to remember it by.

2

—⊹⊹⊹—

one year

Ray looked out the window of the World War II-era amphibian airplane.
The plane flew through squalls of rain and skimmed below gray overcast
skies. Below, he and Barbara could see thickly forested islands separated by
broad expanses of dark green water. At times the airplane's wingtips seemed
to nearly touch the sides of mountains that dropped straight down into the
ocean. It was a long way from the mill towns, coal mines, and soot-coated
landscape of Wheeling, West Virginia.

After considering many offers from around rural Alaska, Ray and Barbara
chose to teach at Sheldon Jackson School in Sitka. They had read about the
rigors of living in more remote areas and decided they were not ready to
completely break ties with modern civilization. Barbara was hired to direct
the school music program. Ray was hired to teach social studies and speech
and act as the supervisor for the junior college co-ed dormitory.

"Alaska! Why do you want to go to that God forsaken place? You will
freeze to death. How will we ever see you?" Ray remembered family and
friends lamenting. Barbara's mother was upset that her only child was moving so far away. "We assured them it would only be for one year. Then we
would return to live a 'normal life.'"

Sitka lies on the western shoreline of Baranof Island on the southeast panhandle of Alaska and is accessible only by boat or airplane. To get there, Ray
and Barbara arrived first in Juneau aboard Pan Am Airlines in late August
1960. Their introduction to Alaska could not have been livelier.

We toured the town somewhat intimidated by its roughhewn characters walking its streets and crowding the many bars. A drizzling rain fell almost continuously, but no one wore raincoats or carried umbrellas. They walked unconcernedly in the rain dressed in damp woolen garments and wearing calf-length rubber boots. In the evenings the bars lining the streets did a land rush business as burly loggers and crusty fishermen jostled one another competing for the attention of the few ladies (who had) the temerity to join in the revelry.

Two days later, they boarded the airplane for their flight to Sitka. The other passengers seemed hardly to notice the turbulence of the ride as the airplane followed the shoreline along Alaska's southeastern coast. Ray described them as "a colorful mix of loggers and fishermen, Indian and white, plus a few stoutly built women holding squirming children with full shopping bags on their laps."

The plane banked into a shallow turn over an island-dotted bay with a small community hugging its shoreline. They saw the onion-domed spire rising from the Russian Orthodox Church that marked the center of Sitka. Small fishing boats huddled on the lee of the island just offshore. As the plane landed in the bay, the choppy water drummed against the aluminum hull. He and Barbara exchanged glances. Their Alaska odyssey had begun.

It rained upon landing in Sitka and for ten solid days afterward. Heavy clouds formed a low soggy ceiling. Thick mist cut visibility to a few miles. The sodden weather had the young couple wondering if they had made the right decision to come to Alaska. Yet when the skies opened and the sun finally broke through, the transformation was breathtaking. Finally they could see where they had committed to spending the coming year and they were not disappointed.

Sitka rests in a natural bowl facing sea-ward. It is flanked by the massive hulks of Harbor Mountain to the north and Mount Verstovia to the south with a snow capped back wall consisting of the saw tooth peaks of the Three Sister Mountains. The community looks out over Sitka Sound, an island-dotted extension of the north Pacific. The westward view is dominated by the perfect frosted cone of a dormant volcano, Mount Edgecumbe.

Ray couldn't help comparing it to the wilderness of his boyhood. If the fishing camps along the banks of a little bass stream in West Virginia could kindle a boy's dreams, imagine what a wilderness of this magnitude could do to a man's soul. The mountains seemed endless here. The sea, with its miles of rugged shoreline, held a wealth of treasures yet to be discovered. Alaska's raw beauty surrounded them on every side, shimmering with life and possibility. In other places nature was often subject to the plow, the bulldozer, and belching smokestacks. The 1950s had also seen a surge of construction in hydroelectric dams that blocked rivers and forever altered the surrounding countryside. But here people seemed small on the landscape and nature was subject to no one. That felt good somehow.

> One Saturday before the formal beginning of classes several staff members and a few students spent the day hiking to the top of Mount Verstovia. We were blessed by good weather and mild temperatures. The trail up the mountain was relatively easy. Near the top we passed the standing ruins of a log cabin that had once served as a World War II military lookout point and then broke out of the tree line onto open alpine tundra. The view was more than worth the effort. Our vantage point put the surrounding land and sea in perspective making it obvious that human presence was less than tiny when compared to the whole of a vast wilderness that stretched beyond view in all directions. We could see fingers of water probing into narrow mountain-lined inlets and fiords. Gazing out over this vista I thought, "There is so much to explore."

Just as captivating to Ray and Barbara as Sitka's surrounding wilderness was the variety of students who attended Sheldon Jackson School, a Presbyterian Mission boarding school. Most villages did not have high schools at that time and so relied on boarding schools to provide children a secondary education. This proved to be difficult for many youngsters, especially since their first language was that of their Native people—Iñupiat Eskimo, Athabaskan Indian, Aleut, and Alutiiq. While the school worked at providing a family-like atmosphere for students, it could not replace the close connections and sense of community that they had left behind in their villages. Back home, everyone knew everyone else and most still practiced traditional lifestyles of hunting and gathering. At home they still traveled by dog team and skin-covered canoes and drew sustenance from land and sea.

Ray and Barbara lived in the junior college dormitory, Condit House, which had a common social room between the men and women's wings of the dorm. Chairs and couches were arranged around a large fireplace and students gathered there to relax and visit. Ray and Barbara's apartment was adjacent to the social room and often became an extension of it.

Both in class and in the more casual setting of the dorm, the Banes encouraged students to tell their stories about the wild caribou that moved across the Arctic plains, and about life in their fish camps and on their trap lines. Ray and Barbara's rapt attention and genuine interest in students' stories helped them develop a rapport with the kids. For the students, telling their stories helped them feel more connected to their far-away village homes. For the Banes, it offered a glimpse into a fascinating way of life. Even the names of the villages were of a world far removed from their lives in West Virginia, names like Metlakatla, Shaktoolik, Kaktovik, Huslia, and Koyuk.

These Native place names were mysterious, more intriguing even than the European place names, which often lauded explorers from England or Russia. Ray and Barbara learned that Russian names began to appear on the map beginning in 1741 with Vitus Bering's arrival on the coast near Mount St. Elais. British Captain James Cook sailed into the area in 1778 after which English names began to appear on the charts. When whalers first entered Arctic Ocean waters through the Bering Strait in 1848, American names were added to the mix.

Long before European "discovery" however, Native peoples had already populated the landscape with names that offered descriptive terms for landmark features. Native peoples were divided into several linguistic groups. Some of Ray and Barbara's students were of Iñupiaq Eskimo descent while others were Athabaskan Indian, and still others were Aleut. From their students, Ray and Barbara quickly learned that there were significant cultural differences between these Native populations. The school was a "cultural stew pot" of Native cultures from around the state. Students of non-Native heritage also attended.

Work demanded most of their time. Barbara had the job of auditioning scores of students for the Sheldon Jackson Choir, directing rehearsals for church services and school functions, and traveling to other southeastern communities for regional competitions and music festivals. She also directed the school band and gave individual piano lessons. Ray was busy teaching, supervising the junior college dormitory, and providing staff support for extracurricular activities.

Ray and Barbara lived in the Condit House dormitory at the Sheldon Jackson mission boarding school, 1960. (Bane Collection)

Even so, Ray still found time to explore nearby mountains. The wilderness never failed to draw him deeper into a sense of place and the mountainous rainforest proved irresistible.

Enjoying the rapport he did with his students, two Native boys invited Ray to go deer hunting with them. Ray had never shot anything larger than a groundhog back in West Virginia. These teens were inviting him into the world they knew best, one in which the group worked together to help provide for the village.

The first segment of the trail ran through thickets of alder, salmonberry, and devil's club before entering a western hemlock-spruce forest. As they climbed up the shoulder of Mt. Verstovia, the terrain grew steeper and they began a series of switchbacks to reach a ridge near the top. Mountain hemlock gave way to brushy meadows and then grassy sub-alpine meadows. Crossing decaying snowfields, they reached rocky alpine terrain near the 2,550-foot summit.

Ray had no problem keeping up with the youngsters; he was only twenty-four himself. The boys treated him as one of the hunting party, not as "teacher." Here, on the mountain, everyone was equal and expected to contribute. Ray enjoyed the young hunters' camaraderie and was happy to switch roles from teacher to student. Excellent hunters and marksmen, the boys shot two deer, and Ray paid attention as he helped them field dress the animals. The boys then slung their quarry over their shoulders and hiked back down the mountain. The young men took pride in donating the meat to the school cafeteria, a tradition in keeping with what was expected back home. The venison also allowed students to eat the kind of fare they were more accustomed to eating in the village.

Ray so enjoyed the hunt that he headed out the following weekend on his own. He told Barbara that he planned to camp in the abandoned cabin just below the tree line. Barbara knew how at home Ray was in the woods and was well aware how he had spent much of his youth hunting and camping, often alone, in the hills of West Virginia. She packed a lunch, hugged him at the door, and wished him luck.

Ray hitched a ride to the trailhead carrying a pack, a sleeping bag and his .270 rifle. Then he climbed up to the old cabin and spent the night. The next morning he put what he had learned the weekend before to work. After

Ray at the top of Mt. Verstovia overlooking Sitka Sound and the city of Sitka. (Bane Collection)

an early breakfast, he hiked the rest of the way up the mountain, shot a big Sitka black-tail buck and field dressed the animal. Then he carried it back down the mountain to the highway.

Ray called Barbara from a nearby tavern and asked her to send someone with a school vehicle to pick him and the deer up.

"Twenty minutes later the school president pulled up and read me the riot act," Ray remembered. "'Don't you know how worried your wife has been with you alone on that mountain?'"

Ray was taken aback. Why would Barbara be in the least worried?

"You've alarmed the entire school staff," the school president continued to rail. "We were considering sending out an emergency search team to rescue you. You could die on that mountain! This country is dangerous. You should act more responsibly."

It turned out that Barbara had attended a social function over the weekend and when asked what Ray was up to, she'd told the women he was out hunting. Alone. Aghast, they had reported back to their husbands who in turn had wondered if there might be some cause for alarm. In the end the Banes learned two things.

One lesson was that it was best to keep their forays into the wilds to themselves. Many of the staff, who were not from Alaska, found life outside the campus to be intimidating. There was no need to create a stir.

Their second observation was that many teachers and faculty viewed the wilds of Alaska from the safety and convenience of their homes and vehicles. They had little interest in exploring the wilderness. They may have come for an experience, but not for adventure. Adventure implied a certain amount of exposure, an element of risk, and the opportunity to stretch to see what might lie around the next bend in the trail.

The Banes learned that the best way to explore southeastern Alaska was by boat. Another teacher at the school, Russell Braun, had mentioned a derelict skiff stored under the school's woodworking shop. A couple of outboard motors also lay unused in a storage room. Russell and Ray dug them out and set to work restoring the boat and repairing a motor. Patched together and working, the little boat gave Ray and Barbara access to the wonders of the coastline and adjacent tidal waters.

The school campus where they lived was just a quarter mile from the beach. Ray kept the skiff tied to a buoy just beyond the low-tide line. He

Barbara served as the music director for Sheldon Jackson School and assisted in producing the musical, "The Mikado," 1961. The cast included students from Iñupiaq and Indian villages across Alaska. (Bane Collection)

used a small boat to row himself and the outboard motor to the skiff at the mooring site. When it wasn't in use, he stored the motor in the school's woodworking building. With their skiff, Ray and Barbara explored the many fjords and islands of Sitka Sound. They harvested butter clams and Dungeness crabs from shallow tidal zones and boiled them in a large pot suspended over an open fire on a beach.

"There were hazards to traveling in southeast, but starvation was not one of them," Ray remembered.

Their newfound mode of transportation gave them the ability to reach small inlets and coves that lay hidden along the seriated coastline. One Saturday, Ray took the skiff out to a place known as No Thorofare Inlet where a local commercial fisherman had mentioned that deer were plentiful. He motored across Sitka Bay and cruised along the rocky shoreline where he found an opening that was barely wide enough to turn the boat around. Ray proceeded cautiously until the passage opened up to a mirror-calm tidewater lake. He continued to explore and found another passageway at the far end of the lake that led to yet a second lake, even more enchanting than the first.

The afternoon was well advanced when I turned homeward. As I neared the upper channel I heard what sounded like a waterfall ahead and was confronted with churning whitewater rushing down a stretch of turbulent rapids. I realized that I had come into the inlet at slack high tide.

In the hours that he had been intently exploring the shoreline, the tide had turned and the lakes were now emptying back into the ocean. The passageways leading to those mirror calm lakes were now torrents of churning water.

"Water slapped over the gunnels and the boat pitched and rolled violently as I was literally spit into the lower lake," Ray remembered. The second passage was a virtual waterfall. Now the little boat was at the mercy of the rapids. Ray hung on as the bow pitched over the edge of the falls. Ocean spray rose up to meet him. Lurching through the shoot, the boat remained upright, but water cascaded in and nearly swamped the vessel. Ray spit out salt water and began bailing.

"After that experience I became far more attentive to tidal charts," Ray said.

As the year drew to a close for Ray and Barbara, it seemed they were just getting acquainted with their new home state. Teaching at a school whose enrollment included students from such far reaches of Alaska had piqued their interest, especially in the Arctic. Maybe they ought to stay another year or two.

"The year in Sitka only served to whet our appetites to see and experience more of Alaska," Ray said. "We knew in our hearts that returning to live in Cleveland was no longer in our future."

In April, Ray attended a regional teacher's conference in Juneau where he looked into other employment possibilities around the state. He was offered an immediate teaching job in a village to fill a vacancy left by a couple who had abandoned their jobs before the end of the school year. Ray declined, saying they still had to fulfill their commitments at Sheldon Jackson. The official working for the Bureau of Indian Affairs (BIA), under which most Alaska rural schools operated, understood and offered positions in Point Barrow beginning in the fall.

Their families and friends would be disappointed but just one year on the last frontier wasn't going to be enough. Ray and Barbara's adventures had just begun.

3

to the top of the world

As Ray and Barbara flew over the Brooks Range on their way to their new home and teaching jobs in Barrow, Ray thought of the Robert Service poem "The Spell of the Yukon."

There's a land where the mountains are nameless,
The rivers all run God knows where. . . .

Although Service actually resided in Canada, he captured the essence of northern wilderness and won favor with many Alaskan readers and new-comers. North and beyond the winding ribbon of the Yukon River, the vast expanse of land seemed to be dominated more than anything else by its remoteness. On the other side of the Brooks Range the topography changed abruptly as it gave way to the Arctic coastal plain.

The land ahead literally seemed to deflate. I had a momentary sense of vertigo. The Arctic Plain is a formless marshy wasteland stretching beyond the horizon. It is a seemingly environmental abyss. There are no trees. With the exception of scraggy patches of stunted willows along sluggish streams nothing grows more than a few inches tall. Countless stagnant ponds and shallow lakes create a Swiss cheese landscape. Streams stagger drunkenly toward a distant icy ocean. The further north we flew the flatter and wetter the country became until it was more liquid than solid. At the coastline we were greeted by a band of low brooding clouds and a curtain of gray fog hanging just offshore.

Not only was this a far cry from West Virginia, it was a world apart from the lush green wilderness of southeast Alaska with its large Sitka spruce, glittering fjords, and rich marine life. The northernmost community in the United States, Barrow, Alaska, is located on the Chukchi Sea of the Arctic Ocean, 320 miles due north of the Arctic Circle. It was traditionally known as Ukpeagvik, "place of the snowy owl."

Barrow's name comes from Point Barrow, named in 1825 by Captain Beechey of the Royal Navy for Sir John Barrow of the British Admiralty. Beechey was plotting the Arctic coastline at the time. Barrow was incorporated as a city in 1958, just three years before Ray and Barbara signed on to teach. As the plane circled over the small village, they could see that the town was a disorganized jumble of unpainted shacks and earth-banked huts.

> Muddy paths and rutted dirt roads wandered aimlessly through the community . . . The tundra surrounding the village on three sides was a drab brown swamp. The ocean was the color of lead, dotted with chunks of dirty ice. The best term to describe the scene was desolate.

At their briefings back in Fairbanks, they had been warned that a teaching stint in a village could either make or break a marriage. Ray looked at Barbara as the plane circled to land. A tear slid down her cheek. He squeezed her hand.

The school principal met them at the plane with a four-wheel-drive utility van and drove them along a rutted beach trail to town. It took them half an hour to drive six miles.

Their home was a small plywood cabin with an oil-burning kitchen stove, their sole source of heat. Open shelving tacked to the walls was scarcely enough to store their year's supply of food. A 55-gallon drum next to the stove held their water supply. Chunks of ice were dropped into the drum for melting and were then ladled out for drinking, cooking, and bathing. To bathe, they stood next to the kitchen stove and used a bucket of hot water.

An enclosed, unheated entry way (qanitchaq) helped conserve heat when going in and out of the cabin. Parkas and other outdoor clothing were hung on nails. A tiny alcove on the side held the infamous "honey bucket," a toilet consisting of a five-gallon pail with a removable toilet seat. The school janitor periodically came and emptied the contents of the bucket. One day Ray returned home from school and found the janitor in their cabin

The Banes lived in a one-room plywood cabin in Barrow. They melted ice for drinking and bathing water and stored meat and other freezable food on the roof. (Bane Collection)

with the honey bucket on the kitchen stove. He was trying to thaw its frozen contents.

Barbara was assigned the first grade and Ray the sixth. The school was bursting at the seams and classroom conditions were appalling. Barbara's room doubled as the staff laundry room. The class was so crowded that students had to crawl under desks to reach the front of the room. Ray's class was held in the attic of the local minister's home. Ray had to stoop to his knees to reach students seated under the low sloping ceiling. When a fire broke out in the house, it was quickly decided that the arrangement was unsafe and they were moved to a building that also served as a local restaurant.

Most of the Barrow school staff, including seven teachers, a principal, and secretary lived in apartments attached to classroom buildings, or in homes that were part of the loosely formed Bureau of Indian Affairs (BIA) compound. Ray and Barbara were in fact happy to learn that as "new" staff, they had been assigned to housing among local residents. Their neighbors were Iñupiat Eskimos and a local bush pilot and his wife. If they were going to enjoy their adventure in the Arctic, they wanted to experience it as the locals did, as part of the community.

"Hey, come on over for a cup of tea?" Sadie Neakok called to Ray and Barbara. Sadie was the daughter of Charley Brower, who had been dubbed "King of the Arctic." He was a whaler turned trader who had settled in Barrow in the late 19th century. His exploits were legendary and Sadie had inherited his indomitable spirit. She'd married Nate Neakok, a village hunter, and together they lived a traditional Iñupiat life. Ray and Barbara spent many evenings in their warmly cluttered home, eating local fare seasoned with laughter. Ray remembered the time with Sadie and Nate as a portal into village life and local Native culture.

In the 1960s Barrow was in the throes of major cultural and economic change. Until recently, the Iñupiat had followed a semi-nomadic subsistence lifestyle. But the modern world had arrived on its doorstep. The building of a Distant Early Warning (DEW Line) radar site and the Naval Arctic Research Lab (NARL) base north of the village now employed local Natives at previously undreamed of wages. A Public Health Service (PHS) hospital, U.S. Weather Service site, and BIA school offered employment and

Weir Negavanna, an Iñupiaq elder, used string figures to illustrate ancient Iñupiaq stories to students. Ray and Barbara encouraged elders to participate in the school program and adapted academic lessons to fit the context of Iñupiaq life. (Bane Collection)

services. The influx of people was straining Barrow's infrastructure to the breaking point.

There was no municipal sewage or water system. By the 1960s, electricity was available only through a mix of private providers, but many homes were still without power. People emptied their waste into 55-gallon fuel drums, which were then hauled out onto the sea ice or simply dumped on the nearby open tundra.

"We knew, even back then, that this way of life wasn't going to last," Ray said.

He described how in the 1960s, modern technologies were beginning to merge with ancient ways. "Imported outboard engines powered traditional skin-covered boats (umiaks). Dog teams transported hunters out onto the windswept tundra, while airplanes landed on the local airstrip. A typical Iñupiaq meal might include frozen raw fish, seal oil and Sailor Boy Pilot Bread."

Ray found it difficult at first to describe the North Slope of Alaska, and initially saw it as a horizontal wilderness.

> *It sprawled over tens of thousands of square miles with minimal vertical relief . . . For someone from the verdant hills and valleys of West Virginia the Arctic plain seemed featureless and empty.*

Ray and Barbara realized that the only way to explore this broad, mostly frozen landscape was the way the Iñupiat had been doing it for generations. They would need a dog team.

In the early 1960s, modern snowmobiles (known in Alaska as snowmachines) were only starting to make their appearance on the scene. At the time, they were prone to break down and could not negotiate the terrain that dog teams took in stride. Dog teams still dominated winter travels and most homes in Barrow had 7–10 huskies tethered nearby.

Ray learned that the local dentist had taken on the care of six young huskies for their owner, big game guide Bud Helmricks, for the winter. The dogs were less than a year old and untrained. Helmricks had left a large supply of frozen fish to feed them. He had also given the dentist a dog sled, lines, and harnesses. The dentist had no interest in running sled dogs and was delighted when Ray offered to take over the task.

Meanwhile, Barbara and Ray saw an ad in the *Alaska Sportsman* magazine for Siberian huskies from a breeder in Oregon. They arranged to buy a six-month-old female. When the pup arrived in mid-October, they named her "Twilight" and she became a beloved member of the family. She eventually grew into a brilliant lead dog and the foundation of their teams for years to come. All that would take time, however.

It was immediately obvious that I did not have a dog team. I had a mob of energetic young huskies with absolutely no idea of what was expected of them. We became a source of great entertainment as I tried to wrestle a gaggle of playful huskies into a working unit. It was like herding geese. In desperation I would tie a line to the front of the pack and physically drag them out of the village onto the beach road. Native villagers came out of their homes to wave at me and laugh themselves weak.

They began to make progress when the cook at the Arctic Research Lab at the far end of the beach road began to keep leftover food to give to the dogs. After that the race was on.

"I had to hang on for dear life as they rushed out of the village running full tilt to get their treats. I no longer had to play rabbit," Ray remembered. "An Eskimo friend finally took pity on me and lent me the use of a lead dog to help me train one of my own. This was done by hitching Twilight next to the leader with a short length of line linking their collars."

By mid-November, Ray and his team were traveling up and down the coastline, occasionally working their way out onto the newly formed coastal ice. Barbara enjoyed accompanying him on evening training runs.

The Bane's interest in running dogs further integrated them into the Barrow community. They learned that laughter dissolves many cultural barriers.

Ray and Barbara became friends with one of the school janitors, an Iñupiat man named Joshua. Like Sadie, he knew the old ways. He had spent most of his life following his nomadic parents as they trailed caribou herds, fishing and trapping their way across the windswept landscape. The family visited villages only briefly to trade pelts for ammunition and other supplies.

Joshua was the first to teach Ray and Barbara the subtle richness of the Arctic's bounty. Ray and Joshua traveled and hunted together by dog team and at one point Ray asked, "Which way to the village?"

Joshua pointed and said, "It's over that hill."

"Where I saw only a uniformly featureless terrain, an experienced Iñupiat traveler could see a land filled with multitude of visual references," Ray explained. It took a year for Ray to distinguish hills and valleys that were obvious to those who lived there.

Joshua invited Ray on caribou hunts where they camped in snow block shelters. The other hunters disdained the sleeping bag Ray brought along. In temperatures more than thirty below zero they simply lay on a caribou hide, dressed in the skin clothing that they traditionally wore.

Joshua seemed to have a remarkable ability to find his way across miles of flat white terrain. When Ray asked him about this, Joshua remarked, "The snow tells me where to go."

Then Joshua showed Ray a principle of Iñupiaq navigation. First he pointed out that most snowdrifts were aligned the same way—they had been formed by the prevailing northeasterly wind.

"With this knowledge, a hunter could set and maintain a given course by cutting across the drifts at a particular angle," Ray said. "Even at night

Dempsy Bodfish of Wainwright at a snow block hut used for hunting and trapping on the east bank of the Kuk River, 1964. The sled in the foreground belonged to the Banes. (Bane Collection)

a musher could drag his foot over the surface of the snow feeling the alignment of the ridges and call out directions to his dogs."

In areas where storm winds may have confused the drift pattern, there was a backup technique. Joshua used his skinning knife to carefully cut out a circle in the hard snow crust. He lifted it away revealing tundra grass that had been flattened by early winter storms. The blades of grass lay with their tips pointing southwest. "The grass will tell you which way to go," he said. Joshua also taught Ray about the moody temperament of sea ice.

> Traveling on sea ice is like walking on the floor of an active volcano. On the surface everything may appear solid and stable, but there are unseen, titanic forces at work. Like a volcano, the ice is a sleeping giant that can suddenly stir and turn the illusion of stability into total chaos.

Different zones of ice behave differently. The shore ice, extending out over relatively shallow water, is stable by midwinter. The shore ice is also called "fast" ice, since it is held fast to the shore. The outer edge of the shore ice is marked by huge piles of ice rubble called pressure ridges. Separating the shore ice and the massive perennial ice pack is the transition zone. Here, ice is constantly forming only to be ripped apart and sent adrift. Lanes of exposed water, called leads, open and close at the whim of the wind and tides. When temperatures are below zero and the air calm, fog forms over the water reflecting the blackness of the sea.

Here in the fickle conditions of the transition zone, marine life thrived and could be harvested from the sea. Seals and polar bears are drawn to open water in the winter. With the coming of spring and summer, they are joined by whales, walrus, and migratory birds.

One day Ray convinced Joshua to take him seal hunting. The newly formed ice was not thick enough for safe travel by dog team, so hunters traveled onto the ice on foot looking for unfrozen potholes where spotted seals often surfaced.

> I walked a few yards behind Joshua mimicking his movements. We followed a winding route trying to walk where ice sheets had overlapped one another creating a firmer surface. The air temperature was near zero, but the top of the ice was damp to the touch. The salt content of the frozen seawater was being squeezed out as the ice aged and thickened. In its early stages sea ice is more elastic and can silently disintegrate to slush under a hunter.

As they traveled, Joshua jabbed the steel tip of his tuuq pole into the ice to test its strength. They spotted a black head lift out of a pothole and Joshua became intensely focused on moving into shooting range. He stopped testing the ice, since the noise would scare away the seal. As Ray followed, he noticed that the ice seemed to be undulating around them.

"Joshua, look at the ice," Ray whispered.

Joshua's eyes widened. He immediately took a crab-like position on the ice, trying to keep as wide a stance as possible. Ray followed suit and they slid their way toward firmer ice, being careful not to lose contact with the surface.

"I could see the ice bend under our weight. It had a rubbery feel," Ray said. "The clammy brine penetrated my mittens, stinging my hands. Had we broken through neither of us would have survived, and our bodies may have never been found."

"Maybe we scared ourselves," Joshua laughed once they were out of danger. They continued their hunt, bringing home a fat seal. But the lesson was not lost on Ray. He and Barbara had a lot to learn, and so much to remember about this vanishing way of life.

Although he and Barbara were teachers in the classroom, they had become happy apprentices outside of it. They worked at acquiring the language. They developed a taste for raw caribou meat dipped in saucers of seal oil. Along with learning to run a dog team, Ray was also managing to hunt and navigate the land and sea ice.

School administrators were less than pleased, however, with the Bane's affinity for the local culture. And it wouldn't be long before the young couple would hear about it.

4

—⁺✢⁺—

going to the dogs

Come mid-winter, cabin fever frayed the nerves of many, especially the school staff. At Barrow's northern latitude, the sun sets on or around November 19, and remains below the horizon for sixty-five days until around January 23. By solstice, on December 20, twilight in the village lasts for a mere three hours. Between the dark and the cold, teachers rarely ventured beyond the walls of their heated apartments or classrooms, which were often housed in the same building. Without exercise, even the dogs became argumentative and took to fighting.

Ray and Barbara's dog team rescued them from winter's common malady. The dogs were a constant source of entertainment and their forays outdoors, even in bitter temperatures, kept winter's gloomy mood at bay. Ray ran the team several times a week, often traveling in the dark by moonlight or head-lamp. On weekends he ventured farther out along the shoreline.

One day, the school principal called Ray into his office.

"Bane, you're new here and I can appreciate your enthusiasm," he began. "But this business of learning the Iñupiaq language to teach your kids English is counter-productive. If these kids are going to be successful, they need to learn English and leave the old ways behind. You're doing them a disservice."

Ray strongly disagreed. And a heated debate ensued.

"Furthermore," the principal said, "it has come to my attention that members of the staff consider your activities running around by dog team and socializing with the Eskimos to be foolhardy and setting a poor example."

"You are entitled to your opinion," Ray countered firmly. "As for the language issue, the standardized test scores from my class speak for themselves. You can't argue with the improvement in their academic achievement."

This quieted the principal, but now disgruntled, he warned Ray to guard against becoming "Bushy," wielding the term as if it were an ailment. He then dismissed Ray with a nod to the door.

Ray continued to run the team, knowing his young dogs still needed a lot of miles and a lot of coaching to become finely tuned. That winter of 1961, distemper swept through Barrow and killed off scores of sled dogs. Ray and Barbara lost two pups. Compared to other teams ravaged by the disease, the Banes had been lucky, but the young team was now down to just four dogs. In spring, Twilight, the Siberian husky pup that they had ordered in October, arrived from Oregon. Eventually they picked up another young dog.

As they worked to buy and raise more dogs to fill out their team, Eddie Hopson offered to loan the use of four of his huskies. Eddie suggested trying the dogs on their own before integrating them into the Bane's younger team.

The Banes assembled a small dog team soon after arriving in Barrow. They raised and trained other huskies and traveled extensively by dog team across the Arctic. (Bane Collection)

"I went over to his house and it was obvious why he made the suggestion," Ray said. "They were huge with almost uncontrollable energy. They looked like long-haired lions."

On an unseasonably warm day, when it seemed spring might not be a too distant possibility, village residents welcomed the new temperatures with open doors. The windows and doors to homes that had been buttoned up all winter were flung open for the fresh air. Ray decided it would be a fine day to harness the four new dogs to his sled and give them a test run.

"The huskies were literally insane with the desire to run. They exploded into a dead run when I released the sled hook," he said. "The sled skidded sideways around the first turn almost flipping onto its side. I tried dragging the sled anchor, but it barely scratched the surface of the hard-packed snow."

He had almost made it to the edge of town when a loose sled dog pup darted across the road ahead. Ray's four borrowed dogs didn't miss a stride in turning a hard right in hot pursuit.

"The pup, now squealing in terror, ran as fast as it could with death literally nipping at its heels," Ray remembered.

People scattered as the runaway team went barreling past. The pup was only a leap ahead of the huskies when it suddenly dove through the open door of a village house. The pup skidded across the floor, seeking refuge under the table of a family who sat eating their midday meal.

"My team never hesitated," Ray said. "They went roaring in too."

The sled was too wide for the door and crashed into the frame, bringing everything to an abrupt halt.

"The fugitive pup cowered in a far corner and five Eskimos were plastered to the wall at the rear of the room," Ray remembered.

Ray became an immediate legend and decades later people from Barrow were still telling the story of the crazy tanik (white man) who drove his dog team into a village home.

In April the sun had firmly reasserted itself in the Arctic sky. Spring temperatures climbed to a balmy zero degrees and daylight hours were increasing by as much as ten minutes a day. By May the sun would not set again for close to eighty-two days, giving the Arctic its moniker, Land of the Midnight Sun. With the arrival of spring, the focus of coastal Iñupiat villages from Kivilina to Barrow and beyond to Barter Island (Kaktovik) is the whaling season. Bowhead whales migrate north to raise their calves and to feed in the nutrient-rich waters of the Arctic Ocean. Like all warm-blood-ed mammals they must breathe air, which means the whales must follow the open leads created in the ever-changing interface between the relatively stable shore ice and the vast, free-floating pack ice.

In 1961, villagers continued to rely on dog teams to transport their gear and themselves to and from the edge of the shore ice and used skin-covered umiaks with men at the paddles for pursuing and retrieving whales.

"They literally lived on the edge of disaster, subject to caprice weather and the ever dynamic and too often turbulent sea ice," Ray remembered.

Ray spent weekends traveling by dog team to the whaling camps. "My visits were met with typical Eskimo hospitality and humor. Whales passed, but they were usually too far out or the sea lane was clogged with floating ice. The whales could be heard blowing even when thick fog hid them."

Finally it happened.

"*Aghavik!* Whale! They've taken a whale!" The news spread throughout Barrow and school was dismissed. People rushed to hook up their dog teams. Men, women, and children piled onto large scow sleds and headed north to the kill site.

Ray took this photo from a skin covered umiak while paddling to help tow in a whale following a successful hunt. The whale was pulled to the top of the ice by villagers using a block and tackle pulley. (Bane Collection)

Ray dashed home and hooked up his own team, following the exodus of villagers traveling out onto the sea ice.

> *We all followed the same trail hacked earlier through miniature mountain ranges of shattered ice, some pieces the size of cars and large trucks. We wound through narrow passes and massive piles of aqua blue ice, frosted with snow. It was frozen chaos.*

When they reached the open lead, the whale was still being towed back to the shore ice. An Iñupiat friend invited Ray to join the boat crew. Grabbing a paddle, Ray took a place in the umiak and did his best to keep up with the men as they paddled through ice-strewn seawater. They swung the umiak into place where a towline had already been secured to the body of the whale.

"It took another hour to drag the whale to the shore fast ice. The crew chanted an Iñupiaq song dipping their paddles in sync with the rhythm of the chant," Ray remembered. "I could not understand the words, but my paddle moved in time with theirs."

It was a medium sized whale, but to Ray it seemed enormous. Adult bowhead whales can reach sixty feet in length and weigh an average of one ton for every linear foot, offering a tremendous food source for the village. The men anchored a block and tackle pulley system into the ice roughly thirty yards from the water's edge. They then secured a thick rope around the tail of the whale.

> *Everyone joined hands to pull the great carcass on the top of the ice. Eventually the massive black bulk lay exposed . . . . Men, wielding long poles tipped with sharp flenses (spade-like knife-blades), began to carve at the whale carcass, slicing through the glistening black skin into a heavy layer of blubber and then deeper into the dark red meat. Great slabs were peeled away. Other men used large hooks to drag the slabs into piles off to the side. Blood poured onto the snow and ice, staining it crimson and oily black.*

Ray helped where he could and took directions from those who knew how. Gas-fueled camp stoves burned under large pots of boiling water from melted snow. Slices of whale meat and blubber were thrown into the pot. There was a seemingly endless supply of tea and coffee for all. Wooden platters full of small chunks of raw whale skin (muktuk) and blubber came around.

"It had an oily walnut flavor and seemed to expand the more I chewed," Ray said. "I was given a small sack of whale meat and some muktuk to take home with me."

A few days after the kill, Ray hooked up his team to return to the sea ice. As he headed out, he saw hunters with their dog teams returning shoreward. They were running alongside their sleds, which carried the whaling canoes. The men held on to the sides of the canoes to steady them and shouted to Ray as they rushed past.

"They seemed to be warning me of something," Ray said. When he looked up, he saw what they were fleeing. "The ice had come to life. It was moving. Big blocks were tumbling over one another advancing toward me like a slow-moving avalanche. Even as I watched, the seemingly solid surface beneath me began to writhe and buckle. It was an ice quake! The dogs were terrified. I rushed to the leader and pulled the team around toward home."

The dogs needed no further urging. A shift in currents and wind had driven the main pack ice shoreward and the huge mass had rammed into the shore ice with incomprehensible force.

Ray continued, "The hunters saw it coming just in time to pull away from their campsites before being ground up in the tsunami of crumbling ice.

Ray stands next to a partially butchered whale on the sea ice north of Point Barrow. The meat, blubber, and muktuk (whale skin) were divided among the members of the whaling crew and village, 1962. (Bane Collection)

As I followed the fleeing whalers, I recalled Joshua's warning, 'Never trust the ice.'"

The school year was coming to a close, but Ray was restless and eager to learn more. Ray had learned from local hunters that if he really wanted to meet Iñupiat people who still followed the old ways he should visit the village of Wainwright. The village lays roughly one hundred coastal miles southwest of Barrow.

Teacher contracts were year-round and leave requests had to be approved by school administration. It was assumed that teacher vacations would be taken to leave the village and visit relatives "Outside" the state or for continuing education.

Ray's idea of continuing his education was to take a solo dog team trip to Wainwright. The principal refused his leave request. Ray had obviously ignored the principal's earlier warning about getting too involved with the locals.

"You'll die out there. This country will kill you," the principal said. "You're not even traveling with the Eskimos."

Ray hounded him relentlessly, saying the leave time was his to use as he saw fit.

"He finally conceded when I threatened to lodge a formal complaint," Ray said.

But their disagreement had delayed the trip by almost a week. Travel conditions deteriorated as rising temperatures and constant sunlight eroded the snow cover and rotted the ice. Pools of melt water formed and patches of tundra lay bare. Trail conditions forced Ray and his team to travel on the sea ice. He had borrowed one husky to round the team to seven dogs but the new dog had shown aggressive tendencies.

On the first night, they camped atop a low barren knoll overlooking the beach. Scattered poles and stakes marked it as a Native campsite. Ray unharnessed the dogs and tethered them to stakes. The new dog snarled menacingly. After feeding the dogs and himself, Ray stretched out in his sleeping bag—on a caribou skin in the bed of the sled—and covered himself with the tarp.

"In the distance I could hear the haunting call of migrating waterfowl winging low along the seaward edge of the ice," he remembered. He couldn't recall a time when he felt more at ease or more delighted to be venturing into the wild. This was far better even than his summer boyhood days camping in West Virginia.

The second day began with a near disaster. As Ray harnessed up the dogs, the new dog lunged, snarling. Ray threw up his arm and the dog clamped down with vice-like force. Its teeth closed through the folds of his parka and sliced into his arm.

"As the dog tightened its grip, I was sure the bones would snap," Ray said. With his free hand, Ray grabbed a wooden stake at his feet and began to fend off the dog, whose grip was unrelenting.

"I swung the club with my full strength across the top of its head and it went down. I thought it was dead, but then I saw it was still breathing. Before it could regain consciousness, I snapped it into its traces. If I had owned the dog I would have killed it on the spot," he said.

Ray cleaned the puncture wound to his arm and although bruised and sore, he decided to continue. The dog wore its harness the rest of the trip and Ray carried a club whenever he approached it. The dog gave him no further trouble.

It took three days to reach Wainwright. On the third day, the overcast sky merged seamlessly with the gray snow on the ground creating a world of eerie quiet.

> Dark spots of dirty ice or exposed tundra tussocks seemed to float suspended in the air. At one point I spotted something grayish white in the distance running toward me. Polar bear, I thought and pulled the rifle from the sled lashings. Then it stopped and gave a sharp yipping bark. It was an Arctic fox. With no reference for distance, I had thought it much larger and farther away.

Then like a mirage, a cluster of dark objects materialized in the distance. They disappeared and then reappeared as the team crossed the rolling tundra until finally the objects remained in place and emerged as buildings. Half an hour later Ray and the team pulled into the village of Wainwright.

"It was the wee hours of the morning. Everyone was still asleep. A chorus of barking and howling dogs announced our arrival. My team shook off their lethargy and broke into a full run," Ray said. He brought them to a stop in front of a rambling school building. The dogs curled in their traces and immediately fell asleep. Ray sat on top of the sled and waited for some-one to come along. Just as he too began to drift off to sleep he heard "Hey ilivich. Kiinyaatin? Sumunkaikavich? (Hey, you. Who are you? Where did you come from?)

Sheldon Segevan, an elder, was on his way to record data from the small weather station mounted on an elevated box near the school building.

"I heard that a tanik was trying to drive a dog team from Barrow, but I didn't believe it," Sheldon said.

The following three days were spent resting the dogs and meeting the people of the village, including Don and Thelma Webster, a missionary couple who had spent three years in Wainwright learning the language and translating the King James Bible into Iñupiaq.

"Unfailingly, I was met with warm hospitality and friendly humor wher-ever I went," Ray said. "Villagers called me into their homes freely sharing their food and ever-ready laughter. They reminded me of the rural farm folks from the hills of West Virginia—unpretentious, independent, and proud of their heritage."

The Wainwright school had a staff of three teachers. The principal and his wife had applied for a transfer. They considered Wainwright to be too isolated, the weather too extreme, and the teaching conditions too difficult.

Ray's return to Barrow was colder, making trail conditions easier to trav-el. But a late winter storm blew in, testing the team and Ray's judgment in trying conditions. He was in the middle of Peard Bay when the full force of a storm descended. Winds swept across the bay at gale force. Snow blew sideways in driving wet sheets. Ray pushed the team, trying to maintain a steady course by reading the wind and snowdrifts. But the dogs were being brutalized by the force of the wind and pelting snow. Ray was worried about becoming disoriented and stumbling onto weak ice. Then he remembered what Joshua or any Iñupiat would do. Ray stopped the team, turned the sled on its side and stretched the tarp out in lean-to fashion. He fed the dogs and they contentedly curled up and went to sleep. Following the team's example, he crawled into his sleeping bag atop a thick caribou skin mat in the shelter of the sled and went to sleep.

When spring storms blow in the Arctic, with its perpetual daylight, it is hard to keep track of time. It seemed the storm raged forever. Moisture

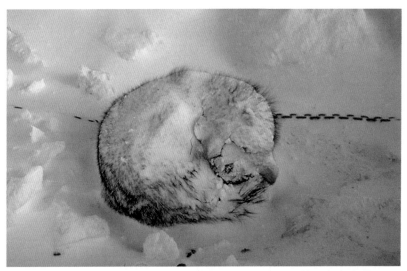

Ray had to teach his younger huskies to get up during storms so they would not be buried by drifts. Every couple of hours, Ray would rouse the dogs from sleep and make them shake off the snow. (Bane Collection)

seeped into Ray's watch and it stopped working. Between naps he drank tea, snacked on crackers, and fed the dogs. When the skies finally cleared, Ray had no idea even what day it was.

Back on the trail toward Barrow, he met up with another dog team with three men hauling a skin boat on their dog sled. In customary Iñupiat fashion they stopped to talk and drink tea. They pulled out meat and seal oil to share and laughed when Ray asked whether it was day or night. It turned out he had been pinned down by the storm for two days.

The dog team trip had offered Ray something of a personal rite of passage. In the past eight months, he had brought up a motley crew of pups molding them into a working team and he had learned enough to earn the nodding respect of his neighbors. He could see that the year in Barrow was just the beginning of a long love affair with the North Country.

A place like Wainwright could draw him and Barbara even deeper into relationship with the people and the old ways of living on the land and sea. No one in Wainwright would question Ray's driving a dog team or hunting caribou or learning the Iñupiaq language. Just one day after returning from his trip, Ray and Barbara put in a transfer from Barrow to Wainwright for the following school year.

When asked what Barbara thought of moving to a place even smaller and more remote that Barrow, she said, "I always loved the people."

Her gift for connecting with people made the Bane's transition to different communities over the years a time of gathering friendships. Pressed about yet another change, to yet a more distant locale—a place considered a "hardship" teaching assignment—she said, "I always knew that as long as I was with Ray, everything would be all right."

Aerial view of Wainwright on the coast of the Chukchi Sea, 1963. (Bane Collection)

5

— ✛ —

becoming eskimo

The morning after arriving to their new home in Wainwright, Ray and Barbara sat down to breakfast and discovered they had an audience.

"The kitchen window was a collage of small fur-lined faces," Ray remembered. "Village children had no inhibitions when it came to satisfying their curiosity about the new teachers. Those were the days before television. We were the new show in town."

The population in Wainwright in 1962 was 280 Iñupiat and seven non-Natives. It would not be long before the third teacher left the village and Ray and Barbara would have charge of all eighty-two elementary students. Many of the younger children spoke only Iñupiaq, making it necessary for older students to serve as translators.

There was a certain irony to the Banes work in the North Country. While the world was quickly changing for the Iñupiat people, the Banes hoped to experience and perhaps even contribute to the continuation of traditional cultural values. Yet schools themselves contributed many of the changes to a culture in transition. Children were required to attend 180 days of classes each year, which tied Iñupiat families to the village—effectively ending their nomadic lifestyle of following game across the Arctic plains. Students were also required to learn English. When children reached the ninth grade, they were sent to Native boarding schools, like Mt. Edgecumbe or the mission-operated Sheldon Jackson in Sitka. Some students traveled as far away as Oregon to attend high school.

Even so, the majority of villagers strongly supported teachers and the school played a central role in the community. The principal teacher was expected not only to teach classes, but also to oversee the operation of the Native cooperative trading post, to serve as an advisor to the village council, and to maintain shortwave radio contact with the hospital in Barrow. Teachers were also asked to help villagers prepare tax forms and other government-related paperwork, and provide hospitality and meals to visiting doctors, dentists, nurses, and government officials. When non-Native outsiders came visiting—often getting weathered in for days at a time—they stayed in the Bane's already cramped quarters, eating meals and digging into provisions that had been purchased and carefully rationed for the school year.

In a way that was counter to the 1960s educational climate, Ray and Barbara incorporated the traditional and environmental realities of their community into their everyday teaching. In Wainwright, they enjoyed the freedom to educate kids in the most germane way possible. Exposing Native students to Western traditions and values was not as important to Ray and Barbara as teaching reading, writing, math, and social studies using the world outside school walls as a springboard for learning. Even the vocabulary needed to be made more relevant. Learning to count 2+2 seals on the ice had far more meaning than learning to count 2+2 goldfish in an aquarium. (Who in the village had ever seen an aquarium?)

The work load for Ray and Barbara was tremendous, but they thrived on being both teacher and student in this welcoming village. Social life in Wainwright revolved around two churches, a small coffee shop, the Native trading post, and the school. The trading post was the town social hall where older men especially, leaned or sat against the walls and exchanged hunting stories and told accounts of the old ways. In the dimly lit store, the men spoke Iñupiaq to each other, but for Ray's benefit would sometimes converse in English.

The trading post was to me, a cultural classroom where I could acquire unique knowledge from the true experts in Arctic living . . . I was able to learn where villagers were focusing their efforts in pursuit of fish and game and why they selected one location over another. They described the many things one had to be aware of when traveling on the sea ice or avoiding hidden hazards along rivers. The weather was a constant topic of conversation. The men discussed signs of changing weather and approaching storms. We talked about the best designs for dog sleds, the best places for putting up

camps, how to approach caribou in the winter, how to predict the end of a
prolonged storm by the howling of sled dogs.

Barbara played the organ and piano at both the Presbyterian and the Assembly of God churches in town. This fed her love for music and nurtured her connection with many village residents.

The village women taught Barbara how to skin a seal, keeping the entire hide intact to form an empty sealskin bag. Seal blubber was placed inside the skin and allowed to ferment and render into oil. While men were the hunters and trappers in the village, it was primarily the women's responsibility to preserve the meat through drying and freezing. Barbara joined them in the task.

Barbara learned to scrape and tan the hides of seals and other game animals. She also learned to sew the fur and skins into clothing. She and the other women would meet at the school where she learned how to use a triangular needle to stitch lightly and to draw the seams tight with thread made of sinew.

> *Another major task taken on by women was the preparation of bearded seal (oogruk) skins and the sewing of the skins to form-fit a boat (umiak) frame. The skins were prepared for sewing by rotting the hides until the hair and surface layer slipped off the skin. It is impossible to describe the smell of the skins at this stage. A number of adult women would work in a heated shed during the sewing phase of the process. I (Ray) recall entering such a shed while the women sat on caribou skin mats on the floor with their legs stretched straight out in front of them. The odor almost knocked me over! They worked and chatted unconcernedly partaking of snacks and treats provided by the owner (umailik) of the boat. This was one job that Barbara was happy to leave to the experts.*

Traditional Native dancing had been a privilege withdrawn by earlier Wainwright teachers. The Assembly of God church frowned on dancing while the Presbyterian congregation saw no harm in it. When asked if they would allow the dancing to resume, the Banes not only said "yes," but also welcomed the opportunity to join in the fun.

At one point Ray and Barbara were invited to join a dance team for the Messenger Feast celebration. The elaborate dance used complex routines and Ray and Barbara practiced with other villagers before the performance, joining in the rhythm and powerful energy of the dance. Drums were made of circular wooden frames with membranes of walrus stomachs stretched across the top. Drummers used a long flexible wand to strike the bottom of the drum, resulting in a deep resounding "thumm." A line of women vocalists sang in a repetitive chant to the beat.

"It was impossible not to be stirred by the music," Ray said.

The Messenger Feast celebration had not been observed in Wainwright for many years and village elders had decided that the festival should be resurrected. Its origins came from days when two or more cultural bands would each send a messenger to exchange an invitation to meet. These gatherings often took place after a bountiful harvest such as the taking of a whale. Dancing, feasting, trading, and story telling were part of the festivities.

As part of the week-long event, Wainwright arbitrarily divided itself into two teams—the Wolves and the Walrus—with households split so that loyalties lay with teams rather than family groups. Competitions of every sort ensued. Athletic endeavors, dog sled races, and feasting made for a time of shared customs and much laughter. One game was a laughing game with

Barbara with Wainwright students, 1963. Each fall, the North Star (background) carried supplies to villages along the coastline of northern Alaska. The Banes had to order everything they would need for themselves and for the school year several months before the ship arrived. (Bane Collection)

the goal to get your opponent to laugh even as they struggled to maintain a straight face.

> At the end of the midwinter games the scores were tallied to determine which team had won. The winning team was given the option of choosing which community service chore they would perform; clearing away the snow from the Kuk Lagoon coal mine or chopping a dog team trail through the sea ice to the spring open-water lead that would form for the passage of the whales. The losing team had to take whichever task remained.

A favorite pastime in Wainwright was dog racing with both men and women competing. At the urging of the villagers, Ray and Barbara entered their team in the races. In a wild free-for-all, up to 20 teams lined up, and then raced pell-mell to a turnaround point, marked by a 55-gallon drum as much as twenty-five miles away. After making the turn, they raced back to the starting point. There were no designated trails, just the wide-open Kuk Lagoon. Sometimes dog teams fought or got tangled up, and drivers wielded their whips trying to keep other teams away. The first sled over the starting/finishing line claimed the title. The trophy was a small cup that winners displayed in places of prominence in their homes.

If the goal to finish first could not be achieved, then at least competitors did not want to finish behind the schoolteacher. At first the Bane's obliged, coming in last or nearly last every time. And each time, the villagers patted them on the back and encouraged them to keep trying. During their three years in Wainwright, the Bane's team grew more experienced and Ray and Barbara's driving skills grew keen. It wasn't long before the villager's encouragement evolved to friendly competition as Ray and Barbara became serious contenders for the cup.

West and northwest beyond the village lay the Chukchi Sea and to the south and east lay the great expanse of the Arctic plain. The land to the south was splayed open by the Kuk River estuary that created an immense lagoon and provided a major transportation corridor for the people of Wainwright. During the short summers, the Kuk River's water offered boat passage deep inland and during the long winter, dog teams could travel the relatively smooth ice for dozens of miles. Reading the lagoon ice posed a special challenge, however. It wasn't a typical river, but neither was it typical ocean ice. Varying degrees of salinity between the salt and fresh water only added to the unpredictability of invisible currents and the movement of tides beneath the ice. As winter approached, the village men watched the development of the ice cover on the Kuk Lagoon in anticipation of beginning inland hunting and trapping expeditions.

One fall day, Moses Nayakik invited Ray to accompany him on a caribou hunt by dog team. The lagoon ice was still in the early stages of freezing with soft and thin ice in scattered locations.

"We left the village on a Saturday morning, crossing the strip of rough tundra separating the ocean beach from the shore of the Kuk," Ray remembered. "Moses' team soon outpaced mine and I fell behind by a couple of hundred yards."

Both teams were following the safe ice along the shoreline of the lagoon. When Moses' team rounded the curve ahead, Ray's team decided to take a shortcut across the cove to intercept them. Before Ray could react, the dogs had loped onto dangerously thin ice.

"As this happened, Moses' team disappeared around another headland," Ray said. "We were in big trouble."

The color of the ice under the sled went from gray to almost black. A traveling wave of soft ice formed ahead of the sled runners.

Ray frantically called the mushing command to move forward. "*Hike!* Come on! Run! Twilight, pull them!"

Even as he yelled, the ice bowed downward around them. Suddenly the rear of the sled broke through the ice. The sudden drag pulled the dogs to a stop. Ray leaped toward the shoreward side of the ice, knowing that his weight at the end of the sled would only make matters worse. The front edge of the sled runners remained precariously on top of the ice with the rear of the sled threatening to sink into the open hole. The dogs, being spread out, stayed on top of the bowed ice. Meanwhile, in his leap away from the sled Ray had broken through where he landed. Within seconds the frigid water soaked through his clothes.

"I desperately pounded at the ice with my elbows, breaking a path shoreward," Ray said. "I knew if I lost contact with the ice, the weight of my water-logged clothes would drag me under. Only pure, fear-driven adrenalin kept me moving."

Finally, his foot touched bottom. As he staggered out of the water, Moses' team reappeared around the far headland. Moses had returned to check on

Ray. Ray's dogs surged toward the oncoming team, dragging the partially submerged sled back onto firmer ice.

After getting the teams straightened out, they headed immediately back to the village with Ray running behind his team, holding onto the sled's handlebars. His wet clothes were quickly solidifying into ice. Ray made it back home before becoming completely hypothermic. It had been a close call. Every year they heard of accidents where people had not been so lucky.

Later in the season, Ray harnessed his team to reach bands of migrating caribou moving south of Wainwright toward the Brooks Range. He went alone, since most other hunters had already filled their ice cellars with caribou meat. With school in session, he had only the weekends to hunt. As he traveled, he happened upon a young caribou standing on a low rise several hundred yards ahead. After setting the sled anchor, Ray began to stalk the caribou. It wandered over the top of the rise and out of sight. Ray followed it, but then heard the dogs barking wildly. The caribou had circled back around behind him and now stood directly between Ray and the team. The dogs were beside themselves. In their lunging and eager excitement, the sled anchor worked its way loose. When the anchor finally lost its grip on the ice, the team took off, chasing the fleeing caribou. Ray made a desperate dive to grab the handlebars, but it was too late.

"I watched the mad race over the bleached terrain, until they diminished into a speck and were lost from sight," Ray remembered.

He was twenty miles from the village and had no food or means of making a fire. He would not be missed for another day. However, he was well dressed and had a gun and a knife. He also knew how to build a makeshift snow shelter. He had two choices. He could walk back home or try to follow the team. Ray knew of Iñupiat in similar circumstances that had accepted the reality of the situation and walked home. A tangled team would likely chew its way free and find its way back to the village. Still, some would likely die of injuries or be run down by wolves.

Chances were slim that Ray would find his team on foot. He had once found a stiff body of a lost husky. It had died of starvation, its skin stretched tight over a frame of bones. He refused to think of the same fate falling to his own dogs. Ray headed toward the horizon where he had last seen the runaway team. After four hours of walking, with no sign of them, Ray wondered if he'd made the right decision. He stopped to reconsider his plan.

Then a faint sound reached his ears. He hurried on and the sound became a far-off howling. Soon a dark dot materialized in the distance.

"Thanking the God who watches over fools, I had found my dogs, eventually seeing the mugs of eleven grinning huskies," Ray said. "My salvation was a bull caribou—still living—beneath a tangled mass of dogs. It had been shot in the foreleg and somehow escaped the Iñupiat hunters. The huskies had given up on the unwounded caribou and instead run this one to the ground. I quickly ended its torment."

He butchered the caribou, eating bits of tallow and meat while it was still warm. When his hands became numb from the cold, he thrust them into the still-warm cavity of the caribou. Just as he finished lashing the meat and skin to the sled he looked up to see a sight that is forever etched in his memory.

> Advancing over the horizon was a moving sea of brown bodies supporting a forest of antlers. It was the main body of the migration. There were literally thousands of them stretching out of sight into the distance. I was watching the last of North America's great game herds passing in review. They were like a living river, a tide moving over the landscape.

Traveling with a partner had its advantages; one being that a hunter could stay with the dog teams while the second hunter stalked the quarry. One day Glen Shoudla and Ray drove their teams out to a distant lead on the sea ice to go seal hunting. Glen shot the first seal. When they spotted another seal in the water, it was Ray's turn.

The hole was a few hundred yards from where they parked the dogs. Ray used his tuuq to test the ice and ducked behind piles of rough ice to hide from the seal. He had walked about a hundred yards when he heard the dogs barking. Ray looked back and saw Glen waving his arms. Ray figured the dogs had been fighting and Glen was breaking it up. The dogs were quiet again, so he continued to stalk the seal.

Ray raised his rifle, aimed, and fired a shot. Success!

What Ray did not hear at the same time that he fired his own gun was the report of a second rifle.

While Ray had been sneaking around the piles of ice, he had unknowingly caught the attention of a polar bear. The bear arose to look around, which set the dogs to barking. Glen waved his arms trying to get Ray's attention.

As Ray continued walking toward the seal, the bear followed him. Glen grabbed his gun and began running toward the bear. The distracted bear turned toward Glen, so he knelt and waited until it came within thirty yards before killing it with a single shot.

"As I headed back I saw Glen bent over a yellowish white blob on the ice," Ray said, "He was skinning out the bear, a young adult male with a beautiful hide. It was Glen's first polar bear and I was really happy for him. The bear was likely curious when it saw me. It certainly could have quickly run me down had it wanted to."

On a November evening in 1963, two years after Ray and Barbara began teaching in Wainwright, Alva Nasholalook, a village elder knocked on their door. He often stopped in for tea and enjoyed sharing his stories of the old days. He patiently answered the Bane's endless questions about Iñupiaq life and customs. On this particular evening though, he was uncharacteristically solemn.

> He informed us that there had been a gathering of the village elders to talk about us. It seemed we did not fit the normal mold of teachers. We behaved more like Eskimos than Whites. The elders decided that something had to be done to resolve this apparent contradiction. We had to become Eskimo.

The elders had decided that to become true Eskimos, they needed Eskimo names. The Iñupiaq name given to a child at birth is often taken from someone who had recently died or an ancestor with a strong spirit.

"Names are passed from one individual to another over countless generations," Ray explained. "Each name carries with it the spiritual blessings and strength of all who have previously possessed it."

The elders had decided that Barbara's name should be Ekalook. The late Ekalook was known for her love of children. Ray's name was to be Otoiyuq, an elder who had been a respected hunter and skilled dog team driver.

"These names would instill in us the power and spirit of the previous holders and help to guide and protect us," Ray said.

From then on in the village, Ray and Barbara were referred to by their Iñupiaq names.

"It seemed that everyone in the village knew of the granting of our spirit names, even before we did," Ray said. The following day nearly every adult they encountered made a point of calling them by their Iñupiaq names.

Wainwright elder, Alva Nashoalak, dancing at a traditional village ceremony. Alva served as the "name uncle" for the designation of Eskimo spirit names for Ray and Barbara. He instructed them in the history and spiritual significance of their new names. (Bane Collection)

"One day I happened to be walking through the community on an errand and saw an elderly Iñupiaq man sitting on the side of his hut, smoking a pipe," Ray said. "He called out 'Hello aapaga!' waving to me." On two other occasions, the man greeted Ray in this manner.

When Ray asked Alva about this, Alva explained, "Oh, he is just saying hello to his father (aapaga). Old Otoiyuk was his father. Now you have his name (spirit). He's just saying hello to his father."

Alva became their "name uncle," serving as their guide and teacher. An Iñupiaq name upholds the memory of all who have ever held it, so that when Ray or Barbara traveled to another village, the relatives of anyone with their names were expected to offer them family-like hospitality.

Ray and Barbara were profoundly moved by the honor of being bestowed their Iñupiaq names. During their second year teaching in Wainwright, the Banes were offered an assignment away from their "hardship" tour. They emphatically declined the transfer.

Life was not perfect in the village. Changes were pressing upon the social fabric of the Iñupiaq people. New technologies were quickly overtaking the many tasks that were once the domain of traditional subsistence skills and culture.

Ray and Barbara felt privileged to be able to see and experience an ancient way of life still largely intact before the encroachment of the modern world. Yet the roar of outboard motors and a new invention called a "Skidoo" was beginning to drown out the strong but quiet voices of the elders. At least for now, Ekalook and Otoiyuq wanted to stick around and listen.

6

— ⋅⊹⋅ —

ekak

Ray heard the walrus before he saw them, low deep grunts resounding across the blue and gray landscape of water and floating sea ice. He sat in David Panik's umiak, part of a five-man hunting crew in a party of two skin boats. Moving slowly through the water, they constantly surveyed their position, alert to the possibility of being crushed or cut off from shore by the restless floes of ice. Then in the distance, they saw large dark objects resting on a pan of ice. Just one hundred yards away, a floe was nearly smothered by the formless mounds of sleeping walrus.

"Thermoses of hot tea and snacks appeared. All the while, the ice pans drifted slowly along, constantly shifting position, softly bumping one another and occasionally grinding together with a soft whisper," Ray remembered. The hunters talked in normal tones, even though the walrus were within earshot.

"Walrus get scared if they hear whispering," Ekak told Ray. "Better to talk."

Ekak, the most elderly of the crew, stood at the bow of the umiak facing the walrus. He spoke to the walrus in Iñupiaq. He thanked them for giving themselves up to help with what the people needed to live. After Ekak was seated, the two boats separated and moved slowly toward the massive hulks lying on the ice.

"I was amazed that the walrus allowed us to get so close before becoming alarmed," Ray said. "They lay in a close-packed pile with their heads resting on the body of other walrus. We were less than twenty yards before they began to show signs of alarm."

Then it began. The men ran to the front of the boat up onto the ice and launched themselves out of the umiak, scrambling to kill the animals before they could slide off the pan. The hunters shot at point blank range into their thick necks as the walrus began stampeding into the water. The walrus called out in high-pitched grunts as they threw themselves into the icy ocean. Blood from those that had been shot stained the ice crimson. It was over nearly as quickly as it began. Within minutes, five walrus lay dead on the pan.

Now the real work began. An adult bull walrus can weight over 3,000 pounds; females average around 2,000. Three of the walrus were butchered on site. Two others were inflated with air using a tire pump. A slit was cut near the naval of the walrus; the air was pumped in, and then plugged with a hand-carved wooden cork. The distended bodies were then lashed to the sides of the boat, serving as outriggers to keep the heavily-laden umiak afloat.

Walrus meat was the mainstay for feeding the dog teams in Wainwright, and a dog team was parked outside nearly every household. Each husky required almost the same amount of food as a human adult. That ranged from less than half a pound of meat a day in the summer, when the work load was light, to as much as six pounds in the winter when the teams were working. Over a year, this averaged out to a daily ration of about three pounds of meat per dog or close to 1,100 pounds per year. A team of seven dogs, like Ray and Barbara's team, consumed roughly 7,700 pounds of food each year.

Ray had joined the walrus hunt to feed his team. As he watched Ekak speak to the walrus in the old way, he was struck again by the rituals and way of life that were so closely tied to the land and sea. So much was changing in the Arctic in the 1960s. Ekak embodied a wealth of stored wisdom—passed from one generation to the next—the value of which seemed immeasurable. The depth and extent of that knowledge were an endless fascination to Ray. Ekak had no formal education yet he was an accomplished scholar of traditional Eskimo skills and Ray said that his insights and intelligence qualified him as a genius.

Cultural change came in many forms and one of the most profound impacts was the advent of the snowmachine. Sled dogs were woven into the fabric of the subsistence way of life. Dogs were self-reproducing and could be fed from the land. Sleds, harnesses, and traces could all be made from

Wainwright elder, Ekak, at fish camp on the Kuk River, 1966. (Bane Collection)

materials taken from the environment. The dogs themselves were a source of hides that could be used to make winter clothing.

Before the introduction of snowmachines, Iñupiat boys went through a period of apprenticeship as they became hunters and trappers. A boy would accompany a father, grandfather, or uncle and together they traveled with a sled pulled by a dog team. Since dog team travel is relatively quiet, the two had the time and the silence of the miles to communicate. The elder hunter instructed the younger in the skills of winter travel, in locating and harvesting game, and in understanding the landscape. The dogs themselves were a tool to interpret the environment.

"When a dog's head was up, you knew he was scenting something nearby. The ice crystals in the air and the wind carried the scent," Ray explained. "When a dog's head was down, he was sniffing the ground and you knew the scent was older and farther away."

Sled dogs slept exposed to the weather in the most extreme conditions and they seemed to feel barometric pressure changes; they often set up a chorus of howling just before a shift in the weather. After days of driving wind and snow, it was a welcome sound to hear the dogs predict the coming end to the storm. Likewise, they often announced the news before a new weather front arrived on the scene.

Drivers, too, needed special skills in handling their teams.

"Every dog has its own unique personality and particular strengths and weaknesses. An experienced musher must be a dog psychologist. The driver must be able to pair up dogs that work well together and avoid canine personality conflicts that can demoralize a team or lead to serious fighting and injuries," Ray said.

Although a few snowmachines had passed through Wainwright, no one in the village owned a snowmachine until 1964. With snowmachines, hunters and trappers could now reach and harvest game before those driving the slower dog teams. Although snowmachines broke down and needed fuel and parts, they didn't need to be fed through the summer months.

I was sorry to see them come in, because I knew the era of traditional dog teams was ending. To effectively compete for scarce resources they had to abandon their dogs and adopt this new technology. Once this occurred, the wealth of information and skills related to the use of dog teams, pack dogs and foot travel would rapidly decay. You don't go from dogs to snow ma-chines without having a great deal of impact and adjustments to the culture.

The noise of the machines alone cut off the communication of boys and elders as they traveled the trail together.

Although these cultural changes happened quickly, dog team races con-tinued as a favorite village activity. Barbara was fine-tuning her driving skills and was a contender for the village trophy that year. Twilight had grown into a fine lead-dog and, unlike many other mushers, Barbara had no need for a whip. The Bane dogs needed nothing more than verbal encour-agement to get the job done.

Ray and Barbara also made friends with a newcomer to the village, Richard (Dick) Nelson. He first came to Alaska in 1961, as a field assistant for a research project on Kodiak Island. He returned in 1963 to work with archaeologists in the Aleutian chain. In 1964, he met Ray and Barbara in Wainwright where he had come to continue his graduate work in cultural anthropology with the University of Wisconsin. Nelson would eventually author several books about the Arctic and the environment. Nelson and Ray became good friends and also fierce sparring partners in table hockey, and sometimes in politics and social ideologies.

"Barbara and I had been largely cut off from the political and social events occurring in the broader world for almost six years. We were children of the 1950s with a decidedly conservative perspective," Ray said. "Dick, on the other hand, had seen and participated in the protest against the Vietnam War that was sweeping college campuses across the nation."

Barbara liked to say of those years, "We missed the Twist!"

Whatever their differences, Ray and Nelson enjoyed venting on any num-ber of issues and both appreciated the tremendous opportunity they had been afforded as they lived and worked in Wainwright—a living portal into a vanishing way of life.

Those late night conversations with Nelson whetted Ray's deepening de-sire to more fully understand the interaction of human culture with the Arctic environment. As the Bane's three years in Wainwright came to a close, Ray decided to continue his education. He wanted to learn more about the Native cultures that both fascinated and at times frustrated him. With

Nelson's encouragement, Ray applied for and was accepted into a graduate program at the University of Wisconsin in Madison for the following year.

Meanwhile some 3,600 miles from Wainwright, on September 3, 1964 in Washington D.C., President Lyndon B. Johnson signed into law the Wilderness Act, legislation that would have a profound impact on Alaska's future and on the course of Ray and Barbara's lives. The Act defined wilderness specifically as:

> A wilderness, in contrast with those areas where man and his own works dominate the landscape, is hereby recognized as an area where the earth and its community of life are untrammeled by man, where man himself is a visitor who does not remain.

The legislation set aside 9.1 million acres of land and offered a mechanism to designate future lands for federal protection. It was a bold and controversial concept for the federal government to set aside tracts of land to remain untouched by human development. When signing the legislation, President Johnson made the following statement: "If future generations are to remember us with gratitude rather than contempt, we must leave them a glimpse of the world as it was in the beginning, not just after we got through with it."

Bold and controversial in Washington, perhaps, but in Ekak's world, the value of wilderness was common sense that needed no legislation or explanation. Land ownership or laying claim to it, was a foreign notion to most Natives of Alaska. The people belonged to the land, not the other way around.

Finally the village women's championship race day arrived. The dog-sled race began at the southwest end of the Kuk Lagoon and extended up river for fifteen miles to a designated turnaround point. The entire village turned out to watch, gathering on the bluff overlooking the lagoon. Fourteen teams lined up to compete for the trophy. The dog teams were strung out between two oil drums, a line that marked both the starting and the finish line.

Barbara sat in a small blue sled wearing a fur parka sewn by Mattie Bodfish, a dear friend and village matriarch. Eager to go, seven of the Bane's fastest dogs barked and lunged in their traces. As team leader, Twilight looked back at Barbara, eagerly waiting for direction.

"Ready! Set!" Someone fired a gun and the dogs were off. Once under-way, the only sounds were the voices of the drivers and the swish of the sled's runners on the snow. On the bluff, spectators cheered. Twilight knew to keep clear of the other teams to avoid getting tangled. Somehow, as they headed toward the turnaround point, the sled managed to overturn, dragging Barbara, who sat in the basket of the sled. In their enthusiasm the dogs hardly noticed. It wasn't until Barbara called out to Twilight to "Whoa!" that the team stopped long enough for Barbara to climb out and upright the sled.

Then they were off again. Making the turn at the end of the fifteen-mile course was the biggest challenge of the race as teams drew closer together to circle the 55-gallon drum. The turn was the place for crashes, overturned sleds, and dog fights. Barbara played the field right, not getting too close, but losing too much ground. Once around the barrel she yelled to Twilight, "Hike! Hike!"

Slowly the distance closed between her team and the one team in front of her. Villagers cheered as both dog teams strained against their harness-es, running neck and neck toward the finish. The crowd went wild as the two teams flew nearly simultaneously across the line. What a race! But who had won?

Race judges conferred and spectators grew hushed. Finally someone from the crowd yelled, "Who won?"

After a pause, *"Barbara!"* was the response.

The entire village poured off the bluff, cheering for their new village champion. Surrounding Barbara with good wishes, they could not have been happier for Ekalook.

During Ray's graduate work, he returned to Wainwright the summer of 1965, to spend three months studying the way the Eskimos used the land. This included an extended stay with Ekak at the mouth of the Kittik River. Ekak's son used the family umiak to carry their supplies to their campsite, some fifty miles inland from the village. Ray would stay for three weeks as part of his research. Ekak would remain until the river froze in September, storing up a supply of caribou meat and fish. Here Ray learned and recorded some of the old ways of the people.

"Ekak taught by example," Ray remembered. "I learned how to make a serviceable knife from the rib of a caribou, make arrow and spearheads from antler and bone, and fishhooks from animal teeth. (I learned) how to make a fire using a bow drill and how to prepare and eat virtually every part of a caribou and other wildlife."

Ekak had an uncanny ability to find animals as they hunted.

"See tulagak?" Ekak pointed to the raven on the horizon. "When he dips his wing, he is showing where to find caribou."

A few moments later, the raven dipped its wing as it flew over a low rise, some 400 yards away from camp. Twenty minutes later four fat caribou appeared grazing peacefully on the ridgeline.

"There," Ekak said. "Tulagak wants us to shoot the caribou so he can eat what we leave. Go do it."

Ray did as he was told.

As they butchered the caribou, Ekak took pains to leave bits of meat to reward the raven for his help.

Together, Ekak and Ray carved net floats from driftwood and made weights from dense animal bones. They harvested caribou for the meat and preserved the pelts that would later be fashioned into parkas, boots, and sleeping mats. They pulled sheets of sinew from between layers of meat and dried them; these would later become tough thread for sewing. They were never idle as they gathered the resources of the tundra and the river.

One day, rain confined them to their tent. As usual, Ekak remained busy carving net weights, repairing clothing, and doing other small chores. Ray worked on research notes. Anxious to maximize the time he had with Ekak, Ray began to question him about the old ways of winter subsistence activities: building dog sleds, traveling, camping, and trapping. Ekak sat quietly, responding only briefly to Ray's inquiries.

Finally with a hint of reproach in his voice, Ekak told Ray that if he wanted to learn more about winter then he ought to come back in the winter. It was now summer.

In effect, Ekak was telling Ray to stay focused and not become distracted by trying to learn about things out of their natural context.

"It was an important lesson in the traditional Eskimo thought process," Ray remembered.

It was also an important lesson in life, being present to the moment.

One evening, as they contentedly sipped hot tea, Ekak recounted how he had traveled overland with his family in the fall months while hunting caribou. They would build shelters made of willow frames covered with sod. Ray wondered about this and asked if Ekak would help him build just such a shelter.

"Ekak was pleased. He said that when the weather turned cold he could move into the sod hut, which would be much warmer than the canvas tent (we were using)," Ray said.

So they set about the project, choosing a place near the tent site but away from where snow would drift in the winter. They marked a five-by-eight-foot oval floor plan. Using a hoe-like tool called an ivroon, they cut slabs of sod from the tundra and arranged them in overlapping rows until the willow frame of the hut was covered. They left an opening for an entryway and covered it with a caribou hide. A small smoke hole at the top of the structure provided a vent for smoke. Before they could use the shelter, Ekak closed the vent and door and set a fire inside, piling on green branches, leaves, and grass. The smoke would get rid of any resident insects inside the hut. They then lined the floor with a springy mat of young willows and coarse tundra grass. They topped this with caribou hides to give it the finishing touches. Ekak was satisfied with the shelter and said he might use it for several upcoming seasons as a base camp.

Ray practicing skills taught by Ekak in building a traditional sod igloo. Built of materials from the native tundra, the small igloo served as a winter shelter for Ekak and other local hunters and trappers. (Bane Collection)

Ekak preserving meat in a caribou stomach. Pickling meat in a caribou stomach with partially digested vegetable matter was considered an Iñupiaq delicacy. Uncooked meat was a common staple. (Bane Collection)

All too soon, their time together came to an end. Ray packed up his notebooks, realizing he had only scratched the surface of what Ekak had to share. As the time approached for him to leave, Ray wondered if he would ever see his old friend again. Now that he and Barbara were back in Wisconsin, who knew what the future held? Once he finished the graduate work, the prescribed path would likely mean life in a university town as a professor. Surely they would be back to visit the Arctic someday but by then Ekak and many of the elders would likely be gone.

He thought back about the last lap around the Kuk Lagoon that he and Barbara had run with the dogs before boarding the plane to leave Wainwright for Wisconsin. The entire village had come to see them off. He and Barbara had stopped at the far side of the lagoon and looked at the crowd waiting to say their goodbyes.

"Why don't we just keep going and forget about leaving," Barbara said.

It was tempting. They loved the people and the way of life that the villagers had shared with them. Yet in spite of their misgivings, they drove the dogs back and boarded the waiting plane.

7

—⊹⊹—

learning to fly

The trouble with Wisconsin is that it wasn't Alaska.

Ray and Barbara had divested themselves of all their sled dogs except Twilight and Big Boy. On their drive to the "Lower 48," as the contiguous Unites States is called by Alaskans, the dogs in the car drew almost as much attention as the sled lashed to the top of the Chevy station wagon. For six years now, the Banes had traveled primarily by dog team, skin-covered umiaks, and on foot. For the first few days on the road, the sheer speed and intensity of motorized traffic took their breath away.

On arriving in Madison, they bought a three-acre property with a small house in a rural area well outside city limits—for the kingly sum of $5,500. The open pastures and farmland helped them feel less confined than city living. Still they felt hemmed in by the presence of fences and "No Trespassing" signs. In Alaska they had traveled hundreds of miles by boat and dog team with only natural obstacles to limit their movements.

Shortly after arriving, Barbara took a job as a teacher and they bought a third husky.

Attending graduate anthropology courses at the University of Wisconsin and interacting with other graduate students gave Ray a greater appreciation of how cultures mold thought processes and become lenses through which people see and evaluate the world around them.

"I had the chance to know individuals who had lived with and studied unique cultures from the far reaches of our world. They opened my eyes, ears, and mind to the rich diversity of cultures and the never-ending effort to understand them. There is no question in my mind that the experience greatly enriched my life and my ability to better appreciate and understand the Native cultures that Barbara and I worked with during our time in Alaska, and beyond," Ray remembered.

Still, they missed the sense of unfettered freedom. When winter set in, Ray hooked the three dogs to a sled and mushed them from a distant campus parking area to school across frozen Lake Mendota, tethering them under a tree outside the Social Science Building. On winter weekends they took the three-husky team to the Nicolet National Forest in northern Wisconsin to drive the dogs and camp.

During their second summer, Ray returned to Wainwright for his research project. These activities helped take the edge off their increasing homesickness for Alaska. Even so, upon his return from Wainwright and especially the time with Ekak, Ray says he knew he was "addicted" to Alaska, especially to life in the Bush.

> The hardest adjustment I was forced to make was to fit into a "normal life" after spending five years freely roaming around the wilds of Alaska. Entire days enclosed in offices and classrooms virtually attached to a small desk made me feel claustrophobic. Driving (by car) each day between our home and the campus consumed more time and energy. I vividly recall standing on a curbside near the Social Studies Building on campus waiting for a bus to take me to a parking lot and being engulfed in a cloud of exhaust as cars, buses, and trucks passed by. In the villages I could step out the door of the school and hook up our dog team for a couple of hours of exercise. On weekends and holidays I would be out with other village men hunting and traveling often sleeping overnight in snow block shelters. In the summers I spent more time sleeping under an upturned umiak than I did in a bed at home. I became increasingly aware that those days of freedom and adventure in Alaska would become rare as I moved into the role of a scholar and, eventually, an instructor in my chosen field. I was simply having a hard time becoming "housebroken" again.

It was late winter 1967 when Ray turned to Barbara and said, "Let's go back to Alaska."

"Okay," she replied. She had one a condition, however. "I want you to learn to fly. We can buy an airplane. I want to see more of Alaska than just the village where we live."

Ray was hesitant. Flying aircraft in Alaska was no casual affair. It required the expertise not only of flying a small plane, but also knowledge of severe weather and extreme topography. Like many in Alaska, Ray had fantasized about being a Bush pilot but wasn't sure he could master the necessary skills.

A couple of weeks after their discussion, Barbara took Ray to the local county fair. One of the most popular activities was the dime-per-pound airplane rides offered by Wendell Bronkow, a local pilot who offered both charter flights and instruction. Barbara presented Ray with a ticket. She had already prearranged for Ray to sit in the left pilot's seat of the airplane.

"The plane had dual controls, so Wendell could fly it from the right side," Ray remembered. "We took off, and then Wendell told me to hold the controls, just to get a little feel for flying. In short order he had taken his hands off the controls and was simply directing how to fly the plane. When we landed, he handed me a flight log book and told me that I had just taken my first lesson in flying."

Ray started formal training the following week and within five days, he took his first solo flight.

That spring of 1967, they sold their home and used the money to buy a used Cessna 170, a single engine, four-person aircraft. Its 145-horsepower engine had a reputation for dependability and low gas consumption. Ray's first long cross-country trip was to meet Barbara in West Virginia where they visited family and friends before departing back to Alaska.

> A thickening industrial haze smudged the sky as I came nearer the Ohio Valley until visibility was perhaps two miles. I had to fly low and search around a bit to find the small Ohio County Airport perched on the top of a hill north of Wheeling. The acrid smell of factory smoke was thick inside the plane. I could feel the thermals rising from the smokestacks of the mills as I passed over them. The experience erased any thoughts I may have had about someday returning to live in the area.

Back in West Virginia, Ray and Barbara answered countless questions about the exotic lives they were living in the north.

"Do Alaska Eskimos really live in igloos?

Yes, but not domed snow houses, they explained. The word "iglu" simply meant house in Iñupiaq. Eskimos sometimes used snow block shelters as temporary camps when they hunted. These could be built quickly as a place to stay during sudden storms. They did build sod igloos for long-term occupancy. Sod houses were still commonly used into the early 1960s.

"Is there any season besides winter in Alaska?"

Yes. Summers are brief, however, and intense with perpetual daylight.

"Is it always dark in the winter?"

They explained how, along the Arctic Coast, the sun sets in mid-November and doesn't rise again in until mid-January. However, even then the sky brightens for a few hours at mid-day, unless there is heavy cloud cover.

One question Ray was often asked was, "Do the Eskimos really swap wives?" Ray was careful to answer this in the appropriate cultural context.

The question obviously attracted a considerable amount of notoriety. I once asked Fred Ipalook, an elementary school teacher in Barrow, if this custom was practiced in the "old days" among the Eskimos. Fred told me that, yes, it was, however it was not the way many Whites/non-Natives seemed to believe. Wives often accompanied their husbands on hunting and fishing trips dividing the chores of camp life and helping in the harvesting of resources. If a man's wife was unable to travel due to pregnancy, health, need to care for small children, or other reasons a male friend's or relative's wife might take her place. This custom could extend to visiting travelers. It should be noted that anyone who took advantage of this favor was expected to reciprocate in kind. The custom was formally recognized in the Eskimo culture. Two men who slept with the same woman were considered to be "related" by the act and expected to help each other and the woman when needed. Children resulting from such unions were told who may have been their biological father and considered themselves to be members of both households. Needless to say, the arrival of Christian missionaries resulted in the overt discouragement of this practice.

Ray explained that as times change so do customs and traditions. "Cooperation and sharing formed the central core of traditional Native life," he said. "Northern Alaska is truly 'hungry country' and prior to modern times it took the entire village to successfully adapt to its hard realities and severe challenges."

He also noted that prior to the early twentieth century women often had minimal control over their personal lives. As it was, Ray said, "We were seeing the tail end of many 'old ways' when we first came to Alaska in 1960."

In August, with Twilight in the back seat, Ray and Barbara pointed their little airplane north. Flying more than 3,000 miles, they were once again leaving civilization behind and entering wild country. The closer they got to Alaska, the more untouched the landscape grew, and the wider their spirits expanded.

Ray and Barbara had been hired to teach in Huslia. The village lies some 400 miles due south of Wainwright and 150 miles east of the western coast of Alaska, a location that puts the village squarely in Alaska's interior. Ray and Barbara knew winters would be harsh with temperatures plunging at times to sixty and seventy degrees below zero. Summers would be brief but equally intense, with temperatures soaring at times into the nineties. They looked forward to this new adventure in a new place.

As they approached the Alaska border in their airplane, they began to get reports of bad weather around Fairbanks. Torrential rains that lasted for days had spilled over the banks of the Chena and Little Chena rivers. Water poured into downtown Fairbanks and outlying regions driving residents to their rooftops. The worst flood in Fairbank's history eventually displaced nearly 7,000 people from their homes. Roads, bridges, and rail lines washed away. Many parked airplanes had been caught up in the floodwaters. Ray and Barbara stopped and spent three days in Big Delta, a United States Air Force base, waiting for the rain to subside. When it did, they flew over the devastation of Fairbanks and nearby Nenana. Warehouses along the Nenana River's waterfront were submerged and Ray and Barbara wondered

Ray learned to fly in Wisconsin. This was their second plane, a Citabria, which could be flown using wheels, skis, or floats. (Bane Collection)

about their year's supply of food they had ordered in advance to be carried via river barge out of Nenana.

"I later learned that our entire winter supply of food had been destroyed," Ray said. They would have to start from scratch, resupplying what they would need for the coming school year in the Bush.

En route to Huslia, they landed in Galena, a small community along the Yukon River. They planned to park the airplane for a few days and catch a commercial flight to Anchorage to attend teacher meetings before the school year began. The control tower in Galena contacted Ray and asked if he would be willing to fly to Huslia to check on an overdue aircraft. Ray and Barbara would quickly learn the important role of their airplane in the villages where they taught. Anyone in a village with an airplane automatically became a taxi for medical emergencies and search and rescue operations.

Ray was glad to volunteer in looking for the missing pilot. As he flew over the landscape he was riveted by this new place, so different from the Arctic coastline of Wainwright.

Ray landed his plane on the upper Noatak River to visit with government officials studying the region for possible national park status. Ray was eventually hired by the National Park Service to assist in the planning of new parklands in the northern region of Alaska. (Bane Collection)

The landscape seemed absolutely bountiful from the air. The presence of trees, thick brush, tall marsh grass and abundance of lakes and streams seemed to speak of vibrant life, particularly when compared to the sparse vegetation of the high arctic. Occasional glimpses of moose grazing on aquatic plants in shallow lakes and marshes reinforced this impression. Surely this was an environmentally rich region.

Like much of Alaska, however, the perception of abundance is misleading. Caribou, like salmon and most birdlife, congregate and move during brief and intense seasons of migration. For the rest of the year, however, wildlife is often thinly scattered over vast tracts of wild untouched lands.

"Overall the region is truly hungry country," Ray reflected. "The interior taiga—marked by black spruce, willows, and alders—forms almost impenetrable thickets in boggy marshlands. Permafrost lurks under much of the poorly drained flats."

When Ray landed in Huslia, several residents walked out to see who had flown into their village. They directed Ray to the church spire rising above the other buildings. It turned out the missing pilot was paying the missionaries a visit and had lost track of time. The pilot apologized that anyone had come looking for him. Ray was glad for the happy outcome of his search and welcomed the opportunity to scout out their new village home.

The people he met in the village were pleased to learn that the new teachers in town had an airplane. The Native people of the area were Koyukon, a distinctly different cultural group from the coastal Eskimos of the North Slope. Following his studies in anthropology, Ray's journals at times took on a more scholarly tone. Along with his natural curiosity, Ray's training had taught him to observe as a researcher and scientist.

The (Koyukon) speak an Athabaskan dialect and share cultural traits with other Native American Athabaskan groups (Navaho and Apache) as far south as the American southwest. They are traditionally matrilineal. They were historically known for being fierce warriors who wiped out an early Russian trading post below the junction of the Koyukuk and Yukon Rivers. However, they are an opportunistic people and substantially adapted their culture to take advantage of new possibilities presented by the arrival of non-Natives in the form of traders, prospectors, missionaries, teachers, medical professionals and others, even adopting the surnames of some of the newly arrived gussaks (white men).

Not long after Ray and Barbara settled into their new community, there was a knock at their door. Fred Bifelt, the school maintenance man stood solemnly before them.

"Hi Fred, come on in," Ray said.

Fred shook his head. "Old George is dying," he said matter-of-factly.

Ray wasn't sure what Fred was getting at—did he need Ray to fly the elder to the hospital in Tanana? It was already dark, so a flight would have to wait until the first light of morning.

Again Fred said, "Old George is dying."

Ray paused. "Do you want us to go with you, Fred?"

Fred nodded. "Yes. Come."

Ray and Barbara followed Fred along the darkened road to a cabin on the far side of the village. People stood outside smoking and sipping cups of hot coffee. They invited Ray and Barbara to go inside. The single-room cabin was crammed with people lining the walls and sitting on the rough plank floor. Men and women called out greetings and invited Ray and Barbara to join them.

"Everyone seemed festive," Ray remembered. "In the back corner of the room was a small bed surrounded by some village ladies. An ancient man with mahogany skin lay covered by blankets with only his head showing. He was obviously in the final stages of departing the world of the living."

Huge pots of strong coffee percolated on the wood-burning stove. Handmade wooden planters heaped full of boiled meat, sourdough bread, and fried sweet bread covered a small kitchen table. Ray and Barbara spent the evening snacking, drinking coffee and tea, and listening to the stories about the exploits of Old George. He had been a renowned hunter, trapper, and provider. Of his many achievements, he was father to a family of leaders including world champion dog team racer, George Attla, Jr.

To the Koyukon, death was a community affair with the entire village gathering to see the person off to the spirit world.

"It was (also) considered "huklnii" (bad luck) to be alone when the spirit of the recently departed person was abroad," Ray explained.

By morning, Old George was gone. School was dismissed so that everyone could attend the funeral. People from surrounding villages chartered flights into Huslia to pay their respects.

The Koyukon had two ceremonies to mark the passing of a loved one; one was the burial and the second was a memorial potlatch, held one year following the death—an event that could last as long as two or three days, especially for someone of Old George's stature.

The year between the funeral and the potlatch was used to collect animal furs, sew skin clothing, create items decorated in intricate patterns of bead-work, and collect the tools, firearms, and other personal items belonging to the one who had passed. All this and more were distributed to friends, relatives, and those who attended the final potlatch.

In the instance of Old George's death, Ray and Barbara were privileged to be invited to participate in an important ritual of the community. This time, their airplane had not been needed.

At other times however, the knock on the door was far different. Rose Ambrose, the village health aide stood at the door.

"Ray, we've got a very sick baby. She needs a doctor. Can you take her to Galena?"

Ray hurried to the plane and prepared it for flight while Rose and the family brought the baby to the airfield. It was growing dark and night would soon be settling in.

"Fortunately there was enough dim light to make my way across the lower Huslia Flats as I homed in on the Galena VOR radio signal," Ray said. "We were met by an ambulance and emergency medical specialist who whisked the patient to an infirmary. They stabilized the infant until (she) could be flown to Fairbanks the next day."

By then it was too dark to return, so Ray and Rose waited until daylight to return back to Huslia. It would be the first of nearly 100 emergency flights that Ray would pilot over the years.

Ray became acquainted with many of Alaska's well-known bush pilots over time including Bud Helmricks, Norm Yager, Paul Shanahan, Bill Fickus, Daryl Morris, Bill Hutchinson, Peter Merry, and others. He would eventually trade the Cessna 170 for a Citrabria on floats. With the change in aircraft, Ray no longer needed a designated paved or even dirt airstrip to land the airplane. Now, any one Alaska's three million lakes or 3,000 rivers could serve as a potential runway. He could use floats in the summer and skis in the winter on these waterways.

"Over the years I became a decent pilot, but I was never in the league of the really outstanding bush pilots . . . I knew my plane, and, more importantly, I believe I knew myself," Ray recalled. "It was like the difference between being a pretty fair fiddle player and a concert violinist. I still stubbed my toe a few times. Hell, I kinda mashed it a couple of times."

December 6, 1969, two years after learning to fly, remains a day seared in Ray's memory. He and a friend decided to go scouting for caribou in his Citabria and after taking off they headed for the Zane Mountains in the Dakli Pass region. The plan was to be back in a couple of hours. About 25 miles north of Huslia, they spotted caribou as they passed over the wind-polished lake. Ray decided to land on the north side of the lake. As he touched down on the ice, rather than decelerate, the plane picked up speed. The wind was blowing the wrong direction and they were heading straight toward a steep embankment. Ray quickly applied power to take off again.

"The plane pulled free of the ice for perhaps three seconds," Ray said. "Another twelve inches of altitude and we would have made it."

Time seemed to slow as Ray watched the crash unfold in surreal detail around him. As they hit the embankment, the plane's metal skis curled back and upward, impacting the main wing struts, ripping them away from the sides of the plane. The wings drooped but were held aloft by the thick mat of willows and alders. The windshield shattered and yet it seemed Ray could see the pieces of glass floating in front of him. The propeller stopped turning, its tips curled back like gnarled teeth. Suddenly all was quiet.

"Get out!" Ray shouted. They forced the plane doors open. Ray grabbed the survival kit from behind the rear seat and they scrambled to get away from the plane before it caught fire.

They waited in breathless anticipation. Ray's head was bleeding.

When the wreckage did not burst into flames, Ray went back, turned off the switches and cut the fuel feed. He then retrieved the rest of the survival gear, including sleeping bags, an ax, hand saw, insulated engine cover, and wing covers.

Ray had suffered a laceration to his head but he was able to stop the bleeding. Otherwise he and his passenger were okay. They set about building a shelter, making a fire, and settling down to do the hardest thing of survival—*waiting*. Even though he had filed a flight plan with the Federal Aviation

With a limited road system, most communities in Alaska are accessible only by boat or airplane. Ray and Barbara used their plane to explore wilderness regions and visit villages across much of northern Alaska. 1972 (Bane Collection)

Administration (FAA) flight service station in Galena, Ray assumed they would have to spend the night before anyone came looking for them.

> All light had deserted the sky when we heard a distant hum of an airplane engine to the south. Then we saw the flashing navigation lights heading in our direction. We quickly got the signal fire going, throwing on plenty of fuel. The plane honed in on the bonfire and dropped low as it approached the lake. It was Norm Yager's Cessna 185. Norm circled and made several low passes. We stood in the light of the fire and tried to show him we were okay . . . Norm made a long approach and touched down on the ice. 'Anyone want a ride home?' he called. Forty-five minutes later we were back in Huslia enjoying a hot meal and looking forward to sleeping in warm beds.

In the days following the crash, Ray, along with a party of village men, returned to the crash site by snowmachine and dismantled the wreckage, hauling it back to the village. He chartered a C-46 cargo plane and had the parts flown to Fairbanks. It never occurred to him not to get back in the cockpit, nor did Barbara have any reservations. She had been the one to encourage him to fly in the first place. She knew he would not be happy without his wings.

While his plane was being repaired, a process that would take six months, Ray poured his extra energy into their new dogs and read Hudson Stuck's classic, *Ten Thousand Miles With a Dog Team*. By the time he finished the book, an idea had begun to germinate in Ray's mind. He and Barbara were enjoying the view of thousands of miles of wilderness aloft from an airplane. What would it be like to view Alaska at ground level, crossing the miles by dog team?

Barbara's insistence that Ray learn to fly opened the door to Alaska for them both. Except for a handful of communities on the limited road system, most of the state's villages appear like disconnected dots on the map. Their only access is by airplane or boat. In over three decades of flying in Alaska, Ray logged more than 5,000 hours of flight time. Not only did it provide personal transportation and offer a line of support for those in need, it would come to play a crucial role in their later work as stewards for the places and as advocates for the people they had come to love.

8

hungry country

The arrival of white prospectors, trappers, and traders in the mid-to-late 19th Century impacted every aspect of life on the Koyukuk River. They brought with them guns and whiskey, trading both to the Native people, along with imported foods, cloth, metal tools, and new means to harvest animals and catch fish.

> *They were lusty men, and soon children of mixed heritage were common along the Koyukuk . . . Some early whites found a permanent home in the wilds of the northern Alaska interior, married Native ladies and raised their families. They were a restless breed and needed lots of space, both literally and figuratively. They merged into the existing social structure of the region. It changed them, and they changed it.*

Ray and Barbara were two of only six non-Native people living in the village of Huslia when they arrived in 1967. The myth and lore of Alaska has always held the notion of strong, independent frontier men and women who fended for themselves in the harsh realities of the North. The stories do not need exaggeration to be remarkable and compelling. Yet the extreme isolation of the north exacted its toll on the hardiest of souls. Anyone who has lived through the winters of Northern or Interior Alaska can attest to Ray's apt description: "The Arctic winter is a stern taskmaster. It tests every living thing, ruthlessly weeding out the weak and foolish and occasionally taking even the best that just happen to be in the wrong place at the wrong time. Nature is neither kind nor cruel. It simply does not care and it doesn't forgive."

Ray and Barbara saw the specter of isolation play out in nearly disastrous detail for a family who had chosen to live beyond even the small comforts of the remote village of Huslia. In the winters of 1968 and 1969, Ray wrote this account of the family's ordeal:

> There was a white man locally known as Blondie, who had married a village lady and moved to the upper reaches of the Huslia River to build a cabin where even the local Native men rarely ventured. Blondie was drawn to live beyond the limits of human settlements. He came to the Alaska bush seeking to restart his life as a modern day version of a mountain man. His (Native) wife was a hard worker from a family known for their skills of making a living off the land. She willingly followed her white husband off into the wilds and ultimately bore him fourteen children while living under conditions most American women—and men—would consider unthinkable. The family came to town two or three times a year to trade furs, pick up basic supplies and visit family . . . .
>
> In mid-May, 1968, the Simon family came to me and asked that I fly supplies and mail to Blondie and his wife, Amelia, at their homestead on

Ray and Barbara established a summer tent camp on this island of an unnamed lake in the Alatna Valley. They spent summer months based out of this camp, ranging out to hike, float, and explore the Brooks Range. (Bane Collection)

the upper Huslia River. They figured that the family would be running low on basics. The ice on the rivers was ready to break up, and boat travel would not be possible for at least a couple of weeks. It was a weekend, and I was getting tired of being cooped up in the village. I agreed. Franklin Simon, Amelia's brother, went along. We removed the right door of the Cessna. We divided up the supplies into canvas bags and loaded them so that Franklin could drop them as we flew over the camp. I secured him with a double safety harness. It was a little breezy, but it did not appreciably affect the flight characteristics of the plane. We followed the winding course of the Huslia River. If it hadn't been for Franklin I would never have seen the cabin.

"There!" Franklin shouted as we passed over a thick grove of white spruce.

I brought the plane around, circled a couple of more times to pick out landmarks and lined up for the first drop. I pulled half flaps to allow for slow flight and tried to visualize the trajectory arc of a falling object thrown from a plane moving at sixty miles per hour. We were at tree top level when I yelled, "Now!" and Franklin threw out the first bag. It took five more passes to complete the drop. We saw people running back and forth as the bags dropped around them. When they ran to one bag I made sure the next one was dropped in a different location. We circled a few times while they waved from the ground, and then we flew back to Huslia.

Later I learned that Amelia had been in labor when we flew over. Her water had burst and the process was well along when we began to bomb them with bags of supplies and mail. Everyone ran outside to retrieve the drop, leaving Amelia alone to bring another child into the world. In the end everything worked out. When they came into town a few weeks later we all had a good laugh about it . . . .

In the fall of 1968, Blondie and his family moved even further up the Huslia River and built a new cabin. On October 7, at the request of Amelia's parents, I flew to their new homestead and dropped mail and supplies. On December 14, I made another mail drop. I had no way of knowing that even as I made the second drop that Blondie was struggling through waist deep snow on snowshoes breaking trail for his dogs to reach Huslia. (Six days later) in the darkness of the evening of December 20th, we heard a commotion outside. People were running and yelling to one another. Fred Bifelt came to our door and told us that Blondie had just arrived in the village.

"He looks like he is dying," said Fred. I pulled on a parka and ran with him to a cabin where an emaciated and almost incoherent Blondie was sitting at a table grasping a cup of hot coffee. His cheekbones protruded sharply from the sides of his face, and his eyes were sunken in dark holes.

Blondie said that his rifle had been broken not long after freeze-up making it impossible for him to take a moose for their fall meat supply. They caught a few pike and ate whatever they could trap or snare, but it wasn't enough. The weather had been unusually bad with deep snow and extreme cold. Finally, the family had used up their food supplies and was forced to eat whatever could be made edible. He had hoped someone would come up from the village on a snowmachine to visit, but no one came. Blondie said that he wasn't sure all of them would make it before help could reach them.

That night villagers put together bags of emergency rations for me to drop to the stranded family. I removed the right side door from the Cessna 170 and had Franklin Simon go along to throw out the bags. The weather was a bit marginal. Flying without a door was brutally cold. We followed the white squiggly line of the Huslia River staying low so as not to miss the cabin.

"There it is!" cried Franklin.

I did a tight turn and came back around virtually skimming the tops of the trees lining the river. We saw smoke coming out of the cabin chimney. As we came around again three figures came outside and stood beside the cabin. More followed.

"Get ready," I told Franklin. He hefted a bag to the door opening while I set up a descending approach to a snow-covered marsh behind the cabin. "Now!" Franklin threw the bag down and away from the plane. Five more times we repeated this process until all the bags had been dropped.

We continued to circle and saw Amelia and her children pushing their way through the deep snow to reach the bags Franklin counted the figures on the ground. "One is missing," said Franklin. Fearing the worst, I set up another low pass. The skis were almost touching the snow as we flew directly past a rear window of the cabin. "There he is!" shouted Franklin. They were all alive.

Several men from the village drove snowmachines to Blondie's cabin, arriving a couple of days after the food drop. They bundled up the family and hauled them all back to Huslia. Amelia came over to thank us and said that when we made the food drop the family was on its last legs. They had a hard time even moving. As the food bags fell in the marsh they could barely walk and stumbled toward them emitting thin cries.

Blondie and his family settled into Huslia to spend the rest of the winter. Blondie, however, soon wanted to return to the upper Huslia to run his trap line. He seemed uncomfortable living in a settlement. Near the end of February he drove his dogs back into the wilds of the Huslia River. (His wife and family) remained in the village.

On March 10, 1969, Amelia came to our house and asked me to fly her and a load of supplies to Blondie. She was worried about him. I agreed. I loaded up the plane and put her in the passenger's seat. We flew back up the river until we spotted the cabin. There was no sign of Blondie. I did spot *what appeared to be a single dog running loose on the river near the cabin. After several passes no one came out.*

The open marshland behind the cabin was covered in deep, soft snow. The snow hid the tussocks and low brush. I skimmed just above the surface looking for possible snags or other hidden obstacles. I came back around and let the skis settle onto the snow keeping up my airspeed and then pulling off near the end of the marsh. I repeated this maneuver each time settling a little deeper packing the snow and also widening the landing zone. Finally, I let the plane settle onto the packed strip and cut the engine. I told Amelia to go to the cabin and check for any sign of Blondie while I wrestled the plane around for a takeoff. She came back reporting that the cabin had been recently used, but no one was there.

Just as we were preparing to get into the plane I spotted a figure moving through the trees at the edge of the marsh. Blondie came walking on snowshoes out of the brush carrying an ax and heading directly toward the cabin.

"Blondie!" I yelled. He kept walking as though we did not exist. "Hey, Blondie. Damn it! Over here."

Finally, he looked up dully and came trudging toward us. Blondie had suffered a breakdown. He was disoriented and rambling. He did not seem to recognize his wife. I decided that it would be best not to place him in my plane for the flight back to Huslia. Besides, it was going to be a tight takeoff with just two of us in the plane.

"Blondie, I am going to leave you here right now. I will send someone to help you."

After flying back to the village I sent some men on snowmachines to retrieve him. However, when they drove to his camp they decided that they also were not equipped to transport him to the village. In the end a state trooper chartered a bush plane into the camp. Blondie received professional help, recovered, and eventually returned to the village to lead a productive life in Huslia.

Blondie's experience was not uncommon. Despite the romantic image of the hearty mountain man living apart from society and wresting a living from the wilds, living alone in the Alaska wilderness can be psychologically and physically stressful. An injury or illness that might be simply uncomfortable or inconvenient in a group setting can be life-threatening when alone. In the back of your mind there is ever the realization that the simple slip of an ax when chopping wood or a knife when skinning game can incapacitate a person who is alone and isolated. Added to this is the lack of human social stimulation, a critical need for people. Intense cold and darkness exacerbate the stress.

Solitary confinement is considered extreme punishment in prison settings, because it deprives a person of essential companionship and can result in psychological trauma. In his book, Alone, *Admiral Richard Byrd describes his struggle to deal with self-imposed isolation in Antarctica, including hallucination and depression. Blondie's experience was no less trying. This in no way detracts from his considerable accomplishments as a skilled woodsman.*

While cold, dark and isolation are the hardships of winters in the Northland, the scourge of summers is the mosquito. During their time in Huslia, the Banes remained in touch with Richard Nelson. In the summer of 1968, Ray and Nelson took what Ray refers to as their "Huck Finn holiday." Barbara went back to West Virginia to visit family for the first part of the summer and joined them for the latter part of their adventure.

The first segment of Ray and Nelson's travels was a long paddle down the Kobuk River in foldable kayaks. "Kobuk" is a mispronunciation of the Eskimo word "kukpuk" or "kuvuk" meaning Big River. Located entirely north of the Arctic Circle, the Kobuk River is approximately 280 miles long and is one of the largest rivers in northwest Alaska.

The river begins its life in the high snowfields of the southwestern Brooks Range and flows from east to west through a broad valley bounded on the north by the proud peaks of the Baird and Schwatka Mountains and to the south by the lesser-forested highlands of the Zane Hills and Sheklukshuk Range. The scenery is varied and inspiring.

As they traveled from Kobuk Village to the villages of Shugnak, Ambler, and Kiana, they were careful to paddle away from the shoreline so as not to disturb the hordes that boiled out of the tundra the moment they came ashore.

As soon as we pulled up to the beach a virtual fog of aggressive mosquitos rose out of the surrounding willows and enveloped us. Even with repellent smeared on exposed skin they covered our clothing and hovered around our head emitting a maddening high-pitched drone . . . The zipper at the bottom of the net was undone allowing just enough room to shove gear bags into the tent and then zipped shut. Finally it was time for us to get in. Dick kneeled at the entrance and proceeded to scrape mosquitos from his front while I smashed the mosquitos clinging to his back. At a signal he unzipped the door just enough to duck in and then closed it again. I then kneeled with my back to the door netting and proceeded to kill the mosquitos on my front while Dick smashed those on my back by pushing against the netting.

They came upon an Eskimo fish camp and an elder couple invited them to stop for coffee and boiled caribou meat. They visited an hour before pushing off to continue their journey. The next day, they were approached by a riverboat with an Eskimo man and woman.

"Hi," the woman in the boat said. "I'm Minnie Gray. My mom and dad asked us to give you this."

She passed a bag filled with dried caribou meat to them. With typical hospitality, the elders had offered generously from their own supply. Although Ray and Nelson had plenty of freeze-dried camp food, the real meat was greatly welcome.

After their paddle to Kiana, Ray and Nelson joined the crew of a barge to Kotzebue, lingered a few days, and then returned on the barge back to Kiana. Following their kayak expedition, they took an outboard boat and traveled the Koyukuk River's surrounding waterways. By the end of July, Barbara had returned and they were set to begin the final segment of their summer-long exploration.

Kuuvangmiut elders at a fish camp gave Ray and Dick (Richard) Nelson dried caribou meat as a gift to replenish their supplies as they kayaked the Kobuk River from the village of Kobuk to the mouth of the river. (Bane Collection)

Ray flew them in their Cessna 170 to Bettles Field, a tiny community located at the base of the rough-cut peaks of the central Brooks Range. They bought fuel and then headed into the mountains, a flight path that took them up the John River Valley and eventually to the Eskimo village of Anaktuvuk Pass.

"This initial flight deep into the heart of the Brooks Range affected me deeply," Ray remembered. "The maze of mountain-lined valleys and primeval wilderness of nameless mountains made me want to see and experience the wonders hidden there."

For all of its challenges, the rewards of living in Alaska were as boundless as the landscape they flew over. Seven years earlier on their way to teach in Barrow, Ray and Barbara had seen these mountains from the altitude of their commercial flight. On this trip, however, they flew among the peaks and through the passes themselves, making short forays into side valleys along the way as they explored the increasingly dramatic landscape. They could see that this was one of the least human-altered landscapes in North America, a place still far beyond the reach of the modern world.

It also whetted Ray's appetite to see it up close.

The sparse remains of a caribou taken by wolves. Wolves, birds and other scavengers completely consumed the caribou carcass leaving only a few gnawed bones and bits of hair. (Bane Collection)

They did not know, on that adventure-filled summer of 1968, that this area of the Brooks Range would shape their lives in ways that they could not yet fathom. For now it was enough to absorb the silence, to feel the magnitude of time in the stillness of those vaulted peaks, and to see the colors of fall begin to bloom on the sweeping valley floor.

9

hog river gary

On December 27, 1967, a fireball of white and yellow flame shot into the Arctic sky as workers lit the natural gas roaring out of a test well in Prudhoe Bay. The flare could be seen for miles. The discovery of the single largest oil field ever found in North America launched a sequence of events that would forever alter the history and the landscape of Alaska. It wouldn't be long before the construction of one of the largest, most complicated, and controversial engineering projects of its time—the Trans-Alaska Pipeline—would begin.

Ten years later, the first barrels of crude oil would flow into the hold of a giant tanker 800 miles away in Valdez, having traveled through a 48-inch pipeline that crosses 34 major rivers, 800 smaller streams, three mountain ranges, and some of the most pristine wilderness on earth.

"We were carried by the current," said Ray, of that time in the history of the state. "The discovery of oil set off a land rush of sorts and brought the promise of enormous economic development. The State of Alaska immediately benefited through the sale of leases. As a consequence, our salary as teachers literally doubled from 1968 to 1969. However, the oil was of no value unless it could be moved in large quantities to markets to the south."

Oil companies would need permits to build the pipeline across those 800 miles to the deep-water port of Valdez. The economic viability of a young state, the federal government's settlements with aboriginal people, and the politics of big oil companies would help steer the course of Alaska's future. In the mix of those powerful interests was the call to preserve wilderness as a legacy and heritage to the Nation as whole.

By 1970, Ray and Barbara had moved to Hughes, a village 62 air miles from Huslia. The Koyukuk River served as the main transportation corridor, but by river miles the distance was easily twice that much as the river looped and double backed on itself. The village consisted of small log cabins strung on a flat gravel bench along the base of a steep bluff. The population at the time was around sixty Koyukon Athabaskans and one Iñupiat Eskimo.

Ray and Barbara, the only non-Natives, lived in a two-room schoolhouse with an attached apartment. Once again they found themselves hosting visiting officials and having school-related activities flow into their living space. Yet they felt a special fondness for Hughes. Ray credits Barbara for their easy transition into new Native villages.

> She radiates a sincerity and kindness that naturally attracts others. It was largely Barbara who made it so easy for us to fit into the tight knit villages of Alaska. Village women would come to our house to visit, and Barbara felt comfortable visiting their homes and sharing their hospitality. The ladies of Huslia and Hughes referred to Barbara as 'sister' essentially adopting her into the village social life.

In the fall, whitefish, the most abundant group of fish found north of the Alaska Range, gather into schools in the Koyukuk River as they get ready to move into deeper water for the winter. Seining was a major source of food for their sled dogs over the winter. Barbara and Ray formed a seining team with their friends Henry and Sophie Beatus. Seining uses a large net with sinkers on one edge and floats on the other so that the net hangs vertically in the water. When the ends are pulled together, the nets close around the fish and they can be drawn to shore. The nets Ray and Barbara used had hand-carved bone and antler for sinkers and balsam poplar bark for floats. They used boats to drape the net in an arc into the river. When they captured a school of whitefish, the water roiled. Ray wrote in his journal:

> Crewmembers rushed into the frigid waters grabbing and throwing the fish onto the riverbank. When we were lucky we could completely fill two large boats to capacity in a couple of sweeps. We went home soggy, tired, and smelling of fish.
> We spread out the fish and let them freeze hard as the fall temperature dropped below freezing. Once the fish were frozen we placed them in a

covered shed. It took several tons of fish to keep a team of working huskies well fed during the winter. To feed the dogs, we cut the fish into chunks and boiled it in a large cauldron over an outdoor fire. As the water boiled, I would toss in kitchen scraps, bits of moose and caribou meat and some-times cornmeal or oats to thicken the stew. . . The dogs virtually inhaled the rich soup. Not having to chew rock hard frozen fish and then thaw it in their bellies saved calories.

After the Koyukuk froze and the ground was covered with snow, Ray and Barbara set out a winter camp in a picturesque valley with an unobstructed view of the surrounding countryside, about six miles from the village. They pitched a 10 x 12 foot canvas wall tent and furnished it with a wood-burning Yukon stove that kept the tent toasty even at minus forty degrees. Unlike the Arctic coastline, wood was plentiful in Koyukon country. Summer and fall months were spent stockpiling the wood supply that provided heating fuel for the winter months ahead. Ray and Barbara kept a supply at their camp and if they ran short, would either cut what they needed or haul dry wood from home.

"Almost every weekend was spent at our camp," Ray remembers. The dogs knew the weekly routine. "We would have the dog sled loaded and the harness lines spread out each Friday. All we had to do after school was hook up the dogs and pull up the sled anchor. I would call, 'Twilight. Camp!' and the team would burst into a full out run and take us to camp without anoth-er command given. On Sunday evenings we simply reversed the procedure."

Ray and Barbara liked the area so much that they began to think of Hughes as a place they might like to make a permanent home. They knew that teachers were expected to rotate every three to four years and they re-alized that they would likely move on to other villages to teach. Yet Hughes could become a place where they could eventually retire. Maybe they ought to build a cabin.

Meanwhile, an impasse had developed in the high stakes bid to develop the oil pipeline. Alaska Natives had long been promised that the federal government would settle aboriginal claims to public lands in the state. The State of Alaska also had legal claim to a set percentage of federally managed lands. Oil companies needed permits to construct a pipeline that crossed the lands involved in these disputes. Ultimately, the permits to build the pipeline could not be granted until the Native claims had been settled.

On December 18, 1971, President Richard Nixon signed the Alaska Native Settlement Claims Act (ANCSA). This act was the first of its kind in the United States' long history of settlements with Native Americans. ANCSA created twelve Native regional economic development corporations in which the stockholders were the Native people who traditionally lived in these regions. These corporations could make profits that allowed communities to prosper, in turn enabling individuals to stay and work in their villages. The intent was to preserve the lifestyles and the heritage of the Native people.

> As Congress considered various versions of the proposed settlement, rumors filtered back to our tiny village of how it would completely change the way people lived. Many of the rumors were dramatically conflicting. Talk of corporations, shares, dividends and allotments were completely foreign concepts that left village people confused and anxious. Most had never thought of property in the legal sense. Virtually no one had a deed to the land where their cabin was located.

Ray decided to use ANCSA as a teaching opportunity for his upper grade students. He wrote to the Alaska department of education and the Alaska Congressional delegation requesting copies of ANCSA-related information. In short order, the mail plane was delivering boxes filled with reams of information, legislation, and reports. Ray spent weeks distilling stacks of government documents into classroom lessons on social studies, geography, reading, and math. The lessons included maps with boundaries of the regions and included games that created classroom corporations where students each owned shares.

Ray's work caught the attention of his friend Henry Beatus, the school custodian and a respected village leader. The students were learning things that everyone in the village wanted to know. Would Ray be willing to share the information about ANCSA with the community?

Word spread to the villages north and south of Hughes and people began arriving by snowmachine and airplane and stayed with relatives. Ray handed out condensed and annotated versions of the legislation, showed maps of lands eligible for Native selection, and explained the process of making individual claims. Villagers brought pots of coffee and snacks to the classes and their apartment became an extension of the classroom.

By day, Ray and Barbara taught school to the kids; evenings were spent studying or teaching what they learned about the provisions of ANCSA to adults. Suddenly those weekend getaways spent at their winter camp were more precious than ever.

The community was grateful for the Banes' help in sorting out the overwhelming and sometimes conflicting information. Ray and Barbara considered the effort a learning experience for themselves as much as for the Native residents. Life was changing dramatically in rural Alaska, and the rate of change was accelerating.

In the early summer of 1972, the river barge from Nenana arrived to offload supplies and equipment. On board was a young man named Gary, who worked as the ship's cook. He spoke at length with Ray, wanting to know about the prospects of living off the land somewhere along the Koyukuk Valley.

"We talked of the possibilities and I tried to explain some of the challenges he would face if he was to realize his dream. I thought little more about it until the following summer in 1972, when he returned on the barge as a passenger. He had a large canoe and a sizeable load of supplies offloaded at Hughes," Ray said.

Gary described to Ray his plan settle on a BLM allotment of land along the Hogatza River. Various options were available to homestead from five to eighty acres. He wanted to settle a large parcel so that he'd have space between him and his neighbors, who he was convinced would flock to the area. Ray doubted he'd have much trouble on that account. The area was largely marsh and scrub brush. Gary was soon on his way paddling down the Koyukuk heading for the Hogatza River, known by locals as the "Hog" River.

Over the next several weeks I kept an eye out for Gary whenever I happened to be flying in the general area. It took him about three days to reach the mouth of the Hog River. Several days later I glimpsed him wading up the Hog with a rope over his shoulder pulling the canoe behind him. The mosquitoes had to be fierce. The banks of the narrow stream were overgrown in thick willow and alder brush preventing him from walking on dry land. I had to shake my head as I imagined what he must be going through.

Within two months, Gary had built a small cabin on an oxbow lake just off the river. When Ray landed on a nearby gravel bar to check on him,

Gary paddled up the river to meet him. The first thing he said was, "Ray, I've decided not to go for sixty acres. I don't think anyone else is coming."

"We both had a good laugh," Ray said. "He had heard me searching for him and grabbed up a bag of letters he wanted to get in the mail. One of the letters was to his wife, Charlene, in Fairbanks telling her to join him at their new homestead."

Ray mailed Gary's letters in Hughes and a few days later at the end of the school day, a Cessna 185 floatplane landed on the river beside the village. Shortly after, there was a sharp knock at their apartment door.

"Bane! Dammit! Where in the hell is Gary's cabin?" It was Tom Classen, a charter bush pilot from Fairbanks who had been flying for more than an hour in search of the homestead. Beside him stood Gary's wife, a petite, well-dressed, and feminine woman. She had hired Tom to fly her to meet her husband and see their new home. The cabin was small and not easily seen from the air, however.

Ray and Tom looked at the map while Barbara and Charlene discussed this new adventure she was about to undertake. Charlene said casually that she would try it for a few weeks and if it didn't suit her, she'd go back to her job in Fairbanks. Barbara asked how she planned to return from the cabin if she changed her mind. Charlene did not seem to understand. Barbara explained that once Tom dropped her off they would be completely cut off from the rest of the world. There would be no way to leave until after freeze up when there was enough snow on the ground for snowshoeing. Even then it would take several days of walking to reach a settlement and temperatures could be too cold to travel.

"She seemed subdued as she returned to the plane with Tom," Ray said. "Over the next few months whenever I happened to be flying near the area of Gary and Charlene's homestead I would divert to check on them and sometimes drop their mail." On November 4, Henry Beatus joined Ray for the flight. As they flew over the homestead a message had been stomped in the snow with spruce boughs on top to help distinguish the letters:

CHAR WANT OUT
CAN U TAKE

Light was fading fast and with Henry in the plane, there was no room for another passenger. Ray wagged his wings in acknowledgment of the message and headed home. For nearly three weeks, poor weather and other emergency medical flights out of Hughes kept Ray from going back. By December 2 when he returned, the couple had patched things up and Char had decided to stay for the winter. By spring, however, she had had enough and the couple separated.

Gary stayed and successfully lived the solitary life of a modern mountain man, trapping and hunting and living the dream he had when he began his canoe trip from Hughes.

"The Koyukon Indians admired him for his tenacity and grit. They considered the Hog River and nearby Pah Flats as 'tough country,'" Ray said.

Local residents began calling him "Hog River Gary." He eventually learned to fly and at one point decided he needed a companion. He found one through a mail-order service and he and his bride enlarged the cabin, installed some conveniences, and raised a family.

The 1971 ANCSA resolved one of the land settlement issues required for the Trans-Alaska Pipeline to go forward. Even before permits were issued, a great airlift was underway as tons of equipment and supplies were airfreighted to the North Slope. DC-3s, Hercules C-130s, small bush planes, and other aircraft brought in drill rigs, pipe, and the people needed to coax the

The isolation of remote bush living took its toll on many couples. Ray flew over this cabin asking assistance to fly a spouse out of the bush, 1972. (Bane Collection)

vast reserve of oil from the ground. Alarmed, conservation groups filed suit to assure the environmental impact of the project would be known before construction began.

Amidst the legal wrangling, events unfolding halfway around the world helped steer the course of Alaska's oil development. In October 1973, Arab oil countries declared an oil embargo on the United States. Within the year, oil prices quadrupled and long lines at the gas pumps around the nation reflected America's first fuel shortage since World War II. Suddenly the need for a large domestic source of oil became urgent.

On November 16, 1973, President Richard Nixon signed the Alaska Pipeline Authorization Act, effectively halting all legal actions and clearing the way for construction to begin. What followed was a boom bigger than all of Alaska's gold rushes combined.

Ray and Barbara watched and wondered how their lives in Alaska were about to change. As important as the Native claims settlement issue was to people living in the bush, the question of how subsequent public lands would be used was equally pressing. Would these lands be preserved in trust as a wilderness for future generations, or would they be developed for their mineral resources? The question became the crux of controversy for years to come and a question that eventually shaped Ray and Barbara's future.

10

—·◦⁘◦·—

in the presence of wolves

Once while driving the dogs to our winter camp I spotted five wolves moving along the side of an open slope perhaps half a mile away. They were moving parallel to my course. When I stopped so did they. When I began to move again they continued to maintain pace with me. There was no indication of any aggressive intent. Wolves are inherently curious. They had access to a bounty of fresh caribou, so hunger played no role in their actions. I felt comfortable with their presence. Before turning around to return to the village I imitated the howl of a wolf. All of them immediately returned my call setting off a chorus of rolling howls that made the hair on the back of my neck stand on end.

—Ray Bane
Not Man Apart magazine, 1972

The Bane's dream to build a cabin persisted, and Hughes seemed just the place to create a home base for their lives in Alaska. The village lay on the Koyukuk River just 62 miles northeast from Huslia by air, but 137 winding river miles by boat. The community was within easy distance of the Brooks Range, which so captivated them, and Ray and Barbara felt accepted by the villagers. Late in the winter of 1971, they approached the village council and asked if the community would support their building a home in Hughes.

The council approved their plan and as it happened, Alfred Attla also planned to build a new cabin. Ray and Alfred joined forces to harvest logs and enlisted several men to help. They pooled their money to buy gasoline for the boats, food, and other supplies for the week it would take to carry out their work.

During the last week of May, the men and their crews took five riverboats and headed from Hughes north on the Koyukuk River into a tributary stream fifteen miles past Allakaket. Village elders from Allakaket knew of the harvest and had suggested the area for their tree-cutting project. The water was high with the spring runoff of melting snow—perfect for floating the logs back downstream toward Hughes.

It took a day to reach the tree-cutting site and set up camp. For several more days, the whine of chainsaws reverberated across the landscape. Once down, each tree had to be limbed and the bark peeled away while the sap was fresh. They wrestled the big logs to the edge of the river using special tongs, pikes, and peeve poles. This time of year, the sky never grew completely dark before the sun rose again to a new day. Even with the hard work, the men maintained good humor with the help of ample supplies of hot coffee, soup, and boiled caribou meat.

The idea was to float the logs down the narrow tributary to the confluence of the larger Koyukuk River. To catch the logs, they first created a log

Ray and a team of village men traveled over eighty miles up the Koyukuk River to harvest trees suitable for house logs, 1972. (Bane Collection)

chain, fastening logs end-to-end across the mouth of the tributary; at this intersection the crew could then lash their harvest of logs together to form a large floating raft. From there they would tow the raft into the main current of the Koyukuk and float it to Hughes, using a motorboat to guide the raft away from shoals, snags, and cut banks.

Once the logs were ready for transport, part of the crew went downstream to fell more logs and create the log chain. Once in place, Ray and the remaining crew pushed roughly three dozen logs into the fast flowing steam and waited to hear that they had safely arrived at the catching point. They held off pushing the rest of their harvest into the water until this test run proved successful.

"It was lucky that we did," Ray remembered, "because not one log made it to the intended destination."

Some two miles short of the main river, as the logs traveled around a sharp bend, the current pushed them into a tangled pile of wood and debris that lay anchored against a cut bank. Rather than bounce around the obstacle, the logs were pulled under it and pinned in place by the strong current. Three dozen prime building logs disappeared into the jam.

"It was too dangerous to retrieve them. There was no other option than to temporarily abandon the project and hope to retrieve the other logs when the water dropped enough to guide them around the drift pile," Ray said. "We resignedly broke camp, loaded our boats, and returned to Hughes, a humbled group."

The weeklong exercise left Ray emotionally and physically exhausted. There was nothing to do now but wait and see what the river would do as the spring runoff melted. Only then would they know if the months of planning, the expense of ordering building materials, and the work of harvesting all those logs would amount to anything.

Ray told Barbara he needed a break and loaded his Citabria to take a few days respite. She shooed him off, knowing some time alone in the wilderness would temper his frustrations. He flew first to Kiana, then Noatak, and when someone at the airstrip at Noatak asked where he was headed, he made up his mind.

"Wainwright," he answered. He headed due north, feeling himself relax as the ramparts of the western Brooks Range stretched into view. He flew across a low ridge and picked up the shoreline of the Chukchi Sea.

Ahead lay the spartan lands of the true Arctic with dark gray seawater, swashed dun-colored beaches and starkly barren tundra bluffs. As I rounded the rugged headlands of Cape Lizborne I was greeted with the yawning vastness of the North Slope tundra plains. The ocean below was littered with broken ice. A shelf of shore ice still clung to the beaches extending out a few miles into the sea. Melting snows along the shore painted dark stripes of mud on the shore fast ice. Shallow lakes and ponds glittered on the tundra. A heavy gray curtain of thick fog hung on the western horizon.

Ray landed on a gravel runway on the tundra next to the village. As he finished securing his plane, a couple of men walked up the gravel road to the landing strip.

"Hey, aren't you Ray Bane?" Homer Bodfish called out.

"Yep," Ray responded. "I came back to collect that money you owe me."

They laughed and pounded each other on the back, exchanging jokes. Word spread quickly and soon Ray was engulfed by a crowd of villagers welcoming him home.

He went to see old Ekak, his mentor and teacher, and dropped in on Raymond Aguvluk, his joking partner. The weariness of the previous week's work peeled away with the laughter of friends. This was the North, a place where setbacks came with the territory; a place where nature could provide everything one needed in one moment and take everything away in the next. Ray had learned from his father early on that the best defense against despair was a sense of humor.

The people living nearest the land seemed to know this and they served it up in generous helpings. He drank gallons of hot tea, consumed platters of boiled caribou, and snacked on bits of frozen raw fish dipped in rich seal oil.

Two days later, he flew out of Wainwright with renewed energy. Although the cabin-building experiment seemed uncertain at the moment, the dream he had long nurtured to take a long distance trip by dog team began to develop in his mind. He resolved that the next time he traveled to Wainwright, it would not be in an airplane.

When Ray returned to Hughes, he learned that during his absence the river had dropped enough for two boatloads of men to return to the logging site. All the logs had been pushed into the stream and safely shepherded to the log chain at the confluence of the Koyukuk River. Even the logs lost in the drift pile were pulled free to join the others. They lashed a massive wooden raft together, leaving a notch in the rear. The men then inserted the bow of the riverboat into the notch and used the boat to steer the raft. The boat kept the raft in the middle of the river and away from cut banks and gravel bars.

Ray picked up his friend, Henry Beatus, in Hughes and they flew back upstream and landed beside the floating raft of logs. Ray tied his plane to the raft and let it float along behind while he and Henry joined the crew and soaked up the sunshine. They enjoyed the passing view for a few miles, then climbed into the Citabria and flew back to Hughes to make preparations for the arrival of the flotilla. There, they built special anchor points along the riverbank, so they could safely stop the raft and secure it when it arrived.

It would be two years before the Banes would begin construction of the cabin itself. Freshly cut logs shrink as they dry and are best aged before using. Meanwhile, Ray and Barbara worked together to landscape their cabin site, dig support pilings, build a smoke house, an outhouse, and small log-cabin dog houses for each of their huskies.

Raft of house logs being floated down the Koyukuk River to Hughes. An outboard driven boat is inserted in a notch at the rear of the raft to help guide it downstream. (Bane Collection)

Like their village friends and neighbors, Ray and Barbara participated in harvesting meat, fish, hides, and fur. The methods they used were a kind of Arctic farming, where nothing was wasted, and something was always left behind so that it could be harvested again another time. So when, during the longer sun-soaked days of spring, aerial wolf hunters began to show up in Koyukuk River country in increasing numbers, villagers were concerned.

Men in the village hunted and trapped wolves for their hides, which were used for ruffs, mittens, boot tops, and parkas. A hunter traveling by dog team had little chance of overtaking a healthy wolf, which made trapping the preferred method of harvesting the resource. The introduction of snowmachines in the 1960s changed hunting practices in dramatic ways. Game could now be pursued on machines, with hunters chasing wolves and other animals over long distances to get a close shot.

The hunter in an aircraft had even greater advantages over the hunter on a snowmachine. Airplanes could travel longer distances, offer a greater field of vision, and soar over rugged terrain.

Ray standing in front of the Banes' new cabin in Hughes. The cabin was built on pilings, giving it an excellent view across the Koyukuk Valley, 1973. (Bane Collection)

"The village hunters could not compete with aerial wolf hunters. They sometimes spent an entire day searching for wolves only to find bloody skinned carcasses," Ray said.

During the 1940s and 1950s, federal agents had undertaken widespread wolf control in Alaska through poisoning, bounties, and aerial shooting. Predators like wolves and bears were considered "vermin" and their eradication, it was surmised, had the benefit of increasing populations of game species such as moose and caribou.

While many Native Alaskans took part in the bounty program, they knew to always leave a lactating female and a few pups behind so that the resource could be harvested again at a later date.

After Alaska became a state in 1959, one of the first actions of the legislature was to prohibit the poisoning of predators. Bounties were stopped shortly thereafter. In 1963, the Board of Fish and Game classified the wolf as a big game animal and a fur animal, which provided the first official recognition of the wolf as a valuable species. This offered limited protection through a system of hunting seasons and bag limits. Even so, the aerial shooting of wolves by the hunting public became common in the 1960s and was increasing in popularity by the early 1970s.

Ray described the process of the aerial hunt:

Aerial wolf hunters flew low over the snow crisscrossing the land searching for signs of wolves. A determined pilot might follow the tracks of one or more wolves for long distances. If wolves were found in heavy forest cover or where it was not possible to land nearby, the pilot would dive on the pack sometimes shooting into them or throwing out lit firecrackers to drive them toward a more open area.

The actual shooting was usually done by a gunner in the rear seat. He would open the side door of the flying aircraft and stick out the barrel of a twelve-gauge shotgun pointing it to direct the fire down and away from the plane. The rear gunner might not even see the intended target. The pilot set up a low pass driving the wolves and then calling for the gunner to fire when he had the wolves lined up. The shotgun fired heavy double 00 pellets that literally sprayed the fleeing wolves. An experienced hunting team could virtually wipe out an entire pack of six or seven wolves using this technique, but it was common for wounded wolves to escape and die a slow and painful death.

Ray and Barbara's experiences with wolves in the early 1970s led to their involvement in the aerial wolf hunting controversy. This led them to cofound the Northern Alaska Environmental Center. (Courtesy Roy Corral)

Village hunters asked Ray for advice about what to do to keep aerial wolf hunters away from rural communities. Ray helped village leaders write a letter to the Alaska Department of Fish and Game requesting that aerial wolf hunting be restricted around rural villages. Other villages joined in asking that the gunning be stopped.

> This action set off a sequence of events that drew me ever deeper into the controversy over aerial hunting. I contributed some letters to the editor of the Fairbanks newspaper and wrote articles on wolves for Alaska magazine and some conservation periodicals. A radio talk show in Fairbanks invited me to be interviewed and respond to callers. I expected and received calls critical of my position, but I was also surprised by the number of callers who supported banning aerial gunning of wolves.

So many outside forces were coming to bear in shaping the future of the North. Oil development had pushed resource development to the forefront and the Banes felt that the voice for the conservation of the land itself needed strengthening. Ray and his friend, Jim Hunter, an insurance adjuster in Fairbanks, and Gordon Wright, the director of the Fairbanks Symphony

Orchestra, decided to form a conservation group that would focus on issues affecting northern Alaska.

"The wolf controversy helped to gel our efforts. We pooled our resources and hired a friend of Gordon's from Wisconsin, Jim Kowalski, to be the administrative head of the fledging group that eventually became the Northern Alaska Environmental Center (NAEC)," Ray said.

On March 14, during prime aerial hunting season, Ray took Kowalski for a flight in the Citabria to do some on-site research into the issue.

"I would land at each site so Jim could get a close-up, first-hand understanding of the process and its results," Ray said. "At one site we found the stripped carcasses of ten adult wolves and the ski tracks of a light aircraft. There was no evidence that any wolves in this pack had escaped. An entire breeding group had been eliminated."

Ray felt strongly about the issue but managed to maintain friendships with the pilots who were skilled in the business of killing wolves. One of those was Bill Hutchinson, who Ray said was one of those "colorful characters that adds spice to the brew of people living in the bush." They

The aerial killing of wolves in Alaska was widespread through the early 1970s. One aerial hunter proudly displayed the hides of a more than 100 wolves taken over the course of a single year. (Bane Collection)

Ray and their husky Kateel. (Bane Collection)

had a friendly, adversarial relationship where they could joke about their opposing positions.

> Bill once told me that if he saw any of my huskies running loose around Hughes he figured he would collect some more wolf skins. I replied that I had been thinking of setting up a shooting blind outside the village where I would stake out a couple of my dogs as decoys and wait for a target to fly by. We would laugh at ourselves, but there was no question that Bill was an absolutely determined aerial hunter. It was part of his identity.

In 1969, NBC aired a program entitled "Wolves and the Wolf Men" documenting the process of aerial wolf hunting in Alaska. The fevered pitch of the issue suddenly leapt from Alaska onto the national stage. Public outrage to the footage prompted Congress to pass the Airborne Hunting Act on November 18, 1971, prohibiting the use of aircraft to shoot or harass wildlife. However, the law left open a loophole allowing states to assign permits for the taking of wildlife for the purpose of wildlife management.

This loophole would be exploited by the Alaska Board of Fish and Game in response to demands by mostly urban hunters to increase populations of moose and caribou for human harvest. It was a flawed victory, but it did help reduce the aerial butchering of wildlife . . . We are fortunate that wolves have never matched the savagery of the men who hunt them.

Wolves would remain, for Ray and Barbara, an enigmatic and beautiful symbol of the Northern wilderness. Once, when they traveled to their weekend camp, they found that wolves had circled their tent just before their arrival by dog team. That evening they heard the wolves serenading from a nearby hill.

"The next day the pack kept abreast of us along a wooded slope for about two miles while we mushed along a frozen stream," Ray remembered. "From their frequent howls we could tell that they would occasionally surge ahead and await our passage."

At no time did the wolves display aggressive tendencies. They were simply traveling along—companions for a while, on what would become the long journey north.

11

- ✤ -

the 1200-mile journey

The Koyukon call it "devil snow." When temperatures drop low enough, suspended moisture falls out of the air as razor-fine crystals of ice.

Ray and Barbara's dog team moved silently across the frigid landscape. Although the day was clear, it was so cold that the team created its own ice fog as they moved down the frozen Koyukuk River. At times the fog was so thick that Ray and Barbara could not see the front half of the team. Minus 60 and dropping. Pulling the sled across devil snow was like pulling the sled through fine sand; the dog's feet began to ulcerate as the abrasive edges of the devil ice packed between their toes.

They were prepared for the cold, but Ray and Barbara wished the beginning of their cross-country dog team trip had begun more kindly. After reading Hudson Stuck's *Ten Thousand Miles with a Dog Sled*, and after years of dreaming of that long distance trip, in 1973 Ray and Barbara decided to take a one-year leave of absence from their teaching positions to pursue their goal.

They had already spent seven years developing and training a team of strong huskies. They had also researched the route by flying to the villages along the 1,200-mile course in their small airplane.

Their newly constructed cabin in Hughes had been celebrated by a traditional open house where elders stood and gave a blessing to their new abode. The main room of the cabin became a workshop where Ray assembled a specially designed 12-foot long dog sled that could withstand the rigors of their journey.

Henry Beatus (left) of Hughes assists Ray in planning the twelve-hundred-mile dog team trip, 1974. (Bob Bellous, Courtesy National Park Service)

Ray also designed a double-walled tent and took it to a tent maker in Fairbanks, who offered to make it at no cost if Ray would allow him to use the design to manufacture more to sell. That year the Banes turned much of their moose meat into jerky to carry with them on the trail. They enlisted the help of local Native women to sew skin parkas, pants, boots, and fur mittens. They also experimented with harnesses and custom-made one to fit each particular dog.

To train and test their equipment, they loaded their sled and mushed to villages both north and south of Hughes. Ray stood on the skis at the front of the sled and held on to a steering device called a gee-pole. When Ray applied pressure, the pole forced the front of the sled to swing right or left. It was a precarious position, perched between the rear dogs of the team but at the front of a moving, heavy-laden vessel. Barbara stood at the back runners.

"Barbara and I worked as a team," Ray said. "She applied the claw foot brake to slow us down if necessary. When we came to a long downhill, she would stop the team while I jumped off the skis and quickly moved to the rear."

For crossing glare ice or wind-tempered snow, Ray invented an inverted U-shaped, hinged metal ice-rudder that, when stepped on, forced the blades into the surface of the ice to prevent the sled from slipping sideways and flipping over.

As they worked to prepare themselves and their dogs for the trip, Henry Beatus and other village men stopped by their cabin to watch their progress and offer advice. They drank hot tea, ate fried bread dough, and snacked on dried meat while recounting stories of their dog mushing experiences.

> *No one had ever traveled by dog team beyond the upper Kobuk River. The land to the west was Eskimo country. I could tell that the idea of driving a dog team all the way to the coast and then north to the top of Alaska was strange to them. More than once I was asked, 'Why do you want to do this, Ray?' Before the trip was over, I would ask myself the same question.*

Villagers weren't the only ones interested in the Bane's upcoming plans. Zorro Bradley, a National Park Service anthropologist, had recently set up shop at the University of Alaska. Bradley was part of a government task force to study federal public lands that were being considered for conservation purposes set out under ANCSA. The clauses in ANCSA that set this land aside were collectively known as "D-2".

These clauses allowed the federal government to set aside large tracts of land for possible designation as national parks, wildlife refuges, national forests, and national wild and scenic rivers. Bradley had heard about the Banes through a mutual friend and wanted to meet with Ray and Barbara before they left on their trip. He invited the Banes to visit him in Fairbanks.

"Zorro and I immediately hit it off," Ray remembered. "We shared similar interests in Native cultures."

Bradley was "a force to be reckoned with, charismatic, and brimming with energy and curiosity." He asked the Banes to document their experiences crossing Alaska and produce a report on Native winter travel routes in northwestern Alaska. In exchange, he promised to find sponsorship from a major dog food company and contact National Geographic. Bob Belous, a National Park Service employee and professional photographer, would travel part of the trail by snowmachine to document their departure and meet them at other sites during the trip.

They planned to begin their trip the first week in February. The returning winter sun would offer longer days and temperatures ranging from ten degrees above zero down to minus thirty degrees below. They fully anticipated that a winter storm might pin them down at some point. What they didn't expect was that even before they set out, the mercury would plummet to minus sixty-five degrees and persist for weeks. One week stretched into the next and by February 12, Ray and Barbara decided to set out on their trip anyway. Surely this cold snap would break soon. The sled had been loaded for days.

It was minus forty-five when they left their cabin at 1:00 p.m., the warmest temperature it had been in a week.

That night they wondered if they had made the right decision. Even as they traveled they could feel the cold deepening. By the time they arrived at a trapper's tent camp the thermometer was dropping to minus sixty degrees, and the dogs' feet had grown sore from the devil snow. The next morning it was minus seventy degrees. As they traveled, a pall of gray ice fog hung over the trail in their wake.

On the first night of their trip, temperature dropped to minus 74 degrees F. In the morning when they hooked up the team, the dogs generated their own cloud of ice fog, February 1974. (Bane Collection)

Barbara with gear for their 1,200-mile trek. Ray designed and field-tested the sled, tent, and other equipment before the trip. (Bane Collection)

It took two more days to pull into Huslia, where they learned that Barbara's father in West Virginia had died. They chartered a plane to Fairbanks so Barbara could fly back to West Virginia to be with her mother. Ray decided to go on alone and hoped that Barbara could rejoin him somewhere along the way.

Men in Hughes gladly helped Ray as he sought directions for the best route to his next objective, the Kobuk River. Cue Bifelt and his nephew offered to guide him by snowmachine to the Kobuk Valley. Their help saved Ray from having to deal solo with two days of gale force winds and whiteout conditions.

Our entry into the village of Kobuk was a bit chaotic. My dogs almost crashed us into Tony Bernhart's Super Cub aircraft parked on the river ice in front of the village. I swore loudly and swung the team away from the plane. Then I realized that I had an audience of Eskimos standing on the riverbank watching and listening to me. Villagers grabbed the front dogs and led the team to a tie-down area. Soon, everything was unloaded and put away. People

*brought out dry salmon and caribou fat to feed the dogs. I later discovered I
had lightly frostbitten the tips of three fingers.*

By February 25, temperatures had returned to normal. At minus 15 and a
north wind of 15 knots, the weather felt positively balmy. It was again time
for a rest, and the short trip between Kobuk and Shungnak followed a well-
packed trail that wound along the river.

*The rugged ramparts of the Brooks Range formed a spectacular backdrop
on the north side of the valley. Lower mountains rimmed the south side.
Temperatures went up to minus ten. A packed trail ascended up the bluff,
and when we turned right into the village schoolyard, Eskimo kids came
screaming out of the building to greet us.*

The welcome Ray received in Shungnak would be typical of every village
along the 1,200-mile route between Hughes and Barrow. People opened
their homes, their larders, and even their stores of fish and meat to help feed
the dogs. Some offered to help ferry some of the gear from the dog sled by
snowmachine to the next stop down the trail.

In Shungnak Ray met Joe Sun, a 74-year-old village elder who told him
about the trail systems around the village. Ray took notes for himself and
also for the report he was writing for Bradley. Remembering his old friend
Ekak, Ray was impressed by Joe Sun's wealth of knowledge about the traditions of the Kobuk Eskimos.

Eleven days after Barbara left for West Virginia, she returned and met
up with Ray in Selawik. Their first day back together was perfect for mushing—clear, minus 30 degrees, with a light wind at their backs. It was good
to be back on the trail together. The dogs pulled steadily as they ascended
a low range of mountains and then rushed down the other side. Ray and
Barbara's respect for the dogs grew with each passing day. They arrived in
Kiana in the late evening.

At one point, somewhere between the villages of Ambler and Selawik,
Ray's right foot began to ache. He enjoyed running behind the sled, but
as he ran on the ice and hard-packed snow, the pain grew more intense.
It wasn't long before it became difficult even to walk. Barbara wound up
having to do much of the legwork and Ray decided that once they got to
Kotzebue, he would have a doctor take a look.

They also decided to cut back on the number of miles they traveled each day. "I found that dog team travel is usually a pleasure for perhaps five hours," Ray said. "After that it became a chore, both mentally and physically. I decided that if we were going to enjoy the trip we would limit our travel to about forty-five miles per day as an average. We were not trying to set records."

On long stretches of easy trail, Barbara sat atop the sled load and Ray stood on the rear runners holding onto the handlebars. Sometimes he perched on the crossbar between the handlebars.

We talked about people, our impressions of the villages, the land around us, our future and our past. Sometimes we were quiet for long spells wrapped in our individual thoughts. We had learned from our Native friends that being quiet together was often more important than talking.

In Kotzebue, x-rays revealed Ray had a stress fracture. The doctor made a plaster brace and taped it. He also made up a medical kit for Ray to deal with the issue. "He advised me to stay off of it, but acknowledged that I was probably unlikely to do that," Ray said.

Before leaving Kotzebue, they arranged for a shipment of dog food to be delivered to a shelter cabin at Cape Beaufort, roughly halfway between Pt. Hope and Pt. Lay. It was impossible to carry all of the dog food they would need for the entire trip and these food drops were critical in keeping them supplied for the next leg of the journey. They mushed on northward passing through the villages of Noatak and Kivilina. Unfailingly they were met with hospitality and help wherever they went.

On March 24, while en route to Point Hope, the winter storm they figured they might encounter materialized, first as a fuzzy line on the northern horizon. Three hours later they were engulfed in a maelstrom of winds gusting up to 50 miles per hour. Billowing clouds of blowing snow cascaded off the mountains. By now they were traveling along the coastline of the Chukchi Sea. Blinded by the blowing snow they mistakenly turned up a narrow valley and found themselves ascending a steep slope littered with broken shale. When they realized their mistake they turned around, and as they maneuvered the turn, the sled rolled over. "Luckily, Barbara had gotten off before we turned," Ray said.

Back along the shore, they continued to fight the wind.

To the left was a jumbled chaos of broken sea ice. To our right, dark shale cliffs loomed over us . . . In a period of ten minutes, the sled flipped over three times. Each time it was a struggle to get it upright again. The wind was so strong that we had to shout to be heard . . . small bits of broken shale from the bluffs became projectiles that attacked us and the dogs like angry bees.

Finally to the right, a valley opened and they saw a cluster of abandoned derelict buildings huddled against the far bluff. Ray went to the head of the team and leaning into the gale, led the reluctant dogs against driving wind toward shelter. What they found against the bluff were buildings well along in the process of decay. Most of the structures had been left open and were packed tight with windblown snow. One, however, was boarded up and offered a chance at shelter. A fine snow dust had blown through the tiny crack between the door and floor, forming a drift inside the cabin that barricaded the door. Ray made his way to a window and used an ax to pry off the boards. He crawled through the window and set about shoveling the rock-hard drift. Once the snow was out of the way, they were able to open the door from the inside.

Later they learned from local residents that the buildings were the remnants of a camp constructed during an experiment known as Project Chariot. In 1958 the U.S. Atomic Energy Commission had planned to excavate an instant harbor at Cape Thompson by detonating thermonuclear bombs. It was part of a larger project researching peaceful uses for nuclear explosives. Initially Iñupiat Eskimos, a small cadre of Alaska scientists, and a handful of conservationists opposed the plan, which was largely supported by Alaska political leaders, newspaper editors, and the university president. The grassroots protest was soon joined by national organizations such as the Wilderness Society and the Sierra Club. Facing increasing public uneasiness over the environmental risks, the AEC shelved the project in 1962.

The abandoned site could not have appeared for the Banes at a better time. Ray said, "It's hard to exaggerate how happy we were to be able to get inside and out of the violence of the storm blowing down the valley."

For five days the wind howled, gusting an estimated 100 miles per hour, shaking the shack nearly off its foundation.

"Wind!! This describes our entire day. I have never experienced such a gale. It roared down the valley all day steadily growing in strength. The

building shudders from the ceaseless pounding causing us to wonder if it will hold together.

We became concerned about the dogs. They needed more shelter. I took a shovel and ax to a nearby storage shed filled with hard packed snow and hacked out twelve dens in the drifts. It was a major chore fighting the wind to move each dog to its new home, but it finally was done. I fed them a light meal of dried fish and tallow. There is enough dog food for perhaps two more nights.

There is no one who could travel in this storm. When I am outside I feel as though I am caught up in mob violence . . . The main concern is for the dogs, although they are much better protected now. All we can do is to wait for this storm to blow itself out, so we can cross the nearby hills and make it to Pt. Hope.

After three days, they were tempted to take their chances, load up, and try to cross the mountains to the north side of Cape Thompson.

The problem is that I am not familiar with the trail. There is too much chance of making a mistake and possibly having an accident in reduced visibility. We have been reminding each other of these facts to sustain our patience . . . The wind picked up during the night again. Barbara crawled up against my sleeping bag and hugged me for comfort. We felt very isolated. I doubt that anyone knows just where we are. Even if they did, there is no way for anyone to reach us. The wind pounding on the walls and stove pipe sounds like distant bombing.

Finally, after four days, on March 28, the wind subsided and they gladly returned to the rigors of the trail. When they pulled into Pt. Hope, Ray was honored to be invited to join a village whaling team, but he and Barbara were eager to reach their old home village of Wainwright. They were soon back on the trail ascending a steep coastal mountain pass, and struggling through a chaos of broken sea ice.

When they arrived at the shelter cabin at Cape Beaufort, they were dismayed to discover that the drop of dog food they had pre-arranged in Kotzebue had not arrived. The four days of being weathered in by the storm had used up their reserve of food for the dogs and for themselves. They were depending on this shipment to get them to the village of Point Lay where they could resupply their provisions. The empty shelter cabin had been used by Iñupiat hunters who had left a few scraps of food on the floor. Ray and

Ray and Barbara wore Native-sewn skin parkas, boots, and mittens for portions of their trip. The sun barely broke the horizon and temperatures were well below zero. (Bob Bellous, Courtesy National Park Service)

Barbara swept the floor looking for any edible debris of food for a meal for the dogs. They could not afford to stop; they needed to make it to Point Lay by the following day or risk the dogs being too hungry and fatigued to travel. By evening they and the dogs were numbly exhausted—with the dogs barely able to eat the meager soup Ray cooked from the scraps.

The next morning Ray and Barbara had a hard time getting the dogs up and out of camp. It would be five o'clock the next evening before they wearily pulled into Point Lay, just in time for another winter storm to descend with a vengeance from the north. This time, however, they stayed at the village school and villagers provided their dogs with all the walrus meat they could eat. It was time for a rest.

On April 12, two months and 1,100 miles after leaving their cabin in Hughes, Ray and Barbara drove their dog team into Wainwright. As they pulled into the community that had bestowed upon them their Iñupiaq names, they were engulfed by smiling, laughing people shaking their hands and greeting them as "Ekalook" and "Otoiyuq." Zorro Bradley was there to greet them as well. In his journal that night Ray wrote, "WE ARE HOME AT LAST!"

They stayed in Wainwright for nine days visiting old friends. They attended Easter services at both churches, joining in the singing and spirit of the occasion. Ray was invited to attend the first village stockholder's meeting and he sat quietly absorbing this new phenomenon in the community. They enjoyed the company of their friends, including old Ekak and many others, who had been patient with them a dozen years earlier when they had arrived as eager young tanik (white) teachers. The community held a dance in their honor.

> Oh, how the beat of the drums gets into your blood! The men and women softly chanted an Eskimo song. Then the drummers struck their drums hard slapping the frames and skins with a resounding "Thum! Thum! Thum!" The tempo picked up and the singing got stronger. First the women members of the village dance team did some free dances. Barbara and I couldn't wait any longer and we joined in. Suddenly there were lots of people dancing. Eventually it seemed everyone was on the dance floor.

The dogs recovered quickly and by April 22, they were on their way for the last and final leg of their epic journey. One hundred more miles would take them to Barrow, where they could load the dogs and their gear and head back to Hughes. Wien Airlines had offered a free ride from Barrow to Fairbanks for them and their dogs and later used a photo of the Banes and their dog team on the cover of their inflight magazine.

They camped at Peard Bay and as they drove the team along the base of Skull Cliffs, their enthusiasm suddenly waned. It had been hard saying goodbye to their friends in Wainwright. Ekak was getting frail and who knew if they would see each other again. There was also the knowledge that the trip they had planned for so many years was coming to an end. They lapsed into a long silence.

Their cloudy mood persisted and late the following day, they came to the site of a monument commemorating the place where Will Rogers and Wiley Post had died in an airplane accident in 1935.

"I stepped on the break and asked Barbara to get off and take a picture," Ray remembered. "She gave me a long look and said, 'You can take that camera and shove it up your ass!' To say that I was taken aback is an understatement. Then I found myself laughing. 'Well,' I said, 'I guess the trip is over.' We both laughed all the way into Barrow."

Before leaving Wainwright, Zorro Bradley had made Ray and Barbara an offer they couldn't refuse. He had arranged funding to support a study into traditional subsistence uses of proposed parklands by the Native residents of the Kobuk Valley. Would they be interested in moving to Shungnak to conduct the field research?

And so it was that the Banes cast their lot with the National Park Service. Their days of being school teachers were over. The long-distance trip across 1,200 miles of Alaska wilderness had been a kind of home-coming, where they had traveled to all the places they knew—and many they didn't—ending where they had first begun their Arctic adventures. It was now proving to be a trip that launched them into a new future, one that tied together their interest in Native cultures, passion for conservation, and the fate of the wild lands of the North.

12

—⋅✢✢⋅—

through ancient eyes

J oe Immuq Sun was 74 years old when Ray and Barbara met him in
Shungnak as they traveled through by dog team in 1974. Sun was born in
1900 at the turn of a century. In the span of his lifetime, technology would
move his people from skin boats and seal oil lanterns to outboard motors,
television, and the computer age.

Ray and Barbara packed up their belongings in Hughes and moved to
Shungnak for twelve months (June 1974 to June 1975) to study the subsistence uses and traditions of Kuuvangmiut Eskimos living along the Kobuk
River. Others involved in the project included their friend Richard Nelson,
Doug and Wanni Anderson, and Nita Sheldon, a resident of Noorvik. The
team later co-authored, *Kuuvangmiut Subsistence: Traditional Eskimo Life in
the Latter Twentieth Century.*

At first, it wasn't easy gaining the trust of people living in Shungnak. This
time the Bane's observations were not held privately in the context of their
teaching experience. Now they were recording and asking pointed, probing
questions of people whom they barely knew.

*Few people are comfortable with the thought that someone is 'studying'
them," Ray said. "While working in Wainwright with Dick Nelson, I learned
the value of showing curious villagers my research notes and sketches. This
helped to put them at ease and encouraged them to correct any mistakes or
omissions in what I had recorded. I made it a practice to carry a small note-
book for jotting down notes and then enlarging upon them in the evenings.
I rough-sketched various subsistence activities and techniques and then
attempted to improve upon them later. Initially, Eskimo ladies would laugh*

and joke with me when I drew diagrams of their fishnets, seining activities, drying racks and other methods of preserving fish, but they soon grew so used to me that they took me for granted.

The elders were more willing to share their stories. Many of the customs, connections, and traditions that had sustained the Kuuvangmiut over thousands of years were fading away. They wanted to share their experiences and insights of the "old ways."

"Until recently the stories told by the elderly had been a major source of entertainment and crucial information needed to successfully live from the land," Ray said. "That role was being eroded. Although television had not yet arrived in Shungnak in 1974, it was obvious that when it did the voices of the past would have a hard time being heard over the din of game shows and soap operas."

Ray recalled when an elder shared stories of the long journeys the men had once made to provide for their families.

"Hey, Otoiyuk! Come on over here." It was Charlie Lee, one of the leading village elders standing in front of his cabin as I walked by. We went inside and sat at his kitchen table sharing strong tea and dried whitefish dipped in a saucer of seal oil. Charlie felt like talking and I was available. He began by complaining that young men were no longer willing to follow the old ways of helping the elderly unless they were paid. Charlie said that the old way was when you saw someone who needed help chopping firewood, building a boat, repairing a house or other work you were never supposed to ask for pay. The person you helped would tell his or her family and friends, and they would help you whenever you needed it.

Charlie then talked of the days when village men would walk into the mountains in July and spend the summer and early fall hunting mountain sheep, caribou, marmot, and other game. The men would go in pairs or small groups accompanied by pack dogs carrying only the bare essentials. They expected to live off of whatever they were able to kill. The caribou stopped coming to the Kobuk Valley in the early 1900s and did not return until the late 1940s. Moose were rare in the valley in those days, so men had to go north to find meat for their families. They made their way north following one of several routes and crossing steep mountain passes. While the men hunted the women spent the summers catching and preserving fish, gathering berries and other edible plants and caring for children.

Joe Sun confirmed Charlie's stories. Both he and Charlie had made these incredible journeys several times.

As Ray and Barbara listened to the elders tell their stories they heard re-peated references to "Aqatuuk" (Howard Pass), "Nukmuktoquak" (Ambler River), and dozens of other Native names. Ray began carrying topograph-ical maps to record the Native place names during his interviews. He was amazed by the concentration of place names along the upper Kobuk River and its connecting tributaries. Invariably they were tied to locations used for hunting, trapping, fishing, and gathering. These names also denoted envi-ronmental hazards, travel routes or places of spiritual significance. He also noticed that the concentration of known place names thinned at varying distances from the village until at some point he was told that if he wanted the place name for that particular spot, he would need to ask someone from villages along the lower Kobuk River.

> *This pattern led to the realization that place names loosely coincided with the subsistence territory of a village or closely grouped villages. The place names reflected a shared cultural map spanning a territory of thousands of square miles. What, to the uninitiated eye, appeared to be a wilderness untouched by man became a cultural landscape rich in history, spiritual values, economic importance, and implications to the development of the Iñupiaq worldview.*

Ray and Barbara lived in a tiny log cabin with their dogs on a small island in the Kobuk River across from the village of Shungnak. The cabin had been offered to them but they'd been told that it "needed some work." They didn't realize to what extent until they arrived. It had a dirt floor and they could see daylight between the loosely fitted cottonwood logs. They spent several days chinking dry moss between the logs to seal up the cabin. Even then they could feel cold air seeping through the walls. When snow began accumulating outside, they shoveled it against the outer walls as insulation to ward against the intense cold.

They covered the floor with loose sheets of plywood to keep down the dust. They spread out camp mats and down-filled sleeping bags. Water had to be drawn from a hole hacked through the river ice.

Each day Barbara walked onto the ice and drew water to fill two buckets and carried them back to the cabin using a yoke laid across her shoulders. She dumped the water into a tub next to the wood stove. During the night, a layer of ice often froze over the top. As winter tightened its grip on the

Kobuk Valley, the river ice thickened and it became a community effort to keep the village watering hole open through six feet of ice. They chopped at the ice using a pole tipped with the blade of a wood chisel.

It took constant effort to keep up a wood supply to feed the cabin stove. The dogs made short round-trips to and from wood cutting sites so frequently that it became routine. They did their job, but they did it without the burst of excitement and enthusiasm they exhibited when we went hunting or traveling to some new area. Like people, dogs become bored with repetition.

Daily living was work and so was feeding their hungry team. Ray and Barbara fished before and after freeze-up learning, as they worked alongside their neighbors, about various Native ways of harvesting fish. As such, the Banes were not just recording the history and ways of the early people; they were getting on-the-job training in living it. Summers were especially busy.

Each day during the height of the salmon run our net would be completely full of struggling chum salmon. The weight of the trapped fish pulled the net to the river bottom. To empty it I would begin at the shoreward end and pull the net across the top of the boat working my way to the opposite end. A stout club was used to stun the struggling fish so they could be untangled from the mesh and dropped into the bottom of the boat. Even as I emptied the net and dropped it back into the river, more fish were becoming entangled in its mesh. The boat filled with their fat bodies making the craft sit low in the water as I drove it back to the village.

The catch was unloaded and placed on a mat of willows at the top of the riverbank near our cabin. For the next several hours Barbara and I were totally occupied with the process of cutting, cleaning and hanging the fish on racks to air dry. We had to keep low smoky smudge fires of balsam poplar burning to repel blowflies and keep them from laying eggs on the still damp flesh. If the eggs were deposited it resulted in maggots consuming the catch. Even with constant vigilance we lost about ten percent of the catch to fly larvae.

It would be late afternoon before we finished the chores of fishing, and we would be covered in fish slime and dog-tired. We washed off in a bucket of water heated over a wood fire and soaked our smelly clothes in a washtub. If there was any energy left we might cross the river and visit families in the village. In the evenings, I would write up the day's notes in my log. We were usually in bed by eight p.m.

In their visits to villagers, they learned about how the upper Kuuvangmiut at one time used fish fences called weirs in the late fall before freeze up. The weir was woven of willow and cottonwood poles that stretched from one bank of the river to the other. Villagers used fish spears, gaffs, and seining nets to harvest the fish that backed up against the weir.

> *This technique was so effective that it temporarily delayed the movement of migrating fish downstream toward Kobuk Lake. The upriver people simply left the weir intact until it was carried off by floating river ice. The lower Kuuvangmiut began complaining that they were effectively being prevented from harvesting a rich supply of fall fish by the actions of their upstream neighbors. By the time fish made it to the lower river, running ice made it impossible for local villagers to harvest them. The upper Kobuk people responded to this pressure by no longer building fish fences across the full span of the river, although they apparently continued using fences to harvest fish coming out of small tributaries.*

Barbara helps pull in the seining nets filled with whitefish, 1974 The Banes participated in a full range of subsistence activities while they studied the lifestyle of the Kuuvangmiut, the Kobuk River Eskimos. (Bane Collection)

Although weirs were less common, seining continued much as it always had and women continued to weave their own seining nets with cord purchased at the local trading posts. The nets were 150-175 feet in length and about six feet wide.

"A seine was made in three sections. Each year the oldest section at one end was removed and discarded and a new section would be added at the other end," Ray said. "As long as this process continued the seine never wore out and could be passed from one generation to the next."

Caribou hunting took place during their brief migration through the area. In addition, Ray helped three men take down a moose and share it with the village.

In the summer and fall of 1974, unusually wet weather resulted in the spoilage of much of the salmon harvest for that year. To replenish their supply, village elders decided to resurrect an old fish trapping technique used during the winter. This offered Ray a rare opportunity to document the use of a burbot (tittaalik) trap, a means of harvesting that was on the verge of disappearing.

A Kuuvangmiut fish camp in the village of Shungnak. The processing and preserving of the catch was a cooperative endeavor. (Bane Collection)

Joe Sun chose the trap site prior to freeze up, a place that required careful study of the lay of the river bottom and the flow of water currents. He looked for "fish trails" where the silt covering the gravel bed had been disturbed by the passage of burbot. The site was chosen, but the trap couldn't be built until later when the river was stable and the ice was sufficiently thick.

During the building of the trap, Ray spent several nights at Joe's camp. It was October and Joe was living near the trap site in a 10- by 12-foot wall tent. The tent was warmed by a wood stove. The wind chill outside was minus 30. They shared meals of caribou meat, frozen raw fish, seal oil, and aqutak (whipped caribou fat mixed with blueberries). The food was accompanied by endless cups of steaming tea.

Ray watched as Joe constructed the "throat" to the trap using soaked, split willow branches as he skillfully crafted a basket-like device. As Joe worked, he told Ray stories of earlier times of the Kobuk people. It reminded Ray of his time with Ekak, when a deep friendship had been forged.

The intelligence and wisdom of these elders captivated Ray. It was hard to fathom how much their lives had changed since the days of their youth. Yet while they may have been perplexed by all the change, it seemed that people like Joe and Ekak harbored no malice. They simply held their wisdom with quiet dignity and when times were hard, the village came to them for guidance. Holding the knowledge of the generations before them, they knew how to deal with adversity and the whims of nature.

One evening, Joe's gasoline lantern malfunctioned and could not be fixed without a replacement part from the village trading post. Joe and Ray had no candles and didn't want to use up the batteries in Ray's flashlight in case of an emergency.

Instead, Joe fashioned a seal oil lamp from a flattened tin can and a wick of dry moss. He poured a small amount of viscous seal oil from a jar into a shallow indentation in the metal and arranged the moss wick so it absorbed the oil. Joe lit the wick and then tended the flame to keep it from producing sooty smoke. The makeshift lamp helped to push back the darkness, although it was still dim.

When he finished making the lamp Joe sat tending its yellow flame with a small twig and continued to share his fathomless store of cultural history. As he spoke, the flame from the lamp produced a yellow glow that flickered across the leathery creases of his face. I lay on a thick caribou skin mat at the rear of the tent. I became absorbed by his voice and dim

lamplight. For a very brief moment it felt as though I had somehow merged
with Joe and was experiencing the world through him. It lasted but an in-
stant . . . However, it left a profound impression with me. For that very brief
moment I felt as though I had been given an insight into the culture and
worldview of Joe Sun.

In less than ten years, Ray would return to Joe Sun's experiences through a follow-up research project. Ray conceived of a project to document the life of Joe Sun. He sought and gained the support of the National Park Service and the Northern Alaska Native Association (NANA) Regional Corporation based in Kotzebue. A major segment of the research was carried out in the upper Noatak Valley where Joe and other Kobuk Eskimo men had once spent their summers on long cross-country hikes in search of game. An ethnographer, Dave Libby, was assigned the job of recording Joe's stories. Ray joined the project for the Noatak fieldwork and served as the pilot of the floatplane used to fly Joe over the country. He also assisted in gathering the data.

Ray and other NPS researchers worked with elder Joe Sun on the upper Noatak River to locate Iñupiaq place names and record Joe's knowledge of the land and cultural history of the area, 1983. (Bane Collection)

For seven days, Ray flew the field party over the vastness of the west central Brook Range. Joe sat next to Ray while the interviewer and his Native assistant sat in the rear. In an article that he wrote for a National Park Service publication, Ray described those days with Joe:

> As the plane wound its way through mountains, valleys and canyons, slipped through narrow passes, and crossed seeming endless tundra plains, Joe pinpointed and named old camping sites; resource concentrations; travel routes; environmental hazards; burial sites; places where battles were fought between Eskimos and Indians of "long ago;" sites for building rafts to travel mountain streams, etc. Behind him the two researchers recorded this information on topographical maps, notebooks, and on tape.
>
> From their tent base-camp on a lake in the upper Noatak Valley, the party had frequent views of wildlife including migrating caribou, Dall sheep grazing on nearby slopes, grizzly bears lumbering across the tundra, and a pack of wolves hunting along the willow lined river. One brown bear made a brief night time visit to the camp disturbing nothing but the sleep of the party . . . A rich cultural blanket that rests gently on the land was revealed through Joe's dedicated desire to share the traditions and environmental knowledge of his people . . . The research party had the rare opportunity to see the natural world through the eyes of an ancient people. From this perspective it would seem that the lure of natural areas to modern man transcends mere esthetic values . . . Perhaps what modern man is really drawn to, is his first and only true home. Hopefully, this perspective and the heritage of the Kuuvangmiit can be passed on to enrich the lives of present and future generations of both Natives and non-Natives.

His friendship with Joe Sun became for Ray an anchor point, a kind of mooring that he would return to when political storms raged. While the winds could often be full of bluster, the land itself was slow to change; so too, it seemed the wisdom of the elders like Joe Sun remained steadfast and sure. In the years and battles ahead, Ray would draw on that friendship and on that momentary flame of seeing through ancient eyes.

13

— ✦✦ —

a place apart

After their time in Shungnak, Barbara and Ray returned to their cabin in Hughes to conduct additional subsistence research with Dick Nelson and Kathleen Mautner among the Koyukon Indians and Nunamiut Eskimos of north central Alaska. They traveled by dog team and riverboat, and used their airplane to visit and carry out research along the upper Koyukuk River and Anaktuvuk Pass. Their work was encompassed in the published report, *Tracks in the Wildland: A Portrayal of Koyukon and Nunamiut Subsistence.* The report recorded the old ways of subsistence lifestyles and helped give planners insight into how proposed parklands could accommodate subsistence use by aboriginal people.

Beginning with their dog-team trip and continuing with their subsistence research, the Banes spent a good deal of time away from their cabin in Hughes. During one absence their cabin was broken into and many of their valuables stolen. The most significant losses were the artifacts and gifts of ivory they had accumulated from their friends over the years.

"While nearly everyone in the tiny village knew who had committed the crime, no one came forward. To do so would have made them a target for retribution, and the nearest law enforcement was a hundred miles by bush plane away," Ray said.

An investigation by state troopers led to nothing. A few young Native men declared they no longer wanted white people in the village. While deeply saddened at the theft, Ray seemed to understand the frustrations of young people in rural areas.

"In a matter of just five or ten years, they saw their culture disappearing. And what did they have to replace it?" he said. "The money from the Native Claims Settlement Act could not stop the decay of the traditional culture. Indeed, it only hastened it. The younger men were particularly frustrated and alienated."

In their two years of subsistence research, Ray and Barbara's commitment deepened toward the concepts they'd discussed with Zorro Bradley when they had first met. Reserving certain wild lands in a natural state—much as they had been for millennia—meant the conservation of a place as wild as it was vast. But it also provided for the continuation of living Native cultures that depended on wilderness to sustain them. National Parks seemed like the right venue to achieve both principles of wilderness conservation and the protection of cultural values.

So in 1976, when Zorro Bradley asked if Ray would be interested in working on a long-term basis for the National Park Service as an assistant to John Kauffmann—who was developing a park plan in the central Brooks Range—he jumped at the chance. No parks had been established yet; it was just the planning phase in anticipation that Congress would enact a bill to settle the d-2 lands issue.

The Brooks Range is Alaska's northernmost mountain range and is located entirely north of the Arctic Circle. The mountain range stretches about 720 miles from Alaska's eastern border with Canada to the Chukchi Sea off Alaska's west coast. The range was named after Alfred Hulse Brooks, chief USGS geologist for Alaska from 1903 to 1924. The Arrigetch Peaks are considered by many to be the most dramatic granite peaks of the western Brooks Range. With an elevation of 9,020 feet, Mt. Chamberlain is the range's highest peak. The Alaska Native villages of Anaktuvuk and Arctic Village, as well as the small communities of Coldfoot, Wiseman, and Bettles were its only settlements.

Ray's duty station would be Bettles, Alaska. Until they could decide what to do with the cabin in Hughes, Ray and Barbara rented it out to the new school teacher in town. Eventually, they sold the cabin to a young village woman, accepting the reality that living as the only non-Natives in a small remote Alaska village was not in their future.

Surprisingly little was known about the Gates of the Arctic area of the Brooks Range. Bob Marshall had explored the Brooks Range in the 1930s

Ray in the Ulaniak Valley during a backpacking trip with John Kauffman, 1976. Ray was hired by the National Park Service to assist Kauffmann in planning the proposed Gates of the Arctic National Park. (John Kauffmann, Courtesy National Park Service)

and had given the name "Gates of the Arctic" to this mountainous portal into the unexplored Arctic. Many of the peaks and valleys remained unnamed.

In his explorations Marshall wrote, "There is something glorious in traveling beyond the ends of the Earth, in living in a different world which men have not discovered, in cutting loose from the bonds of worldwide civilization."

Ray would have that same privilege as he explored the many mountain valleys and passes in the area and became acquainted with the widely scattered villages and individual homesteads within and around the proposed park. When not directly assisting John Kauffmann, Ray would study the area through aerial surveys, and on foot, and by dog team, gathering data and submitting reports to the NPS Alaska Area office in Anchorage.

Ray's surveys were taking place at the same time and for the same reasons that interest in Alaska had suddenly grown keen across the nation. Battle lines were being drawn between those who saw Alaska as a rich resource for oil development and those wanting to preserve some of America's last remaining tracts of wilderness.

On April 29, 1974, construction began on the Haul Road that linked the Yukon River to Prudhoe Bay, becoming the first American highway to cross the Arctic Circle. Truckers would use the Haul Road to eventually transport goods and supplies to the North Slope for construction of the Trans Alaska Pipeline. Eleven months later, on March 27, 1975, construction of the oil pipeline itself began. By the time Ray and Barbara arrived in Bettles in 1976, trucks were rumbling across the landscape as workers began to lay the pipeline's zigzag of steel across Alaska.

Ray and Barbara were warmly accepted in their new community. Barbara volunteered to become the village health aide and went on to receive emergency medical training. She also filled in as a substitute teacher at the school and became a "spark plug" in organizing community dances and other social events.

In his new work for park planner John Kauffmann, Ray noted the complexities of the job.

Planning a national park was far more complex and challenging than I had imagined. Before setting recommended boundaries there must be a careful inventory of the area under consideration. What qualifies this particular place for national recognition and protection? Is it simply impressive scenery and concentrations of charismatic wildlife populations? If so then most of the State of Alaska would qualify. Does it include special cultural resources? What are the primary objectives in establishing a particular park? Is it to accommodate large numbers of visitors or to maintain a more primitive setting in keeping with wilderness values? What are the particular sensitivities of the environment? How much and what kind of use can it tolerate without deterioration? How will the Park Service manage the area if it does attain park status? What personnel will be needed to both care for the park and adequately serve the visitors? What park facilities will be needed? Where will they be placed, and how will they be equipped? John Kauffmann was the chief planner . . . My job was to help him do his job.

One Bettles resident off-handedly commented to Ray, "I guess you are the furthest north park ranger." Ray wasn't a ranger, but at the time he was the most northerly stationed member of the National Park Service.

"When I explained to local residents that my job was to help plan for a new national park in the central Brooks Range, most expressed only mild interest," Ray remembered. "To them I was just another government employee doing some obscure job. There was no park, and most community

Barbara in the Tobuk Creek Valley, 1977. Barbara often accompanied Ray on exploratory trips into the Brooks Range. (Bane Collection)

members seemed of the opinion that it would likely never happen or at least not while they lived there. Events in Washington D. C. were a world away."

In their work together, Richard Nelson had good naturedly accused Ray of having "the bends." Ray was always looking to see what lay around the next bend in the trail. The Brooks Range invited exploration and discovery in a way unlike any other. There were no roads or guidebooks. The only trails were those of caribou and sheep, wolves, and bears who had lived there for generations without human interference.

> Despite its relatively modest ruggedness, the Brooks Range has an appeal that transcends scenery. To me it is a natural mystery. Once you began to explore its secrets it becomes irresistibly captivating. It scatters clues in your path hinting at ever more enticing discoveries over the next ridgeline or around the next bend in a valley.

During the summer of 1976, Ray headed out on an exploratory hike with John Kauffmann, plus three others: author Joe McGinnis, photographer Boyd Norton, and wilderness traveler and writer, Ogden Williams. Kauffmann wanted to explore a potential hiking route into the upper North Fork of the Koyukuk. McGinnis was doing research for a book that would later become his bestselling *Going To Extremes*. Norton would use the photos from the trip for an article in *Audubon* magazine.

One of Joe McGinniss' concerns was the possibility of bear encounters.

"Sighting a grizzly bear on a ten-day hike through the Brooks Range is not uncommon, but close encounters are rare," Ray assured him. "As long as you are alert, keep a clean camp, and take simple precautions it is highly unlikely a bear will pose a problem. We'll be lucky to see a grizzly bear let alone have a close encounter with one."

Ray was wrong. Within the first three days they had three separate encounters with bears, one as close as 25 yards—a sow with two cubs. Ray had packed a .357 magnum revolver and although the bears left without incident or need for the firearm, it was a reminder that this was a wilderness not to be taken for granted.

> 8/10/76: We were up at 7:00 a.m. happy to see the clouds had lifted above the mountain peaks. By 9:30 a.m. we had donned our daypacks and were headed up the valley. It took about two hours to reach the base of the

waterfall. We clambered up a steep talus slope and ducked through a narrow notch in the cliff. My first reaction to the scene that confronted us was awe. It was like entering a massive cathedral empty of people. Before us, almost completely enclosed in light gray rock walls was an enchanted meadow, absolutely level. A tiny lake, like a liquid mirror, was nestled in the soft tundra reflecting the towering grandeur. A small creek meandered lazily through the meadow passing into and then out of the still lake. Approximately one mile west the lush green gave way to gray scree and finally the west end was closed by a rising tundra slope and then by a massive sheer-faced rock wall. The south wall of the basin was formed by rock strata rising vertically towards a climax of thin stiletto-like spires and peaks—some 2000 feet or more above the meadow. The north wall was formed by massive slabs rising less sharply—but still steeply—leaning away from the vertical mountain as though each slab was trying to climb over the one below in a frozen effort to escape the threatening spears of the opposite mountain.

Here in the discovery of Hidden Valley, they found no sign of past human visitation. Although Natives had occupied these mountains for thousands of years, they were a pragmatic people. They invested their energies and attention where they would likely gain the greatest return on their efforts; this valley was remote and concealed with virtually no sign of game. There was the distinct possibility that Ray and his party were the first to see this remarkable place in many generations.

Kauffmann and Ray hiked to the west end of the amphitheater while the others did their own exploring. When they arrived at the base of a rock shoulder, they began a steep, steady climb up a slope leading to the bottom of a sheer-faced rock wall. To the south, a creek tumbled down a rock ravine. Its murky headwaters flowed from the small glacier huddled against a barren mountain slope. As they climbed, they passed a small waterfall plunging off a high cliff to the north. Ray described the astonishing beauty that lay before them:

Once atop the mountain shoulder we had a superb view of the cathedral and surrounding mountains. The west rock wall was a fantastic structure. The rock veins sweep upward and literally bend back on themselves as the top of the jagged ridge is reached. It's like a gigantic ocean wave peaking and just beginning to bend forward to its inevitable collapse. The precipitous mountain wall along the south side of the valley is made up of sharply conflicting rock strata, some of which bend and rear upward to become small, needle-like spires along the rock face.

Perhaps the best way to describe the great swirls of rock strata, splendid spires and ponderous slabs is to refer to it as a symphony in rock. One can almost hear the sonorous chords described by the heavy leaning strata, the soaring crescendos of the peaking spires and the unifying, sometimes hidden, melody of the meadow.

Considering the opposing angles of strata, jagged peaks and ridges and stark shades of gray, one might liken the scene as being in the midst of a petrified thunderstorm. One can almost feel the violent turbulence of conflicting forces, explosive thunder, and wild expenditure of energy.

We felt akin to such past explorers as Bridger, Boone, Lewis and Clark and others who sought out and found the unknown and untainted. Each of us now carried a lasting feeling of accomplishment at being first and regret in knowing that others would undoubtedly follow. But for the next several years it will still be possible to find the unfound and explore the unexplored—here in the Brooks Range.

The group spent the evening relaxing around the campfire, reliving the rewarding discoveries and experiences of the day. Ogden spotted two caribou as he returned to camp.

The following day they carefully cleaned up the campsite, scattering ashes and removing other signs of their presence. On their way out they encountered a party of three hikers heading up the valley. Ray hoped they would have the same sense of discovery and pure joy of an unspoiled natural setting that they had just been privileged to experience. The hikers mentioned that they had come across the tracks of an all-terrain-vehicle (ATV) in the main Itkillik Valley not far from the entry into Cocked Hat Valley. The tracks were likely related to a sport hunting guide's operation based on a small lake in the main valley. Ray figured it would only be a matter of time before those tracks would make their way into the upper Cocked Hat Valley.

"The only thing that might stop or delay what seemed inevitable would be the protection of a national park—or so I thought," Ray remembered.

Their trip was coming to a close, and a chartered plane picked them up at Ulu Lake in the Itkillik Valley and ferried them to Itkillik Lake, a place that put them within walking distance of civilization. The following day they shouldered their backpacks and hiked east to Galbraith Lake toward the site of a pipeline construction camp.

"Well before we came in sight of the camp it was obvious that the modern world had arrived in the Brooks Range. Helicopters and other aircraft busily buzzed overhead and the industrial sounds of a massive construction project reached our ears," Ray remembered. "About halfway to the camp a helicopter circled our party and landed nearby. They informed us that they had sighted a grizzly bear following us and had driven it away. I appreciated the concern of the helicopter crew, but somehow it diminished the wildness we had enjoyed for the past ten days."

It had been a spectacular and educational outing, and Ray felt privileged to live in a place that until recently was so untouched by the mechanisms of man. On the last night of their trek, they camped near the top of the pass near Galbraith Lake and soaked in the austere beauty of the landscape. Each of them was filled with thoughts of the previous days they had spent without a trace of other human presence. No one could escape the sense of impending change.

Ray in Hidden Valley, 1977. Ray and John Kauffmann led a party that included author Joe McGinnis, photographer Boyd Norton, and wilderness traveler and writer Ogden Williams into a hanging valley that stunned everyone with its wild beauty. (John Kauffmann, Courtesy National Park Service)

*The following day we crossed the pass and gazed down on a scene far differ-
ent from what we had grown accustomed to during our long hike. Ahead we
saw the dusty brown line of the North Haul Road and the silver snake of the
elevated pipeline zigzagging its way south. Trucks, buses and SUVs rushed
up and down the road stirring clouds of dust in their wake. Helicopters and
light airplanes droned busily overhead, coming and going like mechanical
bees collecting a winter's supply of honey. The sounds of these activities
wafted up to us, and we knew we had passed out of the wilderness and back
into the domain of man.*

This was just one of the many treks Ray would make to explore and map
out the proposed area of the park. While Ray worked at this dream job
exploring and researching one of the most untouched and scenic regions
in North America, powerful alliances were amassing forces to do battle for
control of those wilderness areas.

14

selby lake

The nation's interest in Alaska was growing as the December 1978 deadline neared for the U.S. Congress to decide the d-2 land issue. The d-2 provision of the ANCSA required that up to 80 million acres of federal lands in Alaska, identified by the Secretary of the Interior for potential parks, refuges, and other wilderness purposes were to be reserved and given interim protection from state selection until Congress could act on the results of more detailed studies.

As Ray explained, "The d-2 lands question drew a line in the sand between those who wanted to see the development of Alaska's resources and expansion of its infrastructure and those who wanted to preserve much of the Alaska wilderness in its pristine state."

A touchstone for both camps was the construction of the Trans Alaska Pipeline.

In 1977, by the time the 48-inch pipeline was completed, it would traverse 800 miles of wilderness, cross 34 major rivers, three mountain ranges, and 800 smaller streams.

Workers thronged to Alaska and the state was awash in money from oil leases. Before oil, the state had struggled to stay solvent; the population was so small and the tax base so limited that even basic services were difficult to finance. The infusion of money into state coffers meant there were funds to pave roads, build schools, and offer handsome salaries to teachers and other state employees. The Banes' teaching salaries virtually doubled with the passage of ANCSA and the beginning of pipeline construction.

Conservation groups, on the other hand, were now focusing energies on making sure that the ten-year study set out in the d-2 provision of ANCSA did not expire without public lands being set aside as national parks, wildlife refuges, national forests, and wild and scenic rivers. Construction of the pipeline galvanized their efforts. Just months after the first pipe was laid down, a subcontractor was found cutting corners by falsifying the x-rays on welds around the pipe's circumference. Thirty thousand eight hundred welds were called into question; it would take a year to check all the x-rays and repair the sub-par welds.

As the deadline for final action on the d-2 lands question grew closer, the debates grew more heated. Pro-development and states' rights activists felt that the resources of the state ought to belong solely to its citizens. Conservation groups, on the other hand, saw Alaska as the one last chance to "do it right" in preserving wilderness as a national treasure.

"Alaska Native organizations were the wild card in this contest with both sides trying to gain support for their position. The promise to protect traditional subsistence was a strong argument for the Native groups to either support the conservationist position or at least not to strongly oppose it," Ray said.

Ray's work in helping to plan new parks was met with friendly skepticism in Bettles. The nearby Trans Alaska Pipeline project had created high paying jobs and given the community easier access to distant urban centers.

"The community liked the existing situation of open access to the land and its resources, and most wanted economic development," Ray said. "They knew that my work contributed to efforts to set aside new national parks, but most did not believe the parks would be created. Residents continued to treat us as neighbors but figured we would eventually have to give up the park idea and find real jobs. They suggested that I apply for the Bettles Field maintenance position under the Alaska Department of Transportation."

As rhetoric on both sides intensified, the media, both national and local, turned its focus on Alaska. The summer of 1978, Interior Secretary Cecil D. Andrus, and other members of Congress, decided to take a fact-finding trip to see some of the proposed parklands and to gauge the concerns of Alaskans. A dozen reporters accompanied the group. Their visit would take them to major communities and key regions of the state. Along with other stops, they would visit Selby Lake on the upper Kobuk River.

Ray accompanied Secretary of the Interior Cecil Andrews (second from left) on a tour of the central Brooks Range including a helicopter landing in the Arrigetch Valley in the proposed Gates of the Arctic National Park, 1977. (Bane Collection)

"Interestingly, no member of the Alaska Congressional delegation came," Ray noted. At the time, Alaska's Senators were Ted Stevens and Mike Gavel. Don Young was Alaska's sole member of the U.S. House of Representatives.

At an Anchorage news conference, Secretary Andrus was asked whether, if he were still Governor of Idaho, he would be willing to have so much federal land turned into parks and official wilderness.

Andrus pointed out that Alaska's Statehood Act of 1958 gave Alaska the right to choose more than 103 million acres of federal lands—nearly 28 percent. This was far more than any other state received in both acreage and proportion. In addition, Alaska Natives were granted 44 million acres.

"The state of Alaska gets four times what my state got. The state of Alaska is not being short-sheeted," Andrus told the reporter firmly. Andrus' home state of Idaho, which entered the union in 1890, was granted only 7.96 percent or 4,254,448 acres from the federal public domain.

Beginning with Alaska's purchase from Russia in 1867, Alaska was a military district of the United States under the control of the federal government. In 1884, the Organic Act allowed Alaska to become a judicial district with judges, clerks, marshals; the federal government appointed limited government officials to help run the territory. The Second Organic Act of 1912 allowed Alaska to become a U.S. Territory with an elected legislature. The federal government still retained much of the control over laws pertaining to the territory's resources and the governor was still appointed by the U.S. President.

At the time of statehood in 1959, the State of Alaska was given the power to "select" a certain percentage of lands not already set aside in federally managed systems such as national parks, national forests, national monuments, military reservations, lands granted to Native tribes, etc. The State did not have to exercise its entire selection at once but was given an extended time span to study the "open-to-selection" federal lands and to make their choice accordingly. It stood to reason that the State hoped to acquire the most valuable and productive lands.

While the Secretary and Congressmen continued their tour, Ray and Barbara were setting up camp for their visit at Selby Lake.

"The Selby Lake visit was an opportunity for an on-site experience in the proposed Gates of the Arctic National Park and to give the group a breather in an otherwise intense schedule," Ray said.

Ray and Barbara arrived beforehand to lie out the tent sites and build a campfire enclosure. Tents, cots, sleeping bags, inflatable rafts, food, cooking equipment, and other camp equipment and supplies were flown in on a government owned Grumman Goose. Other Park Service employees arrived to help prepare the site. Barbara did the cooking.

After their guests arrived, Ray was tasked with answering any questions visitors might have about the Brooks Range, proposed parklands, and subsistence issues. In essence, Ray and Barbara became the tour guides and hosts for the Washington D.C. dignitaries.

"It was a bit intimidating for a couple of West Virginians from an Ohio Valley mill town," Ray remembered. But once everyone arrived and began quizzing him, Ray was not shy about sharing his opinion on the value of keeping wilderness areas intact.

"I'll be very honest with you," Ray told newspaper reporters. "I don't like coming in here like this (by helicopter). I think you have to earn it."

Selby Lake, near the dramatic Arrigetch Peaks of the Brooks Range, could not have been a better classroom for demonstrating the power of untouched wilderness. Without roads or access except by aircraft, the landscape was much as it had always been—vast and soul-stirringly beautiful. It was a place at once tender with its growth of tundra foliage, and magnificent with age-old mountains rising in the mist. Congressmen fished in the clear lake and commented on the long twilight between daylight and darkness. Even time seemed otherworldly with the sun barely dipping below the horizon before it rose again. It was a place too remote and sacred for politics or business—or at least so it seemed.

A couple of days after the congressional party settled into the Selby Lake camp a Cessna floatplane overflew the camp circling as if to land. However, it flew off and landed about half a mile down the lake from our camp. No one thought much about it figuring they were just sport fishermen. The following day a motorized inflatable boat came through the narrows beside the camp carrying men who were for all apparent purposes sport fishermen. They had fishing poles and wore clothes typical of sport fishermen. The Congressmen waved and called greetings. The boats disappeared around a bend in the shore. Several hours later the boats reappeared and returned to their camp. About two hours later we heard the boats driving back up the lake. As they neared we saw that the occupants were in uniform. They were members of the Alaska Department of Fish and Game enforcement division. They beached their boat in front of our camp and got out carrying forms and notebooks.

As the ADF&G officers stepped ashore everyone knew why they were there. Some high level official had directed that a covert surveillance operation be carried out on members of the U.S. Congress camped at Selby Lake with the intent of issuing citations for illegal sport fishing. The fact that none of the Alaska Congressional Delegation chose to accompany the party to Selby Lake seemed a bit unusual. The officers involved had gone to considerable effort to fly to Selby Lake and set up a sham sport fishing camp. They had boated by the camp. Once out of sight from its occupants the officers pulled ashore and climbed up a mountain slope to a hidden vantage point. They used spotting scopes and binoculars to spy on the (Selby Lake) camp keeping notes on people who waded into the lake to cast for trout.

When the officers stepped out of their boat they began to read off descriptions of the fishermen they had observed, telling them to come forward and show evidence of an Alaska sport fishing license. All the Congressmen and their assistants stepped forward and presented their Alaska fishing licenses. Goodloe Baron was wearing waders and still standing in the water up to his thighs casting his lure. He refused to walk ashore requiring that an officer wade out to him. He had his license. It was obvious to everyone this had been an attempt to embarrass the members of Congress and discredit them regarding the pending Alaska Lands Bill. It failed and only served to swing more support to the conservationist cause.

I spotted Morris Udall standing off to the side looking grim. He knew this had been a setup and did not appreciate it. I walked over to him and expressed regret for the event. Congressman Udall's expression softened as he turned to me. "Don't worry, Ray. Just add another million acres," meaning that this rather clumsy effort to embarrass members of Congress would only serve to give leverage to those who wanted to increase the acreage of the proposed conservation system.

"Udall was amazingly calm," Ray said. "You don't threaten the reputation of members of Congress without getting a reaction. Their reputation is everything. In the end, the Alaska Fish and Game effort in trying to discredit the Congressional delegation backfired."

What Ray hoped to impart to the guests at Selby Lake were principles that he and Bob Kauffmann, Zorro Bradley, and others had discussed at length, sometimes in the field and other times at Kauffmann's home in Anchorage. Kauffmann, who lived on Kerchner Avenue, always seemed to have a house full of people passing through on their way into the Alaska wilds; Ray was one of them when he traveled on occasion to Anchorage on business. Known as "The Kerschner Club," the regulars who passed through were writers, naturalists, and adventurers who enjoyed discussing and debating politics, wilderness, and other topics.

One of the topics of discussion was how National Parks in Alaska should be different than those in the Lower 48 states. Many in the group agreed there was value to parks like Yellowstone that were readily accessible and where people could drive through with campers and RVs and see "wilderness" with relative ease.

The new idea of parks in Alaska was to preserve large tracts *without* building roads or facilities to make them more accessible. The idea was to leave the parkland intact as a true wilderness, not just a semblance of one. Visitors, in effect, would have to "earn" the privilege of standing at the Arrigetch Peaks. The only access would be by airplane; travel inside the park would by necessity be on foot, by kayak or canoe, or by dog-team or cross-country skis. Anyone who visited would be encouraged to leave the place as they found it without any sign of human presence.

"Let's save the real parts of Alaska—not just postage stamps," Ray told the group at Selby Lake. "The goal is to manage the land in such a way that a visitor one hundred years from now can experience the same feeling of discovery that we are feeling today, or that Bob Marshall felt more than forty years ago. The parks have to be big if they are to preserve entire wild ecosystems."

The visit to Alaska left an indelible impression on the visitors from Washington D.C. A journalist, William K. Wyant Jr., wrote a series of articles in the *St. Louis Post-Dispatch* following the trip. As he expounded on the controversy between pro-development vs. saving wilderness, of one thing he was certain:

"Whatever may be said of Alaska, it is a land of strange and wondrous beauty and its people are singularly attractive. But its scenic jewels now sit on the gem-cutter's bench, waiting to be fragmented by Congress. In a few years, for better or worse, Alaska will see great change" (*St. Louis Post-Dispatch*, Sunday July 23, 1978).

15

⸺ ⋅✥⋅ ⸺

birth and trauma

No one was to talk outside the meetings about what went on behind
closed doors. The mission seemed overwhelming, if not impossible.

In mid-September, 1978, Ray got a call from the National Park Service
office in Anchorage. He was told to pack his bags. They were sending him,
Zorro Bradley, and others back to Washington D.C. He should plan to be
gone for at least two weeks.

The Secretary of the Interior, Cecil Andrus, had sent out a call to the
National Park Service, Bureau of Land Management, Forest Service, and
the Fish and Wildlife Service to assemble a team of experts in issues related
to the establishment of new federal conservation units in Alaska.

> When we got to Washington, Secretary of the Interior, Cecil Andrus, called
> us together in the assembly hall of a largely deserted government build-
> ing. We were told that our job was to produce an EIS to be used by the
> President in the event that Congress failed to act on an Alaska lands bill.
> President Carter was considering using his authority under the Antiquities
> Act to establish national monuments in Alaska. He explained that it was
> the hope of the President and himself that it would not be necessary to use
> the Antiquities Act authority, but they needed a backup in case the d-2 bill
> failed to reach a vote in Congress.

The Antiquities Act gives the President the authority, by executive order, to set aside land owned by the federal government for protection as
national parks, preserves, and conservation lands. The Act was passed by
the Congress and signed into law by Theodore Roosevelt on June 8, 1906.

Roosevelt used the Antiquities Act to protect the Grand Canyon in 1908 and, since the Act's passage, it has been used more than one hundred times by most Presidents. But never had the amount of land been so vast—in Alaska, 56 million acres; and never had the stakes been so high, as state's rights advocates joined with pro-development and oil interests against a growing cadre of conservation groups nationwide.

The Secretary took questions from Ray's group as they gathered in the room. Ray asked if the Alaska public had been notified about this plan to exercise authority to declare national monuments.

Andrews replied, "No. This gathering is an 'open secret.'"

> He explained that members of Congress on both sides of the issue un-
> doubtedly were aware of the gathering and their purpose. In effect, the
> President and the Secretary were playing a quiet game of political poker.
> The Antiquities Act was their ace in reserve; with the hope that the dead-
> lock in Congress would soon end.

Earlier, in May of that year, and in spite of political crossfire and opposition by Alaska's Republican Representative Don Young, the House had passed an Alaska national interest lands bill. But Alaska's Republican Senator Ted Stevens was ready in the Senate with a counter proposal. Stevens had a powerful position as the minority whip and ranking Republican on the appropriations subcommittee for the Department of the Interior. He also had the support of the Majority Leader, Robert C. Byrd of West Virginia, who agreed not to call the bill to the Senate floor if Stevens and Alaska Democratic Senator Mike Gravel were opposed to it.

Ray and his group worked nearly round-the-clock in the old building to describe the boundaries and national significance of the lands in question. They also reported on the likely environmental, social, and economic impact of the lands' federal protection.

Terry Carlstrom, Chief Planner for the National Park Service, was the overall coordinator for the exercise. The group included 43 members and was divided into teams to address specific issues. Ray was assigned to the team on subsistence and cultural concerns. He also assisted the teams addressing the proposals for Gates of the Arctic, Noatak, and Kobuk Valley.

"We were working against the clock that was relentlessly ticking down to the lifting of the land freeze," Ray remembered. "When we weren't laboring at the task of writing countless rough drafts in the old Interior Building, we were meeting in our hotel rooms to continue the task at hand. There was no time to enjoy the attractions of the Capital. We did attend one social event at the home of Secretary Andrus."

When Ray returned home on October 7, he was completely drained. There was no doubt in his mind that much of the Brooks Range would soon be set aside as wilderness in the form of national monuments.

At home he received a letter from Terry Carlstrom expressing appreciation for the dedicated work of the team during their long hours in Washington D.C. Carlstrom wrote, "I want to take this opportunity to thank all of you for a job well done under adverse and trying conditions. Our efforts have proven to be invaluable since the Alaska legislation did not clear the Senate last Sunday."

Although Senator Ted Stevens had been willing to negotiate, Senator Mike Gravel had threatened a filibuster. The Senate went home in 1978 without action on the Alaska lands bill.

"Well, Ray, it looks like you will be out of a job soon."

Ray and Barbara heard this in various forms from friends in Bettles in the weeks after Ray returned from Washington. Newspapers carried stories saying the Alaska lands bill was essentially dead in the water due to the filibuster threat of the Alaska Congressional delegation and their supporters in Congress.

> I tried to tell folks that the President would not allow the d-2 protection of Alaska federal lands to end without some kind of action. He would use the Antiquities Act to declare national monuments if necessary. Virtually all simply smiled and dismissed my warning saying that Carter wouldn't dare declare national monuments.

Barbara and Ray were exhausted. Barbara had been hauling water and wood, caring for the dogs, working as the village health aid, and undertaking everything else that needed doing in Ray's absence.

They decided to take a vacation and booked a trip to Hawaii. They landed on Oahu in late November and spent the next two weeks lounging on sun-warmed beaches and snorkeling through the crystal clear water of shallow reefs.

"We slept like babies at night," Ray remembered.

Ray assisted a National Geographic Society crew in filming a documentary about the lands recently placed in national monuments, 1979. The crew also filmed the Banes' life in the village of Bettles. (Bane Collection)

Near the end of their hiatus, Ray picked up a newspaper with headlines announcing that President Carter had established huge new national monuments in Alaska. The article described outbursts of public outrage in Alaska including "trespass demonstrations" and protests. Many Alaskans demanded that the monuments be declared unconstitutional and said they would refuse to obey what they believed were illegal laws.

Nearly every elected official in Alaska condemned what the President had done, with Alaska's Congressional delegation claiming that the federal government was at "war" with Alaska. Alaska's Governor Jay Hammond called it a "de facto repeal of statehood" and vowed to sue to stop the act.

Vic Fischer, who had helped write the Alaska Constitution, felt the "hysteria" over the land withdrawals was unjustified. He predicted that the withdrawals would have limited overall effect on Alaska's economy or future development. His was a minority view, however.

In Fairbanks people took to the streets. Hundreds of protestors shouted they wanted to live in a democracy, not a dictatorship. With national television cameras rolling, John Eubank stuffed a set of coveralls with straw and attached a photo of Jimmy Carter's head. He drenched the effigy in lighter fluid and lit it, drawing cheers from the crowd. Alaska Independence advocate Joe Vogler began collecting signatures on a petition for Alaska to secede. A hunting guide made an effigy of an NPS employee and sat it at the entrance to his lodge. He used a moose bone for a leg and clamped it with a bear trap.

Ray and Barbara were coming home to Alaska in an uproar.

"There would be little chance to savor the memories of tropical breezes or white sand beaches," Ray remembered. When they changed planes in Anchorage on their way home to Bettles, Ray called the Park Service office.

"Ray, you and Barbara may not want to go back to Bettles," a senior official said. "There have been some very angry calls from up there, including some not-so veiled threats against you personally. We can transfer you out of Bettles to a job here in Anchorage or some other place if that's what you want."

Many in Alaska saw the federal withdrawal of lands for conservation purposes as a betrayal and feared the state would come to economic ruin. (Bane Collection)

In Fairbanks, President Jimmy Carter was burned in effigy to protest the declaration of monuments in Alaska. (University of Alaska Fairbanks Archives, via www.pbs.org/nationalparks /media_detail/475/)

Ray was firm in his intention to return home. Then he asked for as much information as possible regarding the Gates of the Arctic park including maps and regulations affecting access, private property inholdings, and anything else pertinent to the discussions he hoped to have with residents.

"I was promised that the material would be assembled and expressed to me in Fairbanks before the end of the day. We spent the night in Fairbanks with Zorro Bradley and had the requested material in our hands by mid-afternoon. I spent the rest of the day and most of the night studying the information," Ray said. "Then I put in calls to several people in the Bettles-Evansville community. Some virtually exploded at me claiming that the monuments were an affront to Alaska and that I was little more than a traitor to be working for the Park service."

When he reached Rhoda Musser, a leader both in the Native and non-Native sections of the community, he was told that many in the town considered him an enemy spy of federal government forces trying to take away the rights of Alaskans. She said that some were demanding that the Banes move out of Bettles.

"I asked Rhoda to call a village meeting to take place the following evening so that I could explain what the monument creation meant and respond to their concerns. She agreed but warned that I would face some very angry people. Finally I called Darrel and Neil Morris who were much less agitated. They said that they would meet our plane and have a warm meal waiting for us," Ray said.

> We arrived in Bettles in the early afternoon. As we stepped off the plane we were confronted with handmade posters stapled to poles and tacked to the sides of buildings protesting the creation of monuments and demanding that the National Park Service stay out of Bettles. My name appeared with President Carter and Secretary Andrus on several describing us as communists and demanding that I leave town. We walked to the nearby Bettles Lodge to wait for Neil Morris to pick us up with his van and drive us to their house. Local people we encountered in the lodge either refused to acknowledge our presence or simply glared. No one spoke to us. A copy of a village petition was tacked to the wall. It was signed by virtually all Bettles residents. It rejected any type of National Park Service facility being placed in Bettles or having any Park Service employees living in the community. I was gratified to see notifications of a village meeting at the assembly hall in the evening tacked on the lodge walls.
>
> We spent the few hours before the town meeting visiting with the Morris family. Rumors had spread like wildfire about how the park boundaries surrounded the town and that local people would be completely cut off from hunting, trapping, cutting firewood, traveling by outboard boat or snowmachine, landing airplanes, camping and virtually every other use of the lands surrounding the village. Alaska newspapers and radio featured stories of how Alaskans were being threatened with a Gestapo-type federal land grab that violated their basic rights as Americans and would destroy the Alaska way of life. With no facts to counterbalance [this misinformation, the rumors fed on themselves,] creating virtual mass hysteria.

When Ray and Barbara arrived at the meeting, the FAA assembly hall was packed. People stood along the walls and at the back of the room. Ray walked through the gauntlet of a furious crowd. He carried charts, maps, and handouts. As he made his way through the room, he felt the heat of the crowd's fury pressing in on every side. The room was ready to erupt.

"If the insults had been stones I would never have made it to the podium," he said.

"I hate your guts!" cried the village postal worker, someone who until then the Banes had considered a good friend.

> The next three hours are indelibly imprinted in my memory. Questions and angry comments, often overlapping, flew from the assembly. The maps of the monument boundaries were tacked to a bulletin board and printed material summarizing the proclamations and applicable regulations distributed. People were surprised to discover that Bettles was not surrounded by monument lands. They were relieved to be told that they could still hunt and trap in the new monument, and could continue to travel by snowmachine and motorboat. There were restrictions on the use of airplanes for hunting and trapping, but planes could still be used for non-subsistence access. The monument was closed to new mineral claims, but existing registered claims would be honored. People could camp, but new cabins on public lands could not be built. Commercially guided sport hunting was not permitted. This hit one village resident especially hard, as his primary guiding area was in the heart of the new Gates of the Arctic National Monument. People with private land or a Native allotment in the monument would keep their property and have access to it. I tried not to soft peddle the more restrictive aspects of the new parklands. People needed factual information. There were questions I could not answer. I wrote them down and promised to get the information they desired.
>
> The meeting allowed residents to release pent up feelings and allayed some concerns. However, it did not turn the tide. The fear and anger they felt could not be dissipated in a single evening. Many remained suspicious of Park Service intent and resented the changes that monuments would bring.

A few days after returning to Bettles, Ray drove their dog team out to their woodlot to bring in fuel to heat their cabin. The woodlot was a few miles outside of the village. When he arrived, Ray discovered their entire winter's supply of firewood had disappeared. He followed snowmachine tracks back to the community of Evansville and located the missing firewood between two cabins; his wood had been cut to a specific length with an identifying notch.

Convinced that the Banes would be forced to leave Bettles, and in light of the community's anger over the monument declaration, the wood rustlers apparently felt it was safe to steal from the Banes. Both young men were surprised when Ray knocked on their doors and demanded that they move the wood to his cabin. They had not expected to be confronted. One man's parents lived in Bettles, and Ray said they were hugely embarrassed by their son's act. Before long, the firewood was neatly piled in the Banes' yard.

A few weeks later, a dance was held at the Community Hall. Barbara usually arranged for the music for these events. It was an unspoken rule that whatever differences people might have with one another were left outside the dance hall door. On this evening, however, the rule was broken. Well into the evening a young man from Evansville confronted Ray. His mother was Iñupiat and his father was Caucasian. The young man had been drinking and was in "a mood to express his feelings."

"Why did you take away my dream?" he asked, his eyes glistening. "I just want to live off the land. I didn't want much, but you took it away!"

Ray asked him what it was that he wanted to do. He replied that he wanted to develop a trap line and live off the country. Ray pointed out the window and said, "Then go do it. The best trapping is in the lowlands and foothills, and there is plenty of that to the east, west, and south. That land belongs to the State of Alaska, local Alaska Native corporations, or is still managed by the Bureau of Land Management—just as it was before the monument."

Ray reminded him that he could still go into the monument to subsistence hunt, trap, and fish. In effect, little had really changed for him. The young man looked at Ray for a long moment, mumbled something unintelligible, and walked off to join friends standing nearby.

> The material impact of the monuments to all but a very small percentage of Alaska residents was relatively minor . . . This is not to say that no one was injured by the proclamations. Professional sport hunting guides with prime hunting territories inside the monuments were among those most impacted. They lost the privilege to commercially guide big game hunters on these lands. The filing of new mineral claims was suspended, and it became illegal to fly into the monuments for the purpose of hunting and trapping.

"The turmoil was inevitable. People had good reason for how they felt and had legitimate concerns," Ray said. It was clear to Ray that the only thing to defuse the explosive feelings of Alaskans toward the monuments was to provide factual information. So he, along with Bob Bellous, an NPS management assistant, began to crisscross Alaska to meet with people in towns and villages to explain and open lines of communication.

Barbara remained in Bettles and dealt with the community fallout mostly on her own. The owners of the village store at first refused to serve her. At times village children threw stones. Neither Ray nor Barbara felt any animosity toward them—the kids were just acting out on the frustrations their parents had expressed at home.

"Her good nature and genuine kindness eventually wore the villagers down," Ray said. "Besides, how could they rebuff the person who treated their wounds and gave them medicine for their ailments—always with a smile and kind words?"

Even through the turmoil, Ray and Barbara knew this landmark act of conservation was both historic and monumental. Remembering those moments working on the sod hut with Ekak and that seal-oil lamp lit evening in the tent with Joe Sun, Ray was deeply convinced that his elder friends would agree with the purpose of what had been done to preserve the wilderness they knew as home.

"We were at the birth of a grand National Park," Ray said. "It was a privilege and we felt we had a role in midwifing Gates of the Arctic into existence. It had its moments of intensity, but we wouldn't have wanted to be anywhere else."

The birth had not come easily and the fallout was still far from over. Only in the days ahead would Ray and Barbara realize the depth of some people's anger and their willingness to act upon it.

16

—·✤·—

line of fire

There were many things to occupy Ray's mind but the myriad tasks of daily living in a cabin in the North Country still needed attending to—hauling water, cutting wood, and caring for the team. As Ray harnessed the dogs for their day's work of retrieving a load of firewood from their wood lot, he thought about the challenges he now faced in the community. The adversities on a snow-covered trail were far different from those he was encountering as he and others broke ground in developing new parks in Alaska. It was a new frontier of sorts and he knew there would be some tough days ahead. But Ray liked a challenge and he expected this new journey would be worth the trip.

The wood lot was several miles from the cabin, and as Ray watched his dogs trot in front of the sled he remembered the time several years earlier that he and Barbara had made a three-day training run from Hughes to Allakaket by dog team to prepare for their 1,200-mile trip. Drifting snow had filled in the trail and soft snow made the progress slow and exhausting. After a while, they stopped to give the team a well-deserved rest. Ray didn't bother to set a snow anchor—the dogs were happy to curl up in harness and take a nap. Ray and Barbara dug out a camp stove and cooking pot to heat water for hot soup. Ray rigged a windbreak beside the parked sled and they settled in for a relaxing winter picnic. Then Ray heard one of the huskies whine. He rose up to look over the windbreak and saw a wolf standing over their lead dog, Melozi.

The wolf, gray and gangly, was a youngster "with more courage than brains," Ray remembered.

"Barbara," I whispered. "Look here."

As Barbara rose the wolf suddenly became alert. The other huskies were now picking up the scent and rising from the snow. The wolf backed away turning back up the trail.

"Oh, damn!" I cried, grabbing onto the handlebars of the sled as the team lunged in pursuit. I stomped on the sled brake barely slowing the rush of huskies now in frenzied attack mode. The wolf ran ahead perhaps forty yards and then turned off the trail to wade up a steep embankment. The sled tipped on its side as the dogs tried to follow. Equipment and supplies scattered all over the trail. The wolf easily got away, but we were left with the chore of collecting everything that had been ejected from the sled and then repacking it.

Ray laughed. What wasn't to love about those huskies? These days, rather than dog sledding, much of Ray's travel was by airplane. He and Barbara were the sole representatives for the National Park Service at ground zero in northern Alaska when monuments were created. The nearest park rangers were in Denali National Park, roughly 200 miles away, and they could not spare anyone to assist the Banes. From the time the Banes touched down in Bettles for that explosive first town meeting, Ray was called on to travel around the state to counter hostility and misinformation with the reasoned facts about the new monuments.

Then, on September 11, 1979, in Glennallen, a community that neighbors the Wrangell-St Elias National Park, someone threw a lighted flare inside a Cessna 185 on contract to the Park service. The fire burned the airplane to its shell. No one was in the airplane at the time.

"There had been numerous veiled and anonymous threats to Park service rangers, but this was a first time that actual destruction had taken place," Ray remembered. "The question was would it spread? It did."

Just a month after the firebombing, Ray got up early to fly the Park service Cessna 185 to Anchorage to attend a park manager's meeting.

A light dusting of snow had fallen overnight. As I carried my gear to the plane I noticed footprints in the snow leading away from the tie down site. Then I saw the damage. The plane's tires had been slashed, the door taken off the pilot's side, brake lines and cables had been cut and the interior of the plane vandalized. As soon as I saw the vandalism I avoided touching any surfaces or compromising any [incriminating] evidence. I followed a set of footprints in the snow that led me back into Evansville and past our cabin before being obscured by a snowmachine track. I called the Anchorage office and reported the incident. They immediately sent an FBI agent and Park service law enforcement specialist to investigate the scene. While I awaited their arrival, I looked more carefully at the damage. I discovered that the control cables to the elevator flaps and rudder had been partially filed through. This damage would not have been noticed had the person who carried out the act not resorted to more overt damage. If he had simply partially cut the cable, I might have missed the damage on my preflight inspection. In that case a cable might have failed after takeoff.

I came to the conclusion that the original intent was to cause the plane to crash after it became airborne. At some point in the process, the guilty party realized that if it was a fatal accident, he might be caught. At that point he made the plane unable to fly.

In the end, the attack on the plane shocked the Bettles community and brought people up short. During the day, several residents made a point of coming up to the Banes to express outrage and disappointment. Even with all the heavy-handed talk against the Park service, they did not want their town to be known for condoning violence.

The Bane cabin in Bettles, 1979. (Bane Collection)

Barbara drinks tea at hunting camp. The Banes depended on game meat for food. Each fall they harvested a moose to fill their freezer. The meat was hung to drain the blood before it was packed out. (Bane Collection)

There was never enough evidence to charge anyone for the crime. Interestingly, the short newspaper article about this second act of violence in two months toward Park service aircraft was buried on page three of the *Anchorage Daily News*.

The anti-Federal government sentiment was reaching a fevered pitch around the state. On a spring visit to Fairbanks, Barbara was taking the city bus to a routine doctor's appointment. Friendly as always and interested in the person behind the wheel, she struck up a conversation with the driver. He asked where she was from and she mentioned that she and Ray lived in Bettles.

"Really?" he said. "What has you living way out there in the middle of nowhere?"

"My husband works for the Park Service," she replied.

The man's face darkened and he immediately put the on the brakes.

"You can get off right here," he growled. "The Feds and anybody who works for them can go to hell."

Barbara paused and kept her seat. "Are you really going to make me get off the bus because of what my husband does for a living? Please just take me up the road. I don't want to be late to my appointment."

The driver harrumphed, put the bus back into gear, and continued on in glaring silence. Barbara stepped off the bus at her stop and kindly said to the driver, "Thank you. I appreciate your service."

The summer fair in Fairbanks that year included a booth where people could pay a quarter to throw beer bottles at photographs of their favorite villain: President Carter, Secretary Andrus, Representative Morris Udall, and the Ayatollah Khomeini (who had taken American hostages in Iran).

In his travels around the state, Ray sometimes covered the government decals on the airplanes that he flew with a piece of tape.

Meanwhile, President Jimmy Carter's designation of monuments resulted in Congress revisiting the Alaska Lands Bill issue in earnest. A bill was passed in the House in 1979 only to be stalled yet again in the Senate. The Senate's bill was far less than what conservationists had hoped. The 1980 Presidential election forced Carter's hand however. It was clear that President-elect Ronald Reagan would oppose the Alaska Lands bill, so Carter accepted the Senate version of the bill. On December 2, 1980,

Ray and Barbara depended on firewood to heat their home through the winter months. Their year's supply of wood was stolen in retribution for their involvement in the creation of the new national parks. (Bane Collection)

Carter signed ANILCA into law. Just as Theodore Roosevelt had set aside the Grand Canyon as a national treasure for future generations, Carter's signature set aside 56 million acres of Alaska land for future national parks, preserves, and refuges. Carter's designation of monuments had been the battleground for conservation lands in Alaska, and ANICLA was the peace treaty that followed. And while it fell short of what Carter and conservationists had hoped for, it was still dubbed by some as the single largest act of conservation in United States history.

When rangers and other Park service personnel arrived to work in Alaska's new parks, hostilities flared, but according to Ray and Barbara, it was nothing like what had taken place with the designation of the monuments. They said that much of the fury had settled down by the time Carter signed ANICLA, and many had begun to make adjustments to the new parks and wilderness areas. Many others, however, saw it as the end of a lifestyle that brought them to the Alaska bush in the first place. One of Ray's jobs, for example, was to inform a group of cabin-dwellers along the Yukon and Charley Rivers about the new status of their homesteads. They had illegally built their cabins on federal land prior to Carter's proclamation. With the passage of ANILCA, squatters would be allowed to stay on the land for life, but they could not sell or pass their homes on to family members.

Some of the River People, as they were called in John McPhee's *Coming Into the Country*, had lived in the area since before statehood. Others had arrived in the 1970s with a "back to nature" dream of living off the land. The realities of wilderness living quickly differentiated between those who could endure a challenging apprenticeship and those for whom the wilderness dream was just that. The idea of the few who stayed was to trap enough furs to provide the minimal cash needed for basic supplies like firearms, ammunition, traps, and clothing. Everything else would come from the land itself through hunting, fishing, berry picking, and gardening.

Ray designed and constructed a special dog sled that could be easily dismantled and compactly tucked into a small airplane. In mid-winter, Ray loaded up seven sled dogs, the sled, and supplies for an extended winter trip. He was met at Eagle's community landing strip by Dave Mahalic, Superintendent of Yukon-Charley Rivers National Preserve, and Bill Foreman, Chief Ranger. The next day Ray flew supplies to caches along the trail between Eagle and the northern boundary of the preserve, a distance of approximately 120 miles round-trip.

Ray and Bill Foreman mushed out of Eagle with a heavily loaded sled and seven huskies eager for the trail.

We hugged the west bank of the river as we headed downstream. Freeze up in the Eagle area tends to be a chaotic affair. The strong river current in the upper river tears away ice as it tries to extend out from the shoreline. The river becomes so clogged with heavy ice debris that it finally congeals into a tumbled mass of frozen chaos. I had seen stretches of rough ice along the Koyukuk and Kobuk Rivers, but this made them look like a smooth skating rink . . . Most people unfamiliar with dog team travel have a romantic stereotype image of either riding on the rear runners or in the bed of the sled while the dogs whisk you merrily along over a smooth trail. That rarely happens. More often the person at the rear of the sled is constantly shifting his weight and wrenching on handlebars to guide the sled through piles of rough ice or pushing the sled from the back to help the dogs climb a hill or cross difficult stretches of soft snow. A second person often must run behind to reduce the load on the dogs and make it easier for the driver to guide the sled. Even with temperatures twenty or thirty degrees below zero travelers must guard against getting soaked in their own sweat. They may be running without a parka or jacket to literally keep their cool.

Ray and Foreman were met with guarded hospitality at the cabins and homesteads where they stopped. These were people who had come into the country to escape the trappings of modern society and the intrusion of government controls. The land where they had built cabins belonged to the Bureau of Land Management, who had been largely, as Ray put it, "absentee landlords." Now residents were being told they had to apply for permits to live in their homes and that they would never own them outright.

Ray was not unsympathetic. Arriving by dog sled, and with his own long history of living a rural Alaska lifestyle, he could relate to the daily challenges they faced. Rather than just spell out the rules, Ray asked the River People for their thoughts on how to best define a subsistence lifestyle—a definition that the park could use in future management decisions.

With those kinds of questions, conversations opened, and ideas and ideologies were freely exchanged. It wasn't long before the River People were handing Ray packages of mail to deliver back to Eagle.

The River People had intense beliefs and opinions about subsistence. They tended to be idealistic considering subsistence more than just a lifestyle based on hunting, fishing and trapping. For many it had spiritual significance. They considered it to be a pure way of life that should be perpetuated and encouraged. Some believed that the Preserve should be a type of subsistence lab or training ground for those drawn to the lifestyle. This included banning the use of snowmachines and committing to living on no more than two thousand dollars a year to purchase absolute necessities.

Many of the residents of the Yukon-Charley Rivers National Preserve were young, with the exception of Dick Cook who was in his mid-50s. Having lived there since 1964, he was the acknowledged "elder" of the River People.

"He was more than willing to share his skills and insights into bush living with others who floated down the river to find hideaways to build a cabin and live off the country—as long as they didn't encroach on his trapping territory or otherwise crowd him," Ray noted.

Cook lived in an old 15 by 18 foot cabin, with bottom logs that were beginning to rot into the ground. The furnishings were simple but adequate: a thin metal wood burning stove, Coleman lantern and gas stove, kerosene lantern, a handmade bunk bed, cooking pots and utensils, clothes hanging from nails on the wall, and a revolver hanging from the ceiling.

Dick was more than happy to share his opinions with Ray and many of them were firm and uncompromising. He had little tolerance for technicalities or complexities when dealing with the government.

"He had the tendency to play the devil's advocate and was very direct," Ray said. "I found him to be both stimulating and enjoyable, if somewhat overwhelming and exhausting."

A few years later Dick Cook disappeared into the wilds somewhere along his trap line. Some wondered if he had met with an accident while running his trapline. One June 25, 2001, Cook's body was found in the Tatondik River, a tributary of the Yukon. His wrecked canoe had been discovered several days earlier.

In the days that Ray and his dogs traveled the river and met and mingled with the River People, he came away with some opinions of his own.

To Ray's way of thinking, the greatest impact of the monuments and subsequent passage of ANILCA to Alaskans was psychological. For the vast majority of Alaskans, little of material note had changed—indeed the gift was that great tracts of land could now be left *unchanged* for the discovery and benefit of future generations. Perception, however, had changed. Before the monuments, Alaskans still held a frontier view of no ownership of the land—there were still immense tracts of open wild lands with little or no significant modern development. In reality, virtually all this open land was already under management control of government agencies, both federal and state. However, the illusion persisted that Alaska was still "unowned" and open to anyone who wanted to escape modern civilization and go into the wilds to build a cabin and live off the land.

"A frontier is more than just land," Ray said. "It is the freedom to go wherever you wish and to be able to carve out a life with virtually no interference from governments. Simply by driving a few stakes in the land you could lay claim to a sizeable homestead."

In 1900, the nation acknowledged that the great western frontier officially ceased to exist. It took almost eight decades longer to close the northern frontier in Alaska. With the statehood act, the discovery of oil on the North Slope and the passage of ANCSA, America's northernmost frontier—at least the perception of it—had effectively drawn to a close.

"The creation of large national park and wildlife refuge monuments in 1978 was designed to save significant examples of the last American frontier," Ray said "but they could not save the frontier itself."

17

— ❖❖ —

growing pains

Now that places like Gates of the Arctic National Park and other parks and preserves had been established, these large tracts of land were protected from certain kinds of use. Traditional subsistence hunting was fine, for example, but those activities were to take place from the ground—no fly-in access was allowed. By and large, existing cabins could remain, but new cabins on public lands could not be built inside park boundaries. The question was how would the rules be enforced across more than 43 million acres of new national parklands?

One of Ray's jobs was to fly park rangers on their patrols. For a time, Ray maintained his distance from the law enforcement aspect of park management. One day, Larry, a Bettles resident, asked Ray specifically about the fly-in rules for running a trap line near the Iktillik Valley. Ray explained that the law forbade anyone from flying in to hunt or trap within the park. Traditional subsistence had never been practiced using this kind of modern technology. Larry nodded and then proceeded to leave town for a few days.

On the next patrol flight, Ray wound up flying the park chief ranger, Bruce Collins, over the Iktillik Valley and there, near a privately owned cabin at the edge of a smooth frozen lake was a small human figure standing beside what appeared to be a trapped animal. Ray circled and landed, and there stood Larry with a prime wolverine. The region lays far from any community and Larry freely admitted that he had chartered a flight to get into this remote area. The ranger issued a citation and confiscated the wolverine. Larry accepted the citation but was surprised and angry that he had to forfeit the pelt. Wolverines were hard to come by—a valued prize in the world of trapping.

Back in Bettles, no one differentiated much between Ray's role as the pilot and the park service ranger who issued Larry's citation. In the eyes of the community, they were equal villains of the park service. Ray in particular felt the brunt of resentment since he had participated in citing one of his neighbors for illegally using an airplane and trapping inside the park. This didn't particularly bother Ray. The cited person knew he was breaking park regulations. Transitions took time and these rough spots came with the territory.

In early spring 1980, Bob Bellous called Ray from the park service office in Anchorage. A new director for the Alaska area office was interested in becoming personally acquainted with Alaskans in the new park areas. Bob encouraged the new director to travel by dog team into Gates of the Arctic to meet with local residents. Bob and Ray planned a trip that would take them from Bettles into the John River Valley. The plan was to stop at two remote home sites along the way: the Alman's cabin at Timber Creek and the Fickus homestead at Crevice Creek.

Following the establishment of Gates of the Arctic, the Banes encouraged park management to mount a clean-up effort to remove trash and debris left from abandoned hunting camps, 1983. Tons of garbage were airlifted out by helicopter. (Bane Collection)

During the late 1960s and 1970s, a number of cabins were built illegally on lands that later became national parks and preserves. Some of these structures were removed while others were converted to public use cabins. (Bane Collection)

"I was particularly interested in him spending time with the Fickus family. They were the quintessence of the Alaska bush residents who had successfully carved out a life in the wilderness. Their point of view needed to be taken into account in the management of the Gates of the Arctic," Ray said. Bill Fickus was Caucasian and together with his Native wife, Lil, and their children, they had melded both cultures and were living a successful lifestyle in the North Country.

John Cook and Bob Bellous arrived in Bettles on a crisp morning in February. There was not enough room to carry both men on Ray's sled, so Bellous rented a snowmachine from a local resident to drive ahead of Ray and the dog team. They loaded the sled with gear and enough supplies to last a week on the trail. As they worked, the 11 sled dogs howled and lunged at their chains, demanding to be put into harness.

"We rocketed out of the village onto a hard packed trail leading north. Cook rode on the top of the sled load and clung to the side rails. In the distance the broken wall of the Brooks Range beckoned. The temperature was about minus fifteen degrees, perfect mushing weather," Ray remembered.

Less than two miles out of town, Ray stopped the team to make a minor adjustment to the towline of the sled. The towline is the rope connecting the dog team with the sled and it was an adjustment Ray had made hundreds of times before over many years and miles of dog mushing. The line lay slack, slumped in a coil on the front of the sled.

"Hold them up!" he called, as he made the adjustment. The command directed the dogs to move forward just enough to pull the line taut.

The dogs obeyed but moved forward with the pent up energy of a team ready to run. In a split second, Ray's right hand was caught in the coil of the line as it snapped closed with unbearable force. As the dogs pulled forward, the rope nearly tore his thumb from his hand and partially severed his index finger.

"Whoa!" Ray screamed. By then it was too late. Ray told John to stand on the sled anchor while he worked to extract his mangled hand from the line.

"With my left hand I was able to pull back enough slack to free my right hand. It was not pretty," Ray said. His thumb was dangling by a mere thread of tissue. At first there was little blood, but then it began to spout. "As I looked down, I recall saying to John, 'I sure hope I don't lose that thumb.'"

Since the team was in a difficult place to turn around, Ray directed John to stay with the dogs while he walked back to town. It was only two miles and he told John that he would send someone to help bring the dog team home. Ray packed snow around the severed thumb and finger in an attempt to stem the bleeding and control the pain.

Bob Bellous, who had gone on ahead on the snowmachine, eventually turned around to see why the team wasn't following. By the time Bellous caught up with Ray, he had walked half a mile toward the village and was beginning to stagger on the trail. Ray climbed on the snowmachine and they traveled the rest of the distance into Bettles.

An airplane, carrying renowned wilderness explorer Dick Griffith, had just landed at the airstrip for fuel on its way to Anaktuvuk Pass. Bellous roared up to the airplane on the snowmachine with Ray cradling his hand in a blood-soaked rag. Dick offered his seat on the plane and the pilot agreed to fly Ray to Fairbanks.

"Two hours later I was on an examining table in the Fairbanks hospital emergency room," Ray said. Barbara was notified and after quickly arranging for care of the dogs, she too flew to Fairbanks.

Dr. Bill Wennen, a reconstructive surgeon, tried sewing the thumb and finger back into place, warning Ray that it was a long shot—in the end, he might wind up losing the thumb. One problem was that between a lack of blood supply and being packed as it had been in snow, the thumb was now badly frostbitten.

"It hurt like hell, but it was actually worse when it stopped hurting," Ray said. One cannot feel pain in dead tissue, and he watched as the thumb slowly turned black and necrotic. The surgeon then presented him with several options, one of which was to replace his thumb with his big toe. Ray was not fond of this choice. He needed his feet as much as he needed his hands.

Another option was to remove the thumb altogether. Yet another option was to piece together what was left of the bone and remove the dead tissue of the damaged thumb, leaving the bone exposed. Surgeons would then cut a pedicle flap in his chest and stick the raw bone into the flap where tissue from his chest could adhere and graft over the bone. It would require multiple surgeries and his thumb would literally be sewn to his chest for a period of six weeks. Eventually the flap would be severed from his chest. Ray agreed to try it.

Following six weeks in the hospital, Ray's thumb was surgically removed from his chest.

"I then had a big floppy glob of flesh where my thumb had once been," Ray explained. "Over a period of several months, Dr. Wennen shaped the formless mass into the semblance of a somewhat shortened thumb."

One problem was that the fleshy glob had little tactile sensation, so as part of the reconstruction process, the surgeon moved a flap of skin from the inside of Ray's right middle finger and sewed it onto the front of the new thumb. By keeping the nerve and artery of the patch intact, Ray was able to regain some feeling and was better able to use his thumb to grip.

Ray and Barbara rented a small apartment near the hospital for two months during his initial surgeries and treatment. The most painful part was the physical therapy to regain the use of his arm and hand again. In the six weeks of being sewn to his chest, his arm had shrunken and atrophied, so it too needed mending. In the end, the new thumb became quite functional and Ray kept his fingers and toes intact. There were some slight oddities with his new thumb, however.

"When I touch the underside of my thumb, I feel the sensation on the inside of my right middle finger where the pedicle flap had originally been," Ray said. "Another disconcerting feature of my new digit is that the new skin came from my chest, which is a bit hairy. The thumb will grow a beard if I don't shave it periodically."

Ray and Barbara returned to Bettles with great relief, happy to be back home. It would be several months before Ray could fly again, but by October, he was back in the air. He bought an ATV to help exercise the dogs. He hooked the dogs to the ATV and let them pull the machine along village roads and around the airfield several times a week. The dogs loved it, as did Ray. Already he looked forward to when he could get back on the trail.

The following spring after more time spent traveling to villages around the state to explain ANILCA, Ray and Barbara decided to take a break and get away for a late winter dog-team trip. The trip would serve as park service reconnaissance into the headwaters of the Noatak Valley, where increasing numbers of visitors were beginning to discover its scenic wonders. Like the old days, they would be with their dogs in a wide-open wilderness, enjoying the discovery of new places together. By now Ray was 44 and Barbara was 43 years old.

Temperatures were almost too warm, nearing 30 degrees when they began the trip.

> We passed a band of caribou grazing along the north side of the valley. Feeding craters and trails were abundant throughout the lowlands, indicating a large number of caribou had wintered in the upper Noatak. Fresh wolf tracks and the scattered remains of two caribou on the river told a never-ending story of predator and prey interaction. We saw three moose moving together up the valley. We also saw several flocks of ptarmigan and one red fox. Tracks of wolverine, lynx and hare crisscrossed the river among adjacent willow groves.
>
> The Noatak Valley became dramatically more scenic as we moved upstream. Flanking mountain walls loomed higher and more precipitous. Mt. Igikpak's dark granite face and needle-like spires stood above its lesser, snow blanketed mates like a beacon promising the traveler even greater natural grandeur.

One morning they heard the haunting cry of a wolf some distance up the valley. The howling continued intermittently, gradually moving closer. By mid-morning, Ray and Barbara spotted a black wolf on the far side of the river traveling westward. The wolf stopped and stood intently, watching their camp. Then it disappeared into a willow patch. Later the wolf again howled, this time close to the southeast end of the lake near their camp. Ray imitated its howl, and to their delight they received a mournful reply.

An hour later, a light aircraft circled and landed. It was Joe Abrams, a Fish and Wildlife officer, who said that two Super Cubs were engaged in illegal aerial wolf hunting in the area. One of the planes was reportedly equipped with modified Browning automatic shotguns mounted to each wing strut. The weapons were sighted so that the pilot could line up a running wolf within sights that were marked on the plane's windshield. Once a wolf was in the line of fire, the guns could be remotely triggered by a switch inside the cockpit.

"Joe estimated that this pair of hunters had illegally taken in excess of twenty wolves in the general area of the upper Noatak and Alatna River Valley. They were now thought to be following the tracks of a wolf that had crossed over from the upper Alatna Valley into the upper Noatak, a distance of forty miles," Ray said.

Ray paused. Barbara looked away and steadied her gaze across the valley. She was grappling with what Joe was saying. The wolf who had responded to Ray's call that morning was a lone wolf on the run, probably the only survivor of a pack that the aerial hunters had gunned down.

"The fact that the wolf was within a national park did not make it safe from aerial hunters," Ray said.

As they talked to Joe Abrams, two Super Cubs flew down the south side of the valley, with one flying only 100 feet off the ground. The second Cub flew slightly higher and made a brief swing in their direction before continuing westward. Joe jumped in his plane and took off in pursuit. Ray and Barbara never learned whether Joe apprehended the culprits or not. But suddenly their trip was tarnished by the knowledge of these poachers, intent on killing a creature they had been so thrilled to encounter just hours earlier.

A day later, Nelson and Myra Walker from Kotzebue landed their airplane not far from the Banes' camp to check on a nearby cabin where Myra had a Native allotment. Interestingly, Nelson and Myra wanted to talk to Ray about illegal aerial wolf hunting in the park.

"Nelson said that he knew hunters were shooting wolves in the Noatak Preserve and he was concerned that these illegal activities would result in restrictions being placed on everyone living in the region," Ray said. "He urged me to fly around and prevent these activities. It was hard to explain that I was unable to act as a law enforcement ranger. I did promise to pass on his concerns to the park service office in Anchorage."

After Ray and Barbara returned home from their Noatak trip, Ray made several flights back to the area to look for evidence of aerial wolf hunting activities.

"On one day alone I documented fourteen wolf kill sites, many with the gory remains of crudely skinned wolves or splatters of blood that had stained the snow along with the tracks of ski planes . . . I hoped my flights might slow down the slaughter, but realistically I knew that only the beginning of the spring thaw would do that," Ray remembered.

Ray and Barbara's last extensive dog team trip was up the North Fork of the Koyukuk River to Anuktuvuk Pass in 1982. The village ahead is Hughes. (Bane Collection)

Wolves were, in part, what had drawn Ray and Barbara into the environmental movement to begin with and in no small way had led them to a career change and their involvement in National Parks. Suddenly maintaining a professional distance between his anthropology, subsistence, and piloting work with the park service and the law enforcement aspect of park management seemed like an entirely unacceptable arrangement.

18

—·✧·✧·—

a keeper of the park

Friends within the NPS encouraged Ray to get the additional training he needed to transition into park management. The whole idea in Alaska was to have a "new kind of park" and along with being able to address law enforcement issues, Ray had ideas about how the NPS could be more responsive to people who lived in and near the parks.

With the passage of ANILCA, the addition of Alaska's parkland doubled the size of the national park system. Ray's enthusiasm was admirable, yet some within the ranks subtly cautioned him against trying to make changes to traditional park management. Bureaucracies were notorious for quashing idealism. Still, Ray firmly believed, like many others in the conservation movement, that Alaska represented the "nation's last chance to do things right the first time."

Ray completed advanced flight training and immediately went on to attend a ranger skills academy at the Grand Canyon. He applied to and was accepted by the federal Law Enforcement Training Center in Georgia and after two months became a commissioned park ranger. After returning to Alaska he was offered a position in Kotzebue as management assistant for the Northwest Alaska Areas, encompassing three national park units.

The move to Kotzebue in 1986 was a profound change for the Banes. They had spent the past nine years in Bettles, longer than any other place since they married. They loved Gates of the Arctic, yet for some Bettles residents, Ray was a continuous reminder of the frustration and anger that local people felt when President Carter created the National Monuments in 1978.

"Relations between the community and the park service had improved, but some still had a difficult time letting go of bitter feelings," Ray remembered. "My presence didn't make it any easier."

They felt the time was right to move on. They also made the difficult decision to leave their dog team behind. Ray's work would be more office-oriented and he would not be able to give the dogs the care and exercise they needed. Most of the original team that traveled the 1,200-mile trek across northern Alaska had since passed on and the team was reduced to nine huskies. A trapper living in the village of Old Bettles offered to take them.

"He impressed us as being conscientious and kind," Ray said. "I gave him the whole outfit including harnesses, sleds, and assorted equipment along with a supply of dog food that would last the coming winter. It was the second time we had to leave our dog team when moving and it didn't get any easier."

The community of Kotzebue lies on a spit at the end of the Baldwin Peninsula surrounded on three sides by the ocean waters of Kotzebue Sound. It sits almost directly in the path of what is considered the Bering Land Bridge, a stretch of land that is thought to have connected Asia and North America during the ice age. Originally named Qiqitagruk by the Iñupiat Eskimo, Kotzebue had long been at the crossroads of ancient Arctic trade routes. Kotzebue Sound was named after Otto von Kotzebue, who sailed into the waters while exploring for Russia in 1818.

Kotzebue is the commercial, political, and cultural center of the NANA Region, which serves villages scattered along the adjacent coastline and the banks of the Kobuk, Selawik, and Noatak rivers. With far more services than the community of Bettles, the Banes new home had amenities like a hospital and clinic, elder care facility, and an Alaska State Trooper's office.

Ray and Barbara were not strangers to the area. They had passed through on their 1,200-mile trek by dog team and Ray had boated there with Dick Nelson during their Huck Finn summer of 1968 exploring the Kobuk and upper Koyukuk rivers.

The town consisted of a mixture of small frame clapboard and plywood homes; warehouses; a large rambling building that housed the main trading post; and commercial buildings that housed supplies headed for outlying villages. Modern buildings in town were government facilities and

Main street in Kotzebue. (Courtesy National Park Service)

quarters plus the commercial buildings belonging to NANA. The majority of the town was built on a long gravel bar that was separated from the main Baldwin Peninsula by a shallow lagoon.

Barbara was hired almost immediately to manage a group home of mostly Iñupiat youth.

It wasn't long before Ray's new skills would be put to the test. Ray was piloting the park's Super Cub with district ranger Bob Martin, on patrol of the Noatak Preserve, when they spotted snowmachine trails crisscrossing the upper slopes of mountains on the south side of the Noatak Valley. There were no caribou in the general area and they suspected someone might be pursuing Dall sheep out of season. As they passed over an open alpine meadow they saw blood in the snow and the remains of several dead sheep. Some of the sheep had not been retrieved and still lay in the snow. Others appeared to be missing only their heads.

They followed the tracks of the snowmachines that led back to the Noatak River and to a tent camp set in a grove of trees on the north bank. Circling the plane, they saw that the camp was unoccupied, but they could see sheepskins and meat, and what appeared to be an unskinned wolf hanging from a rack.

They flew back to Kotzebue and contacted Mack Shaver, Superintendent of Northwest Alaska Areas who informed the Alaska State Troopers office.

The next day Ray piloted the Cessna 185 on skis and landed next to the camp with Shaver, Martin, and the trooper. Three local men had just arrived at the camp on their snowmachines. Surprised at the arrival of their visitors, the hunters looked at each other nervously. When the trooper asked the men to put their guns away so that they could talk, everyone cooperated.

We first collected all the firearms in the camp and placed them in a secure location. I was instructed to guard the weapons. The trooper issued them citations for the illegal taking of Dall sheep, wildlife harassment, and transportation of illegally taken wildlife. Everything involved in the actual taking of the sheep was confiscated, including three snowmachines. The men were told that they could drive the machines back to Kotzebue, but they had to surrender them to the troopers' office within twenty-four hours.

The cited hunters had driven powerful snowmachines to the upper slopes of local mountains where they had chased and shot a large number of sheep. The sheep meat was apparently being sold both locally and to

Wildlife poaching was a major problem in the new parks. The remains of wolves and mountain sheep were found at this poacher's camp. A local jury found the accused guilty of a number of hunting violations. (Bane Collection)

communities beyond the NANA region, and ram horns were being shipped to an out-of-town buyer. It was essentially a commercial operation.

The men were brought to trial in Kotzebue with a jury made up of local villagers. The trial drew an audience of residents from the surrounding villages.

This was a test of the mettle of new protections afforded by the park service for public lands and its resident wildlife. Walking through town one day, Ray was stopped by a resident who asked how this all worked.

"You mean to say you can arrest me, Ray?" the man asked.

Ray explained that park rules were like Alaska fishing or hunting laws or rules about driving in traffic. If you broke the rules, you could get a ticket. And if a violation was bad enough, you might even get your license taken away.

"Well, we know what you said about the parks," the man said, referring to the earlier days of community and informational meetings. "We just never thought you were serious."

Ray and others who had taken part in the investigation were called as witnesses at the trial of the poachers, who had plead not guilty to the charges. Ray took a seat in the courtroom. When he was called to the stand, he looked at the jury and figured that the verdict was a foregone conclusion. Many of the jurors were people who either personally knew or were directly related to the defendants.

In the end, he was wrong.

> The jury unanimously voted to convict the poachers. The people serving on the jury listened to the evidence and realized that the violations threated resources that were prized by everyone and an acquittal would reflect poorly on other local residents.

Meanwhile, Barbara came home each night from work more heartsick than the last. Her job at the group home was taking a toll. Rates of alcoholism and suicide in rural Alaska were soaring and each day she went to work, she saw first-hand the carnage of creeping social ills and the devastation of mental illness. She supervised a staff of eight and daily dealt with deeply troubled youth. Many of them had been abused as young children; others had simply been abandoned by their families. What the home could offer these young people seemed paltry in light of their overwhelming needs. The job was exhausting and there were times Barbara came home in tears over the plight of "her kids."

She eventually decided to take a job working for the Alaska State Troopers. It was a job she could do without the lingering ache of despair on her heart each evening.

After their first trip together to Hawaii, Barbara and Ray began to make it a regular vacation getaway. Ray saved all of his annual leave time and took it in mid-winter. Their first trip brought them to three separate islands: Oahu, Kauai, and Maui. They were especially attracted to Maui, and they returned almost every winter to a low-cost tiny condominium within yards of the beach.

On their third trip, Ray noticed people racing back and forth across the ocean water while standing on strange watercraft that appeared to be large surfboards with a mast and sail. It was the early days of a new sport called windsurfing. He was fascinated. It looked like enormous fun. He found a windsurf shop that offered lessons and immediately signed up.

"Each time we returned to Maui I renewed my love affair with windsurfing, eventually building enough experience and skill to do some basic maneuvers and venture further out into the ocean," Ray remembered. "I wasn't particularly good, but I was fixated and having a great time."

If there are two things that Kotzebue has it is wind and water. After they moved to the area, Ray took one look at all that ocean water and the lagoons surrounding the spit and decided he no longer needed to wait for a vacation to windsurf on a regular basis. The water, however, was far from tropical. So he bought a dry suit—an insulated rubberized suit that covered every part of his body except his hands, feet, and head. A rubberized head cap, wetsuit booties, and gloves completed the wardrobe. Getting into and out of the rubber outfit took some effort, but it would keep him warm. He then bought a large windsurf board with a boom, mast, and a collection of sails.

> One mild June day the people walking along the waterfront of Kotzebue were greeted with the spectacle of a crazy white guy standing on a board with a funny looking sail heading out into Kotzebue Sound. Folks stopped and gazed in disbelief at the bizarre scene. Eskimos in outboard powered boats cruised by, slowing almost to a stop when spotting the strange craft and its stranger-looking passenger. Patrons of a shorefront restaurant carried their coffee cups outside to be sure that their eyes weren't playing tricks on them.
>
> Eventually, I fell off the board. Several men at the shore immediately ran to get into their boats to come out to rescue me. Before they could start their engines I had clambered back up on my board and again hoisted the sail.
>
> Most just shook their heads and went on about their business muttering, "Nulugmiut kiinuq!" (White man crazy!)

Over time people became accustomed to seeing Ray sailing back and forth in front of the town or behind it on the lagoons. With the dry suit he could extend his sailing season right up to the edge of freeze-up, which takes place in late September on the coast of the Chukchi Sea.

One Saturday in September he drove to a lagoon on the east side of Kotzebue and launched into the frigid water. He was pushing the envelope; the temperature was below freezing and a crust of ice was beginning to form along the shoreline. The wind pushed his board along at a brisk clip as he sailed out into open water.

He became so engrossed in sailing that he failed to notice the temperature was dropping. He knew this would be the last day of sailing before winter set in and he was eager to wring every moment from the day before packing up the windsurfer for the season. Water sprayed from the board onto the foot of the sail and froze. Meanwhile, slush ice began to form and collect near the shore.

When he finally decided to sail back, he discovered that slush ice extended about thirty yards from the bank into the lagoon, blocking his way to shore. It was impossible to sail through it, and the slush was already too thick to force a path by paddling with his arms. The ice was visibly thickening even as he sat on the board trying to figure a way out of his predicament. He realized there was only one way to get out of this jam.

"Help!" he cried.

He continued calling, hoping someone might be outdoors and near enough to hear his plea.

"Help!"

Finally, he saw someone drive up with a pickup truck towing a skiff with a motor. Walter Sampson, a local Iñupiat villager and official with the NANA Corporation, slid his boat into the water and broke his way through the thickening slush to pull up next to Ray. Walter laughed as he pulled Ray into the boat.

"*Nulugmiut kiinuq!*"

They towed the rig back to shore, both of them chuckling at Ray's improvised rescue. Yet by the time the ice flushed out of Kotzebue Sound the following spring, Ray was once again on the water with the wind in his sails.

Ray had other duties assigned with being a keeper of the park, and his flying responsibilities increased after their move to Kotzebue. The three park units were spread over wide distances and he sometimes flew park biologists to track a collared wolf, muskox, or other animals. Ray enjoyed flying archeologists to ancient sites at Onion Portage on the Kobuk River and to Cape Krustenstern, considered one of the premier archaeological sites in the North American Arctic. The beach ridge complex on Cape Krusenstern is composed of ancient beach ridges containing every known cultural tradition in northwest Alaska from the last 5,500 years. Talking to archeologists and scientists gave Ray the opportunity to see fieldwork in progress. His

Ray kept meticulous notes and journals over the years. (Bane Collection)

flights occasionally took him to the upper Kobuk Valley, and to the home of their old friend, Joe Sun.

> *When time and circumstances permitted I made it a point to visit with Joe Sun and other villagers, refreshing friendships and exchanging stories. Joe and I would reminisce about our time building a winter fish trap, flying in the upper Noatak finding "old places" and his endless supply of stories about the history of the Kobuk Eskimos. His wife, Laura, joined in with stories of the fall fish camps in the upper reaches of the Kobuk and of her relatives who once lived along the Pah River. Other villagers would wander in to drink tea and contribute their memories to the conversation.*

Law enforcement was one of the most difficult aspects of his job, but without it, the establishment of the parks meant nothing. Boundary lines on a map and the rules for the use of protected lands were only pieces of paper unless the laws were carried out. Poaching was one issue for law enforcement. Illegal cabin building was another. Individuals were allowed to hunt, fish, and trap within the parks and preserves for subsistence purposes, but building a permanent structure was usually not permitted. Among other reasons, the use of cabins for subsistence purposes had never been a traditional custom of Arctic peoples. They had relied on wall tents, which could be easily moved to new trapping country when conditions warranted. Cabin building by default gave the owner a preferential claim to the surrounding area, an unfair advantage to others who might also hunt, trap, or fish in the area. Northern Iñupiat groups do not traditionally recognize exclusive individual "ownership" of a given trap line. Permanent structures also have long-term impacts on the land itself.

So when a permit was denied to a resident of Noatak to build a cabin on parkland, Ray thought that would be the end of the matter. The applicant had a Native allotment just a few miles from where he wanted to build a cabin, a place where he could build on his own private property. The individual decided to build on parkland anyway and got to work clearing trees for a log house. In the Arctic, shrubs, trees, and grasses do all of their annual growing in a few weeks of a short-lived summer. A mature spruce tree, just a few inches in diameter, could easily be a century old, and the man had already cut several stands.

Ray avoided taking legal action by meeting with the cabin builder, the council of his village, and NANA representatives. The council and NANA representatives sympathized with Ray's efforts, but were not willing to get involved. The cabin builder was issued a warning about the woodcutting but the warning did nothing to deter him. He continued on with his project.

Finally, Ray flew his plane up the Noatak River and landed on a rough gravel bar.

> I taxied the plane over the bumpy surface to the upper end of the bar. There was a tent camp on the nearby riverbank. An Eskimo family sat around a campfire. I pulled my field pack from the plane and walked into the camp. The subject of my visit stood off to one side apart from the group. Thirty yards away lay a large pile of spruce logs next to a clearing that had been cut from the surrounding cover.
>
> The Native family welcomed me to their fire and offered me tea. I pulled out a box of cookies from my pack to share with my hosts. We sat on the

ground talking idly about the weather, fish runs and wildlife sightings. Finally, the patriarch of the group asked, "How come you stop here, Ray?" It was time to do my job. I reached into my pack and extracted a metal clipboard with a citation form. "I have come to give your son a citation for breaking park regulations," I responded. The others sat quietly while I wrote out the violation notice. When I tried to hand it to him, he walked away. I left it with his parents and thanked them for their hospitality. I climbed into the plane and flew back to Kotzebue.

The alleged violator appealed the citation, which was his right. A local public legal aide represented him before a misdemeanor trial. The judge reviewed the evidence, including the history of efforts by the Park Service to resolve the problem. The judge found him in violation of federal regulations governing the cutting of live standing timber.

Since he had not actually begun to assemble the cabin he was not cited for illegally building a permanent structure on public lands. He was told not to continue attempts to build a cabin at the site. In the end, the man built a cabin on his Native allotment nearby.

Aside from law enforcement work, Ray had an idea about how to manage the parks in a way that involved the communities and residents on an on-going basis. It was a way that would foster relationships and garner buy-in from local stakeholders.

The park service already had a mechanism to do this. Each of the new national parks in Alaska was directed to produce a General Management Plan (GMP) that would set out its primary objectives and describe the goals for the park for a period of four years. Ray had already helped create GMPs for Gates of the Arctic. In Kotzebue Ray was tasked with coordinating three more GMPs for that area.

Ray flew to and attended constant rounds of meetings in remote villages. With park planners and representatives of Native regional corporations, he encouraged local residents to voice their concerns and desires for the new parks. He wanted the new GMPs for each park to be considered a performance contract between the NPS and those who had contributed to its formation.

In carrying out the GMP's plan objectives and management guidelines, Ray suggested there be annual public reports on the progress of the GMP. He also suggested tying accomplishments directly to employee performance evaluations. In other words, superintendents and staff would be held accountable for carrying out the management plan laid out by law and agreed upon by consensus of the entire range of park stakeholders. It would encourage consistency even as changes in park management took place.

When Ray presented this concept to higher agency management, however, it was met with stiff skepticism.

"It turns out that although the park service was legally required to produce GMPs, they were not required to implement them," Ray said.

In his day-to-day work, Ray felt privileged to be a steward of the parks in their infancy. These were unlike any national parks in the Lower 48. No Native Americans hunted, fished, or gathered in Yosemite or Yellowstone national parks. In these new Alaska parks, where such activities were allowed, ethnicity was not relevant as long as users resided within a designated subsistence area and practiced long-established traditions of the region. This meant some often complicated and at times nuanced interpretations of the law.

Ray knew it would not be easy for the park service to carry out its responsibilities to both provide for legitimate subsistence and to protect the wild character of the parks. It would mean constant vigilance and on-going communication with local residents. The adoption of modern technology, particularly motorized transportation like ATVs, complicated park management; the parks had to be protected from encroachments that would degrade wilderness while still allowing for ancient subsistence traditions.

"The General Management Plan for each park laid out the legal parameters for subsistence and access and provided the foundation for working with residents on these sensitive issues; but the plan was only as effective as the park's willingness to use it as a means to confront these issues," Ray said. His observation was that agency culture emphasized the autonomy of individual park management and a largely ad hoc system of dealing with issues. After all of the work and community input of drawing up a park GMP, the document too often just collected dust.

Ray was beginning to wonder if the park service had the flexibility or the political backbone to uphold this new and inspired vision as the caretaker and champion on behalf of Alaska's wilderness.

19

⁓ ✧ ⁓

among bears

The brown bear sow stood in the water on all fours surveying the moving shadows beneath the river's surface. Her cinnamon fur shimmered in the sunshine. Occasionally, she dipped her nose into the water, lowered her head up to her ears, and periscoped while keeping a listening ear on two cubs that romped on the shore. The cubs by turns watched her and then batted at each other in mock battle. The sow, moving with swift efficiency, suddenly dunked her entire head under the fast-moving current and came up with a flopping salmon gripped between her jaws. Water ran off her snout and ears as she padded to shore. She now had the cubs' complete attention. Holding the salmon against the ground with an immense paw, she used her teeth to strip off its skin. Then she ambled back into the water, letting the cubs trounce on the still-moving fish to have their fill.

Every July at Katmai National Park, salmon arrive in huge schools from Alaska's Bristol Bay waters to the estuary of the Naknek River. The salmon swim upstream approximately twenty-five miles to Naknek Lake and from there move into the streams that feed the lake—including Brooks River. The Brooks River meanders for a narrow mile to connect Lake Brooks with Naknek Lake, creating a corridor less than fifty yards wide for salmon working their way upstream.

This concentration of fish draws the monarch of the Alaska wilderness— the coastal brown bear—to feast on the bounty before the onset of the long winter. Their protein-rich diets allow them to grow enormous in size, as much as 1,400 pounds for an adult male.

Aerial view of the Brooks River and Brooks Camp complex. Brooks River Camp is the only developed NPS visitor facility in Katmai National Park and Preserve. The lodge, viewing platforms, and campground are located within a radius of roughly one-half mile. (Courtesy National Park Service)

It was here, in 1987, that Ray was hired to be the Superintendent of Katmai National Park and Preserve. Ray and Barbara looked forward to working in Katmai not only for its charismatic wildlife but also for its dramatic setting among active volcanoes and for the archaeological evidence that indicated people had long been in the area. Ancient peoples had settled in the Brooks River region for the same reason that bears congregate there today—the reliable source of food provided by seasonal runs of salmon. The rich archeological sites of the park were still being discovered in the 1980s as Ray and Barbara packed up to start a new adventure at Katmai.

From Kotzebue they moved some 600 miles due south to the community of King Salmon, which lay sixteen miles upriver from the community of Naknek. King Salmon was their base and winter home, a community built around a U.S. military airfield. The Cold War still smoldered between the superpowers and the Soviet Union just a short distance across the Bering Strait from Alaska. Ray and Barbara often heard fighter jets scrambling to monitor Soviet flights off the western coast of Alaska.

During the summer season, Ray and Barbara lived at the superintendent's cabin at Brooks Camp inside the park itself. The camp was approximately thirty-two miles from King Salmon and could be reached by boat from a docking area at the outlet of Naknek Lake. Ray often used the park float-plane to ferry supplies and personnel between places.

From the beginning, Ray had his work cut out for him. Even before he arrived, many key employees had transferred to other parks, leaving critical gaps in park operations.

"It was as though someone had pulled a plug and with the staff went much of the institutional memory and insight of how and why the park was managed before my arrival," Ray remembered. "We struggled through August, September, and October with remaining personnel often doing double duty."

Barbara worked as a full-time volunteer in the park (VIP), and so most days the two of them went to work together. Barbara's full-time volunteer work proved invaluable. She showed up each morning at the park office to help other employees, especially administrative staff, deal with the heavy workload.

"I often worked late and Barbara was almost always there to walk home with me," Ray said. "Barbara never held a paid position with the NPS but she was happy to volunteer her time because she was committed to the parks and the ideals of the NPS."

When they were not working, Ray and Barbara often took walks on the park road or along the lakeshore. The concentration of bears was greatest in July during the salmon runs and again in September, when spawned-out salmon clogged the river, but bears were known to pass through the area any time during the summer season. Ray and Barbara often found themselves sharing the trail with bruins in which case they simply stepped aside. Bears had the right of way at Brooks Camp.

The standard procedure was to walk off to the side and wait while making some noise to keep from surprising the bear. Ninety nine percent of the time the bear would barely acknowledge you and simply amble by, unimpressed by your presence. Watching a brown bear weighing over a thousand pounds pass within less than twenty yards is truly a humbling experience.

Flying continued to be a part of Ray's work. The park was alternately assigned a Cessna 206, a Cessna 185, and a Super Cub. Depending on the season these planes could be equipped with wheels, hydraulic wheel skis, and floats.

If the flight conditions in the Alaska interior and Arctic coast had been challenging, the conditions were even more so in southwest Alaska. Ray landed and took off on sloping ocean beaches, tidal flats, volcanic ash fields, wind-churned lakes, ocean swells, and even on a small lake nestled deep inside a volcanic crater.

Severe weather frequently forced Ray to fly low while ferrying supplies and personnel between King Salmon and Brooks Camp. During those low flights, he noticed what appeared to be rutted all-terrain vehicle (ATV) trails cutting deep inside the park boundaries. From the air the physical impact appeared considerable. Later he walked a ridge line, known as Pike Ridge, just inside the recently ANILCA extended park boundaries, and found that ATVs had caused widespread damage to low growing vegetation and heavy erosion of soil. Small trees had been pushed over and the area was littered with trash and other debris. He also found evidence of illegal hunting. Many of the impacts along the ridge line appeared to have been going on for some time, likely before the extension of the park boundary in 1980. However, more recent trails were now extending into long established pre-ANILCA park lands. This coincided with the virtual explosion of ATV use throughout rural Alaska, particularly over the past couple of years. The longer these illegal incursions went on the more entrenched and difficult it would be to correct the situation. When winter snows fell, he followed ATV tracks and discovered winter trap lines had been set well into the park. He later discovered ATV trails were also entering the park from the north, originating from villages located along the shore of Iliamna Lake. While hunting and trapping were permitted in the northern preserve section of Katmai, no subsistence or sport hunting was permitted in the park itself.

Ray learned that a number of residents from the village of Naknek and King Salmon, including military personnel from the Air Force base, had been driving ATVs along Pike Ridge for several years before the ridge had been incorporated in the park. Now, however, local ATVs had become far more powerful and versatile, and residents were extending their forays deeper into park lands. This technology posed a serious challenge for park management. In addition to impacts to natural resources, the ATVs posed a serious threat to archaeological sites barely hidden beneath a thin layer of soil. The more Ray investigated the more damage he found. Recreational use of these machines was only beginning to ramp up. Ray felt something had to be done.

In the fall of 1987, Ray and his Katmai park staff developed an ATV management strategy, which they then took to the public. Handouts of boundary maps were distributed to local residents and posted in conspicuous places. Park employees attended public meetings to explain regulations, answer questions, and respond to concerns about local uses of the park. Boundary markers were placed in areas of heavy ATV use. The park staff worked closely with the U.S. Fish and Wildlife Service, King Salmon Air Force Base command, local Native organizations, and the regional Fish and Game Advisory Council. Rangers were sent out into some of the most impacted areas of the park to contact users on the ground and ask for their cooperation. Numerous flights were made to map the full extent of ATV use and its damage.

Large concentrations of brown bears annually congregate along the Brooks River, a small stream joining two large lakes. Dozens of bears show up for an annual feast of salmon, drawing thousands of bear-watchers from around the world. (Courtesy National Park Service)

Public reaction to restrictions on ATV use was decidedly mixed. Some were grateful that something was being done about these loud and destructive machines. Others, however, felt that the park was being heavy-handed and some complained to their local, state, and even Congressional representatives. Feeling the heat of political pressure, the park regional office contacted Ray and encouraged him to discontinue his ATV program, or at least tone it down a bit.

Ray pointed out that he was clearly working from the park's General Management Plan. The GMP was meant as a guide for all decisions for the park, a kind of handbook and bible written over time with input by local residents, stakeholders, and the general public. Draft copies of the GMP were sent for review to state agencies and the offices of state and federal elected representatives. The same held true for every other park in Alaska.

Katmai's GMP laid out three objectives with regard to ATV use:

1. Generally prohibit ATV traffic and related activities within the park and preserve boundaries.

Hallo Bay in Katmai National Park is important bear habitat. The bears graze on the marsh grass and feed on clams in the intertidal zone until salmon begin to migrate up the local streams. Hallo Bay was heavily impacted by the *Exxon Valdez* oil spill. (Courtesy Mitchell Silver)

2. Only allow ATV use by special use permit for well-defined and legitimate purposes (i.e. access to private inholdings) when it could be shown as the least damaging means of access.
3. Work with neighboring landowners and local residents to resolve ATV concerns.

Ray emphasized to regional officials that no citations had been issued; instead he and his staff were focusing on communication and voluntary cooperation.

> It took two years to finally turn the tide. Public sentiment gradually shifted as reflected in a formal resolution of support by the Bristol Bay regional Fish and Game Advisory Council. The King Salmon Air Force Base personnel formed a volunteer Wildlife Ethics Committee to assist park rangers in preventing illegal ATV incursions and in protecting park resources. This group evolved into an invaluable source of volunteer labor maintaining park trails and facilities. Illegal ATV incursions into the park dropped to a small fraction of what they had been.

It was a slow process, but a satisfying victory in educating people about the damage that ATVs wreaked on the landscape. The timing could not have been better since the popularity of these machines was soaring. Ray was frustrated that the park service had flinched under political pressure.

Ray was determined however, and decidedly uncompromising in his protectiveness of parklands like Katmai. As far as Ray was concerned, "A caretaker who knows of or suspects illegal and damaging activities taking place on federal parklands while opting to look the other way for political or personal convenience is a poor excuse for a park superintendent."

One day in early summer, Ray flew the Super Cub to make an aerial patrol of the park coastline. The beach adjoining Hallo Bay along the park coastline is a level grassy plain. Before the arrival of the summer salmon migration, bears often frequent the inner bay, grazing on marsh plants. A cache of aviation fuel in bear-proof, five-gallon cans near the western edge of the bay allowed park service pilots to make extended flights along the coastline without having to turn back for fuel. As he circled to land, he spotted three adult bears about a quarter mile from the fuel cache. They seemed to be preoccupied with grazing.

Ray landed and taxied over to the cache. From the ground, the bears had disappeared from view. Standing on the plane's large tundra tires, he lifted two cans of gas to the top of each wing and then climbed onto a wing to begin refueling his airplane. From his slightly higher vantage point, he discovered that the three bears had moved much closer.

> It seemed they were playing some type of game chasing one another. One of the bears was obviously a fully-grown adult male. Suddenly the large boar aggressively charged a second bear, setting off a brief battle. The two combatants roared and circled each other, mouths agape displaying stout fangs and heads turning to the side. Drool dripped from their lips. The larger bear bit and slashed the smaller male. It escaped the attack and ran off across the meadow. The large male bear now turned its full attention to the third bear. I realized then that I was watching a mating ritual. The two lovebirds continued to move toward the airplane while I sat watching from the wing.

Ray quietly lifted his dangling feet and tucked them out of the way of the oncoming bear. Ray held his breath as the boar passed directly underneath him.

"When I looked down on that enormous mass of fur and muscle it again reminded me that out here I was just part of the food chain and I wasn't necessarily the top link," Ray remembered.

The big boar's focus was on the sow, however, and he paid no attention to Ray or the Super Cub. The female ambled toward the beach and the male followed intently. They eventually rounded a nearby point of land and disappeared.

Ray finished fueling the plane and continued on his way. He never tired of the unexpected pleasures of his job.

Bears often grazed on sedges growing along the meadows and tidal flats of Hallo Bay when salmon were not in the river. Ray noticed that at low tide, when expanses of tidal lands were exposed, bears would walk out onto the smooth wet sand and nose around. Curious, Ray landed a few times to see what the bears were up to. It turned out they were searching for clams.

> When a bear discovered the location of a clam it would furiously dig down and uncover the succulent shellfish. The bear would then delicately insert a claw from either paw and pry the shells open so it could use its tongue and dexterous lips to transfer the contents to its mouth. They went to quite a bit

of effort for a relatively small reward. I came to realize that the beach line did not limit the area the bears exploited. Their habitat extended well off-shore. Whatever affected the coastal waters of the park had a direct impact on the bears, foxes, wolves, eagles and other predators and scavengers.

All of which pointed to the complex web of life and the interdependence of species and habitats. The land, sea, mountains, and wildlife of Katmai were for Ray and Barbara a cathedral of nature at work.

The ebb and flow of life in Katmai National Park was a reflection of the best of what Alaska had to offer—volcanoes, glaciers, mountains, ocean, wildlife, and four million acres of unspoiled wilderness. It was at once a peaceful sanctuary and a dynamic, vibrant ecosystem that never failed to captivate the Banes. Never in their wildest dreams did they foresee how the actions of a single captain on an oil tanker 350 miles away would threaten the entire coastline of a place they called home.

20

⸺ ✛ ⸺

exxon valdez

On March 24, 1989, at 12:26 a.m., the Coast Guard received a message at the Valdez, Alaska, traffic center, "We've fetched up, ah, hard aground, north of Goose Island, off Bligh Reef and, ah, evidently leaking some oil and we're gonna be here for a while and, ah, if you want, ah, so you're notified."

Captain Joseph Hazelwood radioed that message from the supertanker *Exxon Valdez*, a call that would announce the beginning, to date, of the largest oil spill in United States history. The 987-foot ship, second newest in Exxon Shipping Company's fleet, was loaded with fifty-three million gallons (1.2 million barrels) of North Slope crude oil bound for Long Beach, California.

When the *Exxon Valdez* ran aground at Bligh Reef, eight of its eleven cargo tanks ruptured, discharging some eleven million gallons of toxic crude oil into Prince William Sound. The timing of the spill, the remote location, the thousands of miles of rugged and wild shoreline, and the abundance of wildlife in the region combined to make it one of the worst oil spill disasters in the world.

Four hundred miles southwest of Bligh Reef, in Katmai National Park, Ray and Barbara heard reports about the spill from the news and the park regional office. There was momentary disbelief, followed by short-lived assurance that a concerted oil spill response would be forthcoming. It had been twelve years since oil began flowing through the trans-Alaska pipeline without major incident. Surely safety measures were in place and oil containment booms were standing by. But no one had planned for a spill of this

Fifteen hundred miles of coastline were impacted by the oil spill. With every tide, a new
raft of oil was delivered to the shore. (Alaska
State Archives)

magnitude. As the oil disgorged like blooming poison onto the clear blue
waters of Prince William Sound, it became clear that oil would soon slam
the shorelines of some of the most pristine wilderness areas in the world.
The Sound was the premier habitat and breeding ground of whales, salmon,
sea otters, sea lions, seals, and dozens of species of birds.

Because it was closest to the spill, it appeared that Kenai Fjords National
Park might be the most severely impacted. There was still the hope that
the oil might be carried out to sea and dissipate as it flowed out of Prince
William Sound. Anne Castellina, Superintendent of Kenai Fjords National
Park, went straight to the residents of the small, nearby town of Seward
and warned them of the upcoming possibility of an oil-slicked shore. What
could they do together as a community to mitigate the damage? The town
and the park service rolled up their sleeves.

Ray got a phone call from the Assistant Regional Director in the NPS
Anchorage office. "Ray, I want you to come into Anchorage for a few days
and travel to Seward. We're pulling in other park superintendents and some
regional staff to give you a chance to see the Incident Command Team system at work on the oil spill. Some day you may have to work with it."

On April 9, I flew the Cessna 206 from Anchorage to Seward with other NPS personnel on an aerial tour of the coastal areas that would likely be impacted by the spill. I spent a couple of days in Seward visiting the main headquarters for local spill response. It was a busy hive of involved officials, staff and groups, including representatives of the Exxon Corporation. A fleet of leased boats had been dispatched to stretch floating booms across the mouths of streams and seaward openings of fjords hoping to hold back any oil that might drift by. The Park Service had imported a number of employees from the Lower 48 who were trained in the management of large-scale disaster events to work with other agencies. Special funding to support spill response efforts had been arranged.

As I walked around the assembly hall I happened to wander by a series of maps tacked on the wall. I idly stopped to study them. They included charts tracing the progression of the main oil slick, coastal topography, sensitive habitat, tidal zones and other features that had to be considered when directing response efforts. One of the displays showed the prevailing currents of the seawaters stretching from Prince William Sound to the Alaska Peninsula and extending along the Aleutian Islands. As I stood gazing at the chart it suddenly dawned on me; Katmai was going to be clobbered by the oil spill. The ocean currents marked on the wall chart would carry the

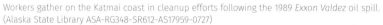

Workers gather on the Katmai coast in cleanup efforts following the 1989 *Exxon Valdez* oil spill. (Alaska State Library ASA-RG348-SR612-AS17959-0727)

*primary bulk of crude oil past Kenai Fjords, possibly hitting the extreme
tips of headlands projecting out into the ocean. It would pull the oil in a
broad left hand curve past the entrance to Cook Inlet and then propel it
through the Shelikof Strait likely pushing it against the coastline of Katmai
from Cape Douglas in the northeast to Katmai Bay in the southwest. Only
major storm winds might alter this scenario.*

Ray stared at the maps. The arrows of the currents looked like a slingshot,
a looping catapult with the trajectory landing squarely against the western
coast of Shelikof Strait and Katmai National Park. The oil was going to soil
the coastline all the way down to Aniakchak. Based on the speed of the
current, Ray estimated the oil would hit Katmai National Park within days.

He pointed out his observations to the park service team in Seward.
People were plenty busy with the efforts at Kenai Fjords and besides, they
suggested, wasn't Ray overreacting a bit?

Although Ray had years of practicing diplomacy as he traveled to explain
public lands after President Carter's designation of monuments, he had never been shy about expressing his opinion. The team's glib dismissal was not
going to cut it for Katmai National Park. He lost his temper.

"This is bullshit!" he said. "Katmai is going to be hit and something has
to be done to prepare for it."

He flew to Anchorage and cornered the park's head of natural resources
and asked for a meeting with the acting regional director, Dave Ames. At
the meeting, Ray showed charts of ocean currents and demonstrated why
Katmai needed immediate assistance in developing an oil spill response.
The park service knew almost nothing about the resources and environmental conditions of the Katmai coastal area.

"We had to survey the existing pre-spill setting to be able to accurately
measure the oil spill's impacts and set realistic goals for effective mitigation," Ray explained.

The group listened attentively and then the natural resources person
spoke up. He pointed out the cost of such an endeavor. The effort at Kenai
Fjords had already consumed most of the available funding. Work there
was going well so far and the park service had garnered public and political
support for their effort.

"Besides," the person said. "Even if the oil reaches that far, no one visits
Katmai that much anyway."

Ray's response was apoplectic. "I did not endear myself to park service staff," he said.

Dave Ames, however, had listened thoughtfully to Ray's presentation.

"I support Ray's request," he said. "We need to shift some resources and personnel to Katmai."

"I could have kissed the guy," Ray remembered. But it would take time to assemble and deploy people to the site. In the end, scientists were almost at a dead run trying to stay ahead of the advancing oil as it spread down the park coast.

"It was like taking inventory while the house is burning down," Ray said.

Katmai National Park includes some 400 miles of coastline with deeply incised bays and fjords and dozens of wilderness islands. Its beaches range from broad bands of white sand to jagged rock cliffs. Periodic fierce storms drive ocean waters well inland, flooding salt marshes and the lower reaches of streams that flow into the sea. In places like Hallo Bay, tidal shifts alternately expose and cover extensive shallow tidelands where brown bears and other animals forage for food. Wolves, foxes, eagles, and a host of other animals scavenge the tidelands and beaches for dead fish, seals, birds, otter, and even whales.

"Whatever the sea brought to Katmai and Aniakchak ultimately impacted life far inland," Ray said.

What the sea brought to Katmai and Aniakchak in the days ahead was oil. On April 16, less than two weeks after the spill, Ray flew the Super Cub along the Katmai coast to look for oil. At first, as he looked out over the coastal water, he thought that maybe they would be lucky. But as he got closer to the water he saw large reddish-brown patches that turned out to be giant rafts of oil.

"The oil was everywhere," Ray said, "like a slow-moving avalanche."

Ray landed on several beaches and found gobs of brown pasty oil washed up on the sand. A thin sheen drifted in the waters near the shore.

Within days the floating oil came in close-packed rafts of ugly brown mousse extending from the shoreline seaward into the hazy distance of the Shelikof Strait. From the Katmai shoreline it seemed to virtually fill the entire width of the strait. I saw a skimmer ship designed to scoop up floating oil. It was well offshore of the park coast moving north through an enormous oil slick. From my vantage point [in the Super Cub] it looked like a tiny water bug cutting a razor-thin line through the massive expanse of oil-fouled waters. It was having absolutely no measureable effect on the volume of oil being carried down the Shelikof Strait.

The effort to save the coast of Katmai and Aniakchak ran into problems from the start. Every boat in Alaska that was capable of supporting the cleanup effort had already been leased to Exxon or other agencies now at work in Prince William Sound and on the Kenai Peninsula. Katmai needed an estimated 10,000 feet of booming material to protect some of the primary resources of the park. That, too, was hard to come by.

Bad weather also impeded progress. Although the oil moved relentlessly forward, boats and aircraft to get personnel and supplies to the area had to return to their bases and wait for better conditions.

Efforts were made to reduce oil contamination in important salmon spawning streams by stringing floating booms across the mouths. However, storms often washed the oil over and around the barriers. (Bane Collection)

"Ultimately, we obtained a tiny fraction of what was needed," Ray said. "By the time that small amount was deployed, the damage had already occurred."

The oil came ashore at the worst possible time. Brown bears were still coming out of their winter dens ravenously hungry, drawn to the beaches in search of carrion and seaweed. Migratory shore birds were nesting in the lowland marshes. Eagles and other birds of prey searching for food and material to build their nests. Colonies of sea otters, sea lions and other coastal creatures were setting up housekeeping on the rocky islets. When a bird became fouled by the sticky oil and died, its body would be picked up by a fox, wolf or other scavenger not knowing they were ingesting poison. I saw bears walking through thick patches of oil in search of food. It was one of the saddest and most frustrating experiences of my life. I kept thinking that I should have been more aware and acted sooner than I did. I had been appointed the primary caretaker of the park. I knew that I had no responsibility for the spill. However, I should have recognized the importance and vulnerability of the coastal regions sooner and been more effective in coordinating mitigation efforts.

The heartbreak was beyond anything he or Barbara had ever experienced. It was like a lingering death of a beloved friend, a time they both describe as "a death in the family." They watched as the limp bodies of birds and otters washed ashore. Twice a day, the tide delivered a new mat of oil to the coastline. And every day the bears of Katmai waded in and ate from the foul-smelling water and sands of their oil-slicked home.

On May 1, I accompanied Boyd Evison, NPS Alaska Regional Director, on a helicopter flight to the Katmai coast. I directed the pilot to sites where heavy impact had already occurred. Boyd was shocked by the scope and severity of the damage. We passed over a sow brown bear with cubs digging around in obviously contaminated beach sands searching for food. The copter touched down at Hallo Bay where we were greeted with mats of thick crude oil washed up on the once-pristine six mile long beach. There were shapeless lumps in the oil in the beach surf. As we drew closer it was possible to see the lumps were hundreds of dead seabirds. Most were diving birds that had suffocated when they could not clear their beaks upon surfacing. We came upon a bald eagle flopping helplessly near a small stream, its feathers matted with tar. A grungy red fox seemed confused as it trotted aimlessly back and forth along the inland edge of the beach. Large patches

Ray observes a dead bear that likely died of poisoning following the oil spill. Bears, eagles, foxes and other wildlife along the Katmai coast scavenged oiled birds and animals that washed ashore as a result of the spill. Clams, seaweed, and marsh grasses were also contaminated. The full scope of the wildlife impacted by the spill is unknown. (Bane Collection)

of rainbow-hued sheen floated on the waters along the shores. Mats of sickly brown sludge drifted with the current. In places the oil in the water was so thick that the waves breaking on the beach came down with a dull leaden thud.

As the ecological disaster unfolded, Alaskans and the public looked on with horror. Hordes of people arrived in Alaska to help with the cleanup.

"Cleanup efforts were largely a Laurel-and-Hardy exercise," Ray said. Every day hundreds of people on beaches in Prince William Sound would wash rocks and scoop oil from the sand. Workers sprayed hot water from high-pressure hoses to clean oiled rocks along the shoreline of Prince William Sound. And every twelve hours the tide would deliver another raft of oil. It was nearly impossible to remove oil that had already seeped inches deep into the sand.

The physical cleanup work was largely accomplished by laborers using hand shovels to scoop mats of oil and tar balls off the sand. Exxon and the Coast Guard had proposed using intrusive methods of removing the oil from the park. This included using hot steam pressure hoses to scour oil from the rocks and caustic chemicals to flush it off the beaches. On the basis of recommendations of the park resource specialists and simple common sense I protested these methods. They would only increase the damage from the oil. I was also informed that there was a plan to bring in a special incinerator ship that would anchor in Kukak Bay. Collected oil debris would be carried to this vessel where it would be burned. Again, after conferring with park specialists and doing some personal research on the process I adamantly refused to support it and suggested that the park would lodge a formal complaint if it were attempted. The burning of the oil mousse and other contaminated debris would produce and release dioxins and other toxins into the air. Kukak Bay is sheltered from strong winds from the south and north by a low range of mountains. The toxins would likely concentrate in the bay, possibly causing severe environmental impacts that could last for decades.

By September, fall weather began to take hold. Storms off the north Pacific made cleanup efforts increasingly difficult and hazardous. It was hardly human effort that cleaned the beaches, but rather the steady drumbeat of tides and weather and pounding surf. At least it appeared that might be the case; at least it was the hope of those who saw the futility of spraying hot water on rocky beaches.

On September 30, 1989, Ray flew the Super Cub to Hallo Bay where bears had once passed directly under his airplane wing when he stopped to refuel. He made several low passes and saw there was still a sheen of oil in the water near the beach. He landed. At first glance, the beach appeared to be almost back to normal. As he walked around, he found a few scattered tar balls, but not the large concentration of oil he'd seen earlier in the summer.

"Maybe the coast really will recover," Ray thought.

He pulled a short-handled shovel out of the plane and began digging in the sand. Six inches below the surface, his hopes were dashed. A thick vein of oil oozed up from the hole.

"As the sun's rays touched the oil, it began to weep toxic tears," Ray remembered. "I walked up and down the beach for hundreds of yards digging test pits and having the same results. The tides had simply buried the oil, concealing it from view. But it was still there."

This oil would continue to leach into nearby streams and coastal waters. It would be ingested by clams and other sea life and contaminate seaweed.

Storms would carry some of it ever deeper into marshes and stream outlets. The toxic brew would continue to make its way inland in the bellies of bears and on the beaks and talons of eagles. Only time, lots of time, would eventually break its poisonous hold on Katmai.

In the end, more than 1,500 miles of shoreline were impacted. Twenty-five years after the *Exxon Valdez* oil spill, an *Anchorage Daily News* article corroborated conservationists' worst fears: "Today, government studies confirm that most of the populations and habitats injured by the spill have not fully recovered, and some are not recovering at all . . . Government studies report thousands of gallons of *Exxon Valdez* oil still in the beaches today, that the oil is still nearly as toxic as it was the first two weeks after the spill . . . The remaining oil will take decades and possibly centuries to disappear entirely. (Tests on near-shore animals "indicate a continuing exposure to oil" *Anchorage Daily News*, September 16, 2013).

As winter approached, Ray and Barbara were raw with emotion and exhausted from the work of trying to mitigate a disaster while still running the park's normal day-to-day operations. The staff was also on the ragged edge. Everyone had been impacted by the oil spill, directly or indirectly. People who cared about Alaska felt a loss beyond what words could convey.

Whatever measures had been taken to assure safety of the transport of oil when the Trans Alaska oil pipeline had been built, they hadn't been enough to keep a tragedy from occurring. In the years since the pipeline's construction, the interests of oil and gas companies had largely paralleled the interests of the State and its citizens. People in Alaska had benefited in measurable ways from the oil industry's presence in the state. With oil money flowing, it had been easy to be complacent about the oil industry's safety practices; and easier still to trust the agencies tasked with monitoring those practices. So it was not just environmental degradation that the public was grieving. It was a spiritual landscape that felt both culpable and betrayed.

"It was our innocence that we lost," Ray said. "Katmai was one of the most unspoiled wilderness areas of Alaska. If you took one place that encapsulated everything that Alaska had to offer—mountains, volcanoes, the ocean, glaciers, and wildlife—Katmai had everything that makes Alaska special."

He paused, searching for words.

"I don't want to overstate this," he said, "but it had been perfect."

21

— ❖ —

katmai carnival

Ray was not making friends in high places. During the *Exxon Valdez* oil spill, he demanded that Katmai National Park receive its fair share of protection and mitigation efforts before the oil fouled its shoreline. During the cleanup efforts, Ray was often interviewed by the press and was encouraged to be more positive regarding his assessment of the spill impacts to Katmai. Alaska's Congressional delegation was doing more than just dealing with an oil spill. They were mopping up a public relations nightmare with a nation outraged by the devastation they were seeing on nightly television news.

"The Kenai Fjords National Park efforts were handled superbly by Superintendent Anne Castellina," Ray said. "It was a storybook rendition of how you deal with an oil spill. It helped that, except for the tip of rocky headlands, the impacts at Kenai Fjords were limited."

This was what the Congressional delegation wanted to hear. Success stories.

The news out of Katmai National Park was not so rosy. "They wanted positive comments, but to my way of thinking, what I was seeing painted a much less positive picture," Ray said. "I tried not to overstate it, but in some cases it would be hard to overstate how bad things were. I was warned that certain powers-that-be were not happy with the news emanating from Katmai."

Years later, the official 1995 NPS report on the *Exxon Valdez* oil spill, *Lessons to be Learned: The National Park Service Administrative History and Assessment of the* Exxon Valdez *Oil Spill*, conceded that the greatest impact had been on Katmai. Compared to the forty miles of Kenai Fjords

National Park, more than 300 miles of Katmai National Park's coastline were oiled. By the season's end more than 7,800 oiled bird carcasses had been recovered. Cleanup crews removed an estimated seven million pounds of oil and oily debris from Katmai beaches—a fraction of what had actually washed ashore.

As the oil spill response wound down for the winter and Brooks bear viewing camp was closed, Ray met with his staff to set priorities for the coming year of 1990. Everyone was worn to a thin edge by the demands of the summer's oil spill cleanup efforts. With so many resources devoted to spill cleanup, the day-to-day operations of running the park had strained personnel to their limits. Long hours and frayed nerves found many staff members welcoming the end of the season.

At the meeting, Ray was surprised at his staff's low emphasis on the Katmai coastal region where oil had significantly damaged the park. He was also disappointed that more emphasis wasn't placed on monitoring the damaging effects of ATV access in the park.

The staff discussion focused on how the park's primary goal was to provide visitors an enjoyable bear-viewing experience. One key staff member stated matter-of-factly, "Visitors equal money and we are here for the visitors."

Ray was taken aback. Was the purpose of the park service simply to provide entertainment for visitors?

The National Park System Organic Act, which created the park service in 1916, set the purpose of the park system: "The fundamental purpose of the parks is to conserve the scenery and the natural and historic objects and the wildlife therein and to *provide for the enjoyment of the same in such manner and by such means as will leave them unimpaired for the enjoyment of future generations*." (emphasis added)

While important, recreation was never intended to be the sole purpose of the national parks. The words, "unimpaired" and "future generations" had a deep meaning to Ray. The discussion with his staff left Ray with the feeling that he was out of step with both his staff and the park service in general.

I went home that evening and lay awake much of the night reviewing the meeting and my thoughts about what had been said. I had initially been drawn into the Park Service largely because of a desire to protect and preserve wilderness areas in Alaska, especially the Brooks Range. I was not particularly thinking of how many visitors might come to see the park, although I hoped that visitors would come and enjoy the park on its own terms and gain a sense of completeness and adventure. To me Brooks River was an important part of Katmai but only a very tiny part. I believed the bear viewing opportunities should be managed to allow for a relatively natural population of bears, including minimizing conflicts between human and bear uses.

While Brooks River was special for its bear viewing, it was no more special to Ray and Barbara than Hallo Bay, Kukuk Bay, the Aniakchak Crater, and many other unique and dynamic locations found within parklands across Alaska. To Ray, the number of visitors who annually see and use an area of the park did not determine its relative value. Park status was often determined by visitor numbers. Yet, Ray wondered, was this the best way to measure the value of a park?

"In the case of Katmai, the success of the management of Brooks River was being measured in how many visitors we were packing into a relatively confined area to see the bears," Ray said. "Those numbers and all that they signified were overwhelming what should have been a respectful and educational experience. Brooks River was degenerating into a carnival-like atmosphere with the bears as the main sideshow. "

Floatplanes lined the beach wingtip to wingtip along Naknek Lake. Ropes were tied from the tails of the aircraft to the tree line. In many instances, bears had to navigate around human obstacles to get to and from the salmon stream to feed. In one photograph, a gauntlet of ropes kept a sow and her two cubs from traveling unimpeded along the shoreline. The mother and her two infants had to swim into the lake and paddle just beyond the airplanes' propellers to get to the other end of the beach.

To Ray, the photo was an insult to the core ideals of the park service, the least of which was to "do no harm."

"Every one of those airplanes was contributing to the congestion and environmental impacts that the NPS was supposed to be controlling," he said.

Even before the oil spill, Ray had been working to complete a Development Concept Plan (DCP) for the park. Brooks Camp was located squarely on top of one of the Alaska Peninsula's largest pre-contact cultural sites. According to anthropologist D.E. Dumond, an expert on Eskimo and Aleut village settlements, the area contains some of the richest prehistoric and proto-historic cultural resources in the greatest concentrations in Alaska. Foundations of

A sow grizzly abandons efforts to walk on the beach at Naknek Lake and swims around the planes while her cub clings to her back. Rapid visitor growth placed increasing pressure on bears at Brooks Camp in Katmai National Park. (Courtesy National Park Service)

more than eighty sod houses have been identified in the area. Ray was in-credulous when workers, doing repair work on a water line, began digging up obvious remnants of an archaeological site.

"It was like building commercial visitor facilities directly on top of Stonehenge in southern England," Ray said.

Through a DCP, Ray envisioned moving the existing camp to a nearby, less intrusive location. The new area would be less than a mile away from the river, which would serve as a buffer between the activity of people and the movement of bears. The river itself would become the boundary between people and bears. Less habituated and more sensitive bears would have a relatively undisturbed retreat from human intrusion on the north side of the river. The camp's move to the south side of the river would also protect many ancient archaeological sites from damage.

As it was, bears and people used the same trails and fished the same ar-eas. "Problem bears" that showed aggressive tendencies were run off and conditioned against interacting with people by rubber bullets and hazing.

By default, this limited the rich nutrition and calories of the salmon run to those bears willing to tolerate the pressures of human contact. Bears too shy to approach the swarm of activity at Brooks Falls would not have the opportunity to partake in the bounty.

"We are not supposed to manipulate animal behavior to accommodate visitors," Ray said, "We're here to manage an ecosystem and protect the resource in its most natural state. The goal is to provide viewing opportunities without forcibly altering the natural behavior of the bears and other wildlife."

Ray felt that a DCP would offer a blueprint for good stewardship and a "firewall" against future development that did not make good sense. The document was still on the drawing board when Ray got a call from the regional director.

"Ray, Senator Ted Stevens is considering adding a rider onto proposed legislation in the U.S. Senate that would direct a considerable sum of money to Katmai," the regional director began. "He wants the money used to

Human remains found during maintenance on utility lines at Brooks Camp in Katmai National Park. The Brooks Camp visitor facility is located directly atop a major archeological site which includes ancient burial sites of Native Americans. Such intrusions are contrary to official NPS policy. Circa1987. (Bane Collection)

expand the bear viewing opportunities at Brooks and to add a platform at Lake Camp near the outlet of Naknek Lake."

Ray listened with growing apprehension. The Senator also wanted a permanent bridge to connect the north and south sides of the Brooks River. Rather than separating bears and people these projects would have the effect of throwing people and bears into even closer proximity.

The regional director continued, "As the park manager, we need you to support these projects."

Ray paused. "Give me a little time to think about it, and I'll call you back."

Ray pulled out the park's GMP, research documents about bears, and then got on the phone and talked to resource management specialists and other park staff. He flew his airplane over the areas where Stevens proposed the new structures. Two days later, Ray returned the phone call to his boss.

"I can't support Senator Stevens' proposal. It goes against the recommendations of the park's GMP and is contrary to what we are trying to accomplish in the way of bear management," Ray said. "Before we add additional structures, we should first complete the DCP for Brooks River and a separate DCP for possible developments at Lake Camp."

There was a long silence at the other end of the line.

A terse "thank you" ended the call.

Apparently, Senator Stevens' office, anticipating a positive response from the Park Service, put out a news release announcing the pending construction of new facilities at Katmai. When a reporter contacted the Park Service to check on the release he was informed that the park superintendent had declined the offer. That set off a political firestorm that embarrassed the Senator and the regional directorate. It didn't help when the Anchorage Daily News *published an editorial cartoon showing caricatures representing Senator Stevens and a park ranger battling atop a bear-viewing platform with bears watching the action. The title read, "Animals Gather at Sen. Stevens' Wildlife Observation Deck".*

Not long after the cartoon was published I happened to be in the Alaska Regional Office on business and stopped by Dave Ames' office. While we were talking Dave pointedly asked, "Ray, when you leave Katmai where do you want to go?" I was caught off guard.

"I haven't thought about that. There's still lots I hope to do at Katmai, and I have no desire to leave Alaska."

He nodded his head and changed the subject.

ANIMALS GATHER AT SEN. STEVENS' KATMAI WILDLIFE OBSERVATION DECK.

Anchorage Daily News, January 13, 1990

Not long afterward, a friend who was a division head saw Ray walking through a hallway in the regional office and called him into his office. He closed the door.

"Ray, you got problems," he said. "The folks upstairs are pissed at you. I've been directed to contact people on your staff and encourage them to share any dissatisfaction with your leadership. The word is out that you will be moved out of Katmai. I think it is bullshit, but it's going to happen."

Ray had seen these things happen before. The sequence of events to remove a superintendent from a park usually began with an "operations evaluation," which in turn set the stage for an involuntary transfer. A few weeks later, Ray got short notice that Katmai would be the subject of an operations evaluation.

It was a strange thing, knowing the end of their time at Katmai was near. Ray flew to Hallo Bay, a place that was to him nearly mystical. Even damaged and tarred now by oil, its beauty would forever haunt him. He thought about his boyhood in West Virginia and the wild places that had brought him so much solace.

He remembered a time when he was about eleven years old, when he had set up camp near the bass stream where he spent his summers as a boy. He woke up one unusually cold morning to find a deadly copperhead stretched out along the length of his blanket, enjoying the warmth of Ray's young body.

Ray lay perfectly still, knowing any movement might cause the snake to startle and strike. He was a long way from home or help. So he lay there alone, breathing, watching the snake. He stared at the walls of his tent and listened to the calm, steady beat of his own heart. A fly buzzed. A mosquito landed. Eventually, the sun came up and the tent warmed. Only then did the snake languidly slip out of Ray's tent.

Ray remembered that he had not been terrified. His father had taught him to respect wildlife. The best thing he knew to do was to stay quiet and let the snake leave on its own.

Ray knew he couldn't stay quiet about the construction of the new bear-viewing platform. He simply couldn't "go along to get along." In light of the archeological trespass and the human pressure on wildlife, if Brooks Camp did not already exist, it would not be allowed to exist—it violated the very rules that were the foundation of good National Park management. Even so, Ray was not naïve enough to think that power, politics, or money—like a snake in the tent—would simply go away of its own accord. Maybe he couldn't change the world but at least he would stand true to his own ideals and convictions. Still, he couldn't help feeling deeply disappointed.

In the time we had spent with Katmai we had grown to love it. It is, without question, one of the truly great parks in the national park system, and it deserves far better than it often receives. We had tried to address and resolve issues that directly affected the basic resources and character of Katmai. We were leaving just as it felt as though positive change was taking place . . . As park superintendent I had failed in my part of carrying out the stated goals of the park GMP and others identified by the park staff. I could only hope that succeeding superintendents and other park personnel would not allow the progress made over the past few years to slip away. The park deserved better. Unfortunately, the path of least resistance too often was chosen as the preferred direction for the management and care of Katmai.

In the end, the bear-viewing platform was built and growing numbers of visitors continued to pour into the park for the bear-viewing spectacle. In 1989, the park saw over forty thousand visitors, most of which came during a brief three-month period to see bears at Brooks Camp. In the years since, the number of visitors has, in some instances, doubled to more than eighty-two thousand people.

In May of 1999, Dr. Barrie K. Gilbert, a Senior Scientist at Utah State University and noted bear biologist who had directed studies of human-bear interactions along salmon streams in Katmai National Park, responded to plans to further expand the bear viewing facilities at Katmai. Dr. Gilbert urged the National Park Service to avoid exacerbating an already stressed situation at Brooks River. He expressed concern for the welfare of less habituated bears, especially sows with cubs, driven from the area by aircraft traffic, intrusive structures, and human use.

Gilbert chastised the NPS for an "environmental assessment" that failed to include critical research findings compiled by him and other biologists. He also lamented the failure to assess the impacts of other wildlife species that depended on Brooks River as a critical feeding ground. Not surprisingly, the NPS supported the construction of these additional facilities.

In his analysis Gilbert wrote, "(Brooks River is) a biological hotspot of productivity and diversity of species. Therefore, of any place in the park, this area should receive the greatest protection from human impacts . . . The

Following the Banes' departure from Katmai National Park, additional platforms and walkways were built to maximize public viewing opportunities. Biologists are concerned that increased human activity is driving more sensitive bears away from the Brooks River fishery thus altering the natural dynamics of this highly productive feeding area. (Bane Collection)

riparian corridor is an oasis of productive biological processes based on incredible infusion of salmon from the sea. How can our national parks fail in their mission of protecting such treasures? How can an agency claiming to maintain some semblance of America's heritage, fail to cap visitation while expanding the [human] built environment— little different than [that of] a private concern exploiting massive public demand for recreational opportunities?"

Gilbert urged the park service to expand the scope of the environmental assessment with a supplemental Environmental Impact Statement (EIS) to fully address the serious concerns raised by the proposed facility expansion.

Gilbert's request was denied.

22

—✵—

reining in the rebel

In February of 1990, Ray and Barbara moved to Anchorage. Ray was given the opportunity to "voluntarily" transfer to America Samoa to become the superintendent of a new national park unit being created with joint United States and Samoa management. The Banes briefly considered the job but declined. Both Barbara and Ray wanted to stay in Alaska, at least until they retired. Ray was given a "redirected assignment" to work in the Alaska Regional Office as a management assistant.

They bought a modest home a few blocks from the Alaska regional office. Barbara quickly found an administrative job with the Alaska Department of Transportation at the Anchorage International Airport. She loved her work and enjoyed her fellow employees.

"Although the transfer had not been a surprise, I have to admit that it was heartbreaking to both of us," Ray said. Katmai was a jewel of a park, a place they loved fervently enough to stand up to defend. To be reined in by the agency that was tasked with protecting it was a hard pill to swallow.

Yet in typically optimistic fashion, Ray and Barbara made the best of their circumstances.

"You don't want to waste time feeling sorry for yourself," Ray said. They adapted.

> Anchorage was an ideal medium-sized city with virtually all the urban amenities plus nearby scenic natural areas. Our home was in a part of town known as Rogers Park, which gave us quick access to a trail system that stretched for miles along the high coastal bluffs snaking off into the

*surrounding hills and low mountains. For me it was virtually a lifesaver, giv-
ing me the opportunity to escape the pressures of being confined to a formal office complex five days a week and the intensity of urban life. I took up
cross-country skiing in the winter and switched to a bike during the summer
months. Barbara and I joined a health club and met during our lunch break
to pit ourselves against the exercise equipment.*

Ray found another outlet for exercise and adventure. One Saturday in late
spring, Barbara and Ray were driving along Turnagain Arm just beyond
the city's confines. The "Arm" as it is often referred to, cuts a thin, mostly
shallow lane of seawater some sixty miles long, almost severing the Kenai
Peninsula from the mainland of Alaska. Thirteen miles wide at its juncture
with Cook Inlet, Turnagain Arm averages four to six miles wide for most
of its length.

"My God!" Ray exclaimed as they rounded a bend along the winding
highway that hugged the mountains along the shoreline. "Look out there.
Those are windsurfers!"

He pulled the car off to the side of the road and watched six surfers speed-
ing back and forth on brightly colored sails, their shiny boards skipping
across heavy wind chop. They wore black rubber suits, rubber gloves, caps,
and insulated boots. The water temperature was barely above freezing,
and the air temperature was about sixty degrees. A week later Ray joined
their ranks.

*Sailing the Arm was a giant step above my past experience windsurfing. I
had sailed in frigid waters north of the Arctic Circle, but the winds had been
comparatively gentle and the currents almost non-existent. The Arm was
the difference between grade school and graduate school when it came
to windsurfing. A local shop carried basic windsurf equipment, so I picked
up a couple of sails and a buoyant board to add to what I already had. The
Turnagain sailors welcomed me into their midst, but they let me know that it
was my responsibility not to venture out too far and to have a basic survival
kit to deal with emergencies. The Arm had already taken the life of one local windsurfer who had sailed beyond the view of his friends. His body was
eventually found snagged on an oilrig far down Cook Inlet.*

Turnagain Arm experiences the second highest tidal shifts in North
America. The Arm nearly empties at low tide, exposing a broad floor of
muddy glacial silt. The silt bars intersect with meandering channels of tidal

Ray windsurfing in
Turnagain Arm (1992).
(Bane Collection)

waters that are still draining even as the incoming flood tide approaches. The tidal bore, a tsunami-like wave with a foaming face, sometimes rises to heights of five feet as it moves up the Arm then disappears in deeper pools only to dramatically rear up again in shallow waters.

"In addition to its dynamic hydraulics, Turnagain is also a powerful natural wind generator. When the winds exceed forty miles per hour, they create a phenomenon windsurfers call liquid smoke," Ray explained. "Sheets of water are lifted into the air and carried with the wind like a low layer of heavy fog."

Windsurfing in Katmai and Kotzebue had been tame compared to this. Over the next nine years, windsurfing on Turnagain Arm became an outlet that never failed to exhilarate Ray.

"I frequently sailed with Peter Toenies, a German expatriate and retired electrician living in Anchorage. He and I were often the only windsurfers on the Arm," he said. "I also became acquainted with Steve and Janis Tower. Steve is a respected orthopedic surgeon and Janice is a professional cycling coach and superb athlete. We began a friendship that deepened and continues uninterrupted even now, twenty-three years later."

Shortly after their move to Anchorage, in early February of 1991, the chief law enforcement ranger for the Alaska region asked Ray to take charge of an internal investigation involving alleged misuse of government property. A formal complaint from a private citizen alleged that a ranger was using park aircraft for personal purposes. The investigation centered on a particular aircraft. Theoretically available to all Alaska regional park operations, this plane tended to be used almost entirely by one park and the Alaska regional office in Anchorage. Ray collected the flight logs for the aircraft and other documentation and transposed the data into a spreadsheet.

"What evolved from the exercise was a pattern that raised questions about the appropriate use and efficient management of aircraft on a regional basis," Ray remembered.

He submitted his findings in the form of a preliminary progress report to the chief of law enforcement and suggested expanding the investigation to determine if additional charges or disciplinary actions might be warranted. The questionable actions, as it turned out, lay not solely with the park ranger in question, but rather, officials higher in the chain of command.

> The investigation ended abruptly. I was directed to turn over all the data collected. The ranger who had been the original focus was quietly transferred to another park. A senior official mentioned in the report accepted a management position in the Lower 48. I was moved from my fourth floor office to a desk in the corner of an obscure room and transferred into the Subsistence Division.

Ray felt right at home in the Subsistence Division. The division chief, Lou Waller, was a strong believer in the original intent of ANILCA for subsistence management in the new parklands. He had come to the park service after a long career in the Bureau of Land Management and was willing to take on controversial issues related to this sensitive topic.

"I asked Lou for permission to take on an issue near and dear to my heart, the use of ATVs on parklands in Alaska. Lou said that as long as I could handle the workload he had no objections," Ray remembered. "I took him at his word, distributing questionnaire survey forms designed to develop a comprehensive overview of ATV uses and impacts on a NPS Alaska region-wide basis."

In early 1991, Ray compiled the results of his survey plus the summaries of ATV research, and legal and policy considerations into a region-wide report. The report was submitted to the Alaska regional director through the chief of the subsistence division with copies given to all involved parks for review and comments. The essence of the report was that ATV's constituted an immediate major threat to several national parks and posed serious concerns for virtually all park units. Recommendations included forming a regional ATV management taskforce to research and make recommendations for regulations that would mitigate ATV impacts in the parks.

"The longer corrective and mitigation efforts are delayed, the more difficult it will be to bring the problem under control," wrote Ray in his report.

Although it generated a number of comments, no action was taken to address the report's concerns or issues. One superintendent, who was a good friend, stopped by Ray's office to talk about the report's findings.

"Ray, it's a good report. What it says is true. The parks, including my own, are being clobbered by ATVs. But if you think that anyone is going to take it on, you are whistling Dixie. No superintendent wants to end up where you are now," he said.

Those words stung. Ray realized that he had come to serve as a walking warning to other park managers who might challenge the status quo in tackling difficult park management problems.

"It also made me mad," Ray said. "As long as I 'played by the rules' most of my efforts would simply be ignored, buried in some obscure file cabinet, likely to never again see the light of day. I had become a curmudgeon."

Ray decided then and there that if he was going to be a curmudgeon, he would be an effective one. "I gave the bureaucracy some indigestion," he said.

In a nationwide initiative, the Director of the National Park Service had introduced a program called "Campfire Talks" encouraging NPS employees to share their thoughts and concerns. Ray took him at his word and sent a condensed version of the ATV issue paper he had written for the Alaska region office and its member parks. Ray asked that the Director review it and take appropriate action to protect parklands from mounting ATV damage.

"I sent similar letters to the Secretary of the Interior and Assistant Secretary for Fish, Wildlife, and Parks. Everything in my letters was taken directly from research and surveys that had been earlier submitted to the Alaska region directorate," Ray said.

> A couple weeks later Steve Shakelton, an assistant in the Law Enforcement Division, walked into my office, pulled up a chair and sat down with a heavy sigh.
>
> "Ray, I need your help. The folks upstairs gave me this letter from the Director and told me to prepare a draft reply from the regional director." He handed the letter to me as he spoke. It included a copy of my letter to the (national) director and directed that the Alaska regional office draft an answer and send it back to Washington so the (national director) could respond to me.
>
> "I don't know enough to draft a response letter. It looks to me that what you wrote is pretty much on the money," said Steve.
>
> "Are you asking me to write a response to my own letter?" I asked incredulously. He resignedly nodded his head. I burst out laughing. "O.K.," I said finally. "But you had better expect more to follow, because this is not the end."
>
> The regional office "downsized" the Subsistence Division, and I was moved again. This time I was assigned a desk in the Cultural Resources Division and given the title of Cultural Anthropologist.
>
> I had come full circle in my NPS career.

During his time in Anchorage, Ray twice volunteered for two extended assignments in Washington, D.C. Barbara understood Ray's desire to be more involved in influencing change on behalf of the parks. Ray spent time in the NPS legislative support office helping to review proposed legislation affecting national parks and drafting testimony for NPS officials to present to Congressional committees. Along with other assistants, he sat in on committee hearings to assist NPS officials in their testimony.

A second assignment took him back to Washington as a special assistant to the Assistant Secretary of the Interior for Fish, Wildlife and Parks. He helped to review various proposals for policies, land exchanges, outreach to communities and interest groups, and researched other facets of federal conservation efforts.

During his stay in Washington D.C., Ray lived in a hotel apartment complex across the Potomac River in Alexandria, Virginia. He commuted to work on a bicycle, touring through Arlington Cemetery and the National Mall, past the Lincoln Memorial and the Vietnam Wall.

It was my morning psychological cup of coffee that helped to inspire me for the rest of the day. When I left work I would often cycle around the Mall and take a ride along the Chesapeake and Ohio Canal before returning to my hotel. On weekends I explored Washington and took extended rides up the towpath of the C&O Canal or out into the rural farmland of northern Virginia. A few times I cycled to Mt. Vernon, the home of George Washington, or found some Civil War Battlefield where I could absorb the historic character of the region.

Barbara was able to get time off to fly to Washington and spend a week with me exploring the city. We haunted the Smithsonian Museum and visited virtually every notable site in the city and its outskirts. On the evening of the Fourth of July we gathered on the south bank of the Potomac along with a mass of others who stretched for roughly two miles along its banks. We watched the brilliant fireworks displays and heard the muted music of the military bands.

For a brief time Ray and Barbara toyed with the idea of transferring to D.C. to work at a mid-level position in the Washington office. By the end of his second assignment, however, Ray realized that he was not suited for urban life or the political pressure cooker of Washington, D.C.

"Whatever contribution I could make to the agency and to the parks which I cared deeply about would be best made where I had the most familiarity with the issues that Alaska parks faced," Ray said. "I would go back to Alaska to finish out my career as a curmudgeon."

Over the years Ray had kept in touch with Joe Sun, his primary research informant and a close friend from the village of Shungnak on the upper Kobuk River. Advancing age had forced Joe to move from his village to an elder care facility in Kotzebue. He periodically came to Anchorage for medical care.

"He always had his family call to tell me when he was in Anchorage so I could visit him at the Alaska Native Hospital," Ray said.

On August 13, 1993, Ray and Barbara got a call from Joe's oldest son. "Ray, Dad died this morning. He told us to let you know when he went. We will be holding the funeral on the fifteenth. We hope you can make it."

Ray immediately went to the regional director and asked that someone from the Kotzebue NPS office be sent as an official representative of the National Park Service to Joe Sun's funeral. Joe had been the primary Native contributor to the pioneer study, *Kuuvangmiut*, one that had substantively contributed to the inclusion of subsistence in ANILCA. Joe had shared invaluable insights into the subsistence of Native cultures and enriched the ability of the park service to interpret Native history in the parks of northwest Alaska.

"It seemed appropriate that the park service should officially show its gratitude and respect to this Native elder so esteemed by Natives throughout northwest Alaska," Ray remembered. "But the request was denied."

Ray took personal leave and caught a scheduled flight from Anchorage to Kotzebue, then connected with a local mail flight into Shungnak. The plane was full of local Natives traveling to Shungnak for the funeral. Special charters were being flown in from villages throughout the NANA region. As he stepped off the plane a four wheel ATV pulled up. It was one of Joe's grandsons.

"Over here, Ray. Throw your bags on the rack and jump on," he said. He whisked Ray into the village and delivered him to Joe's son's home.

The cabin was packed with local villagers and visitors from distant villages. I joined the crowd of Eskimos who filled the house partaking of platters of Native food and pots of hot tea. Joe's son saw me and came over to talk to me. "Dad's out in the shed where it's cool. If you want to visit him go ahead. You will be sleeping here while you are in town."

I walked out to the log shed and opened the door into its dim, cool interior. Joe Sun occupied a locally constructed casket supported by two workhorses. He was dressed in the clothes he would have worn to attend church. His creased leather-hued face was peaceful. I sat beside him, and we had our last talk. I told him how much he meant to me and reminisced about how we had worked together building the winter fish trap and spending cold winter nights camped on the nearby riverbank. In my mind I could still hear his soft voice spinning stories of walking the upper Noatak Valley and shooting the rapids of the Reed River to return home. He had been both a friend

and a teacher who I would cherish for the rest of my life. Joe would be buried
the next day, but he would continue to live in my mind and my heart.

The next morning everyone gathered at the village church for the funer-
al. It was completely packed when I got there, with people standing out-
side. I squeezed my way into the interior and stood near the rear wall of the
church. Joe Sun's immediate family was seated in the front pew. Just before
the service began I saw his oldest son stand up and begin to look around
the room. When he spotted me standing at the back of the room he pushed
his way through the crowd to me. "Come up front, Ray. Dad wants you to sit
with the family!" It was the highest honor I had ever been paid.

For all of Ray and Barbara's tribulations in their work with the NPS
during Ray's latter years with the agency, the affirmation by Joe Sun's family was a testament to the value of their time spent preserving wilderness and
gathering the memories of elders like Joe.

Ray remembered backpacking in the late 1970s into a remote valley in
Alaska's central Brooks Range.

"I found no trace of earlier human presence," he said. "The head of the
valley formed a natural amphitheater. On a whim I shouted, 'Hello!' and
heard my call repeated three times as the sound waves bounced from one
rock wall to the other, each greeting fainter than the first—the final being
almost below the range of human hearing."

It occurred to Ray that he and Barbara had spent a large part of their lives
in Alaska seeking and attempting to preserve echoes. The echoes included
the unique voices of Native cultures that lived in close relationship with the
natural environment.

"We had the privilege to sit with elders who had been born in the late
nineteenth century or very early twentieth century. Clear-minded seniors
told of a lifestyle little changed from ancient times when tools and weapons
were crafted from stone, bone, ivory, and wood and when travel was depen-
dent on the muscle power of men and dogs," he said.

The land itself reverberated with echoes.

In Alaska there are still remnants of true wilderness, where the complex
web of natural life has not been shredded by the mechanical extensions of
man. It is no accident that ancient subsistence-based cultural echoes tend
to be found in close association with surviving wilderness areas. Humans

have spent well over ninety-five percent of their existence in a wilderness. Absent this natural stage, the cacophony of modern life quickly overwhelms those cultures more closely rooted to the land.

The passing of Joe Sun had silenced a voice from an ephemeral era. Yet his stories could continue through the years because of his willingness, during his lifetime, to share them. Ray felt privileged to have collected many of those stories in *Kuuvangmiut*. He was grateful to have played a part in keeping some of Alaska's wilderness intact. And most of all, he was humbled to have held in trust, the friendship of a remarkable man.

23

---✦✦---

citizens of the natural world

Somehow Ray and Barbara managed to stay positive in the face of what at times felt like a culture of retribution at Ray's workplace. He intended to make a difference in whatever capacity he could, and he continued at the National Park Service in Anchorage for eight years with stubborn grit and optimism.

"We had no reason to be angry. We were accomplishing things," he said. As Ray said this, however, his eyes flashed a fierceness born of his tough West Virginia upbringing. They didn't call his father "Battling Bill Bane" for nothing, and Ray was his father's son.

In one instance, Ray was invited to help with the recovery of an aircraft that had crashed and flipped upside down into a lake in the Noatak River National Preserve. Three park service rangers had escaped the crash and were found freezing but alive thirty-two hours after they swam to shore. The crash took place in September 1992, shortly before freeze-up. The Cessna 185 on floats was worth a great deal to the park service and Ray and another NPS employee, Janis Meldrum, were sent to the site to determine if the airplane could be recovered.

They flew by helicopter from Kotzebue to the small lake where the plane lay inverted seventy-five yards from shore. A thick and growing layer of ice had already formed around the aircraft. Expecting to be on thin ice, Janis and Ray found themselves on a firm surface able to support the weight of several people. If the weather stayed cold it would be possible to land a small plane on it within a few days. It was obvious that conditions had passed the point where the plane could be easily extracted from the lake. It would take a well thought out plan with special equipment and a team of workers to pull the plane onto the top of the ice. It had to be done within a few days, or the thickening ice would break the plane apart and lock it in for the winter. The freeze and thaw of spring breakup would complete the destruction. Time was not on their side.

Ray's apprenticeship with the Iñupiat and Koyukon had taught him to be innovative when dealing with the forces of the Arctic. He went back to his office in Anchorage and drew up a plan. He knew the ice would soon be thick enough to support the crew and equipment needed to extract the plane. They would need to cut the ice around the airplane in two stages. Then they could use a bipod pulley and winch system to pull the airplane out by the float struts and tail rod, slowly flipping it back to an upright position onto the ice. He wrote up the plan and sketched each step on paper. Once the aircraft was out of the water, the plane would be drained and slung beneath a helicopter for transport to Kotzebue.

Ray's diagrams illustrated each step of the process including the construction of a special bipod, placement of pulleys and wenches, removal of ice cover in planned stages, and the steps needed to minimize further damage to the aircraft. It even directed the draining of contaminated fluids from the aircraft engine to prevent internal damage. If carried out as planned within the next several days, there was a good chance that the plane could be returned to service within a few months.

Ray presented the plan to the regional directorate who submitted it to the Office of Aircraft Services (OAS) for evaluation. They enthusiastically signaled their approval. It looked like an inventive and workable solution to recover the plane. When the time came to carry out the plan however, Ray's request to be included in the extraction crew was pointedly turned down. Members of the recovery team later came to Ray and told him that his plan had worked like a charm. From his Anchorage office, Ray later read an article in the newspaper about the success of the operation. The recovery team was presented with special awards for their work. Ray's name was never mentioned.

"Barbara and I never felt like we were sacrificing anything over the years," Ray said. "We were working on behalf of something we valued. The parks to us were like the children we never had; so whatever happened to the parks, I took personally."

It was why Ray never stopped pestering and pushing and making a nuisance of himself when he felt that the park service could do better. Ray freely admitted, "I was a pain in the ass."

"Managers come and go and what happened to me was of no consequence," Ray said. "What mattered is what happened to the parks."

In the fall of 1997, Barbara and Ray retired from their jobs in Alaska. Barbara was sixty and Ray was sixty-one years old. The Anchorage International Airport staff gave Barbara a send-off that included a special scrapbook highlighting her life in Alaska. Lou Waller hosted a going away party at his log home overlooking Cook Inlet and Turnagain Arm.

Ray and Barbara began the next chapter of their lives on the island of Maui, Hawaii. After all their years and passion for Alaska, many people wondered why they chose to leave their beloved home state.

> One of the reasons we left Alaska is that we felt it was time to step aside. We had been intensely involved in Alaska issues, including education, cultural studies, conservation, and land management for over three decades and it had taken its toll. If we stayed in Alaska we knew that we would continue to be drawn into the maelstrom of controversy, particularly involving the care of national parks. Perhaps selfishly, we wanted to save the "golden years" for the simple enjoyments of being together and doing things just for the fun of it again.

Ray reflected that perhaps Edward Abbey put it best when he wrote, "Devoted though we must be to the conservation cause, I do not believe that any of us should give it all of our time or effort or heart. Give what you can, but do not burn yourselves out—or break your hearts. Let us save at least half of our lives for the enjoyment of this wonderful world which still exists."

While Barbara enjoyed her walks and quiet evenings reading, windsurfing became a major focus of Ray's retirement. He was 61 years old, devouring the wind and surf with fervor.

> Flat water sailing seemed mundane once I acquired the skills of catching and riding waves that towered over the tip of my sail mast. A truly thrilling

ride was to get on a "double mast high" wave, often in excess of twenty feet high, and toboggan down its liquid face while curving back and forth to find the "sweet spot" and avoid outrunning the watery avalanche. The immeasurable power of the wave radiated up through the board to my legs. Timing was absolutely crucial, because the wave eventually collapsed in a liquid explosion. I occasionally screwed up and paid the price of being pummeled by tons of turbulent seawater that pushed me down and held me underwater. While being swept across jagged coral, I was spun like a rag in a giant washing machine. I paid the price in both equipment and a battered body, but I was hooked on the adrenalin rush.

Eventually I came to the realization that while the waves were ageless, but I wasn't. Traveling to and from the beach plus the time spent rigging equipment and actually sailing used up virtually an entire day. I (began to) spend less time windsurfing and more time cycling. I found that I could get on my bike to spend a couple hours riding and still have plenty of time to do other things.

In September 2002, Ray joined his cycling friends John Hirashima, Roger Krom, and a few other Maui cyclists for Cycle Oregon. The annual weeklong fall ride through Oregon traverses more than 500 miles of scenic and historic attractions around the state. Ray trained for the expected challenges of the ride. Although not a race, it did require training and good physical conditioning.

Everything went well until the last day of the trip. While still clipped in the pedals, Ray ran off the side of the road, tumbling—still attached to his bicycle—over a steep embankment. He ended up with compound multiple fractures to his right ankle. An ambulance rushed him to a local hospital where surgeons reassembled the broken bones with metal plates and screws and then sewed him back together. Two days later he was on an airplane heading home to Maui.

Almost two weeks after the accident, infection set in, sending Ray into shock and back to the emergency room. He spent three months confined to a hospital bed as doctors struggled to save his leg. Barbara brought him a laptop computer and, ever the optimist, Ray began researching options for a prosthetic lower leg that would allow him to continue biking and windsurfing.

The leg survived but the windsurfing habit did not. His range of motion would not allow the flexibility he needed for windsurfing maneuvers. Ray considered the leg for the windsurfing a fair trade off. He would just have to focus on cycling.

In the end, moving to Maui would not be the end of the Banes' environmental conservation work. In the summer of 2000, Ray and Sierra Club Alaska Representative Jack Hession talked about the value of studying how government agencies manage the use of all-terrain vehicles on public lands. Hession had been Sierra Club's Alaska representative for thirty-four years and like Ray, worked tirelessly during the tumultuous days that marked the 1971 ANCSA and the 1980 ANILCA. Hession was no stranger to controversy. In the heated days before ANILCA passed, he received bomb threats and was routinely ridiculed in Alaska newspapers. In his bestselling *Coming Into The Country*, John McPhee said of Hession "When you're the Sierra Club's man in Alaska, bears are the least of your problems."

Hession enlisted the support of Deborah Williams, Executive Director of the Alaska Conservation Foundation (ACF). A graduate of Harvard Law School, Williams had at one time represented the National Park Service and served as a special assistant to the Secretary of the Interior for Alaska, where she advised the Secretary in managing over 220 million acres of national lands. As Executive Director of the Alaska Conservation Foundation, Williams embraced the idea for a report that studied the impact and management of ATV access on public lands in Alaska.

"We needed this resource and Ray was exactly the right person to write this report," Williams said.

Now all of Ray's work on ATV issues in Katmai National Park and in the NPS regional office in Anchorage was coming full circle. He spent much of the late winter of 2000 reviewing research reports and other literature about ATV access, particularly how it affected Arctic and subarctic lands. He knew from his own experience in the Bush what these machines did to landscapes ranging from dry upland terrain to boggy lowland tundra. In the thirty years since their early use, the machines had only grown more powerful and far ranging.

What Ray discovered in his research and later in the field study was far worse than he first imagined.

ATVs do more than just cause ruts and mar the esthetics of affected wild lands. The cleated tracks and lug tires of these machines grip and tear

The use of ATVs exploded in Alaska in the late 1970s and 1980s. Ray documented the severe impact of ATVs in his 2000 report "Shredded Wildlands." This report can be viewed on Amazon.com. (Bane Collection)

fragile vegetation cover, exposing the dark underlying ice-rich soil. Tundra soils exist in a delicate balance maintained primarily by the insulation of plant cover. Once this vegetation blanket is crushed or torn away, the sun and mild summer air immediately set off recurring rounds of thaw that spread like a cancer, radiating outwards to adjacent lands and often damaging streams with erosion contaminated runoff. Permafrost land literally bleeds when its fragile protective skin is cut.

In one field experience, Ray followed heavily rutted ATV trails branching off the Nebesna Road into Wrangell-St. Elias National Park. Well inside the park, the NPS had placed special matting materials across heavily rutted trails to test their ability to reduce ATV impact. Small signs and a brochure stand explained the purpose of the test strips, and asked ATV users to remain on the trail to aid in the research. The stand had been knocked over, and ATV users had compounded the damage by churning new trails around the test strips. Black spruce and other vegetation had been crushed all around the matting material—making a mockery of efforts to control the expanding environmental damage.

Ray's Alaska fieldwork concluded with a low-level aerial survey of the lower Kenai Peninsula in a floatplane flown by friend and wilderness advocate Page Spencer. Page and Ray took off from Anchorage and flew down the peninsula searching for signs of ATV activities.

> *From the air we saw dramatic evidence of almost unimaginable environmental damage and an obvious failure of responsible land managing agencies to protect the lands and resources under their care. The Kenai Peninsula, however, was only a tiny tip of the ATV iceberg in Alaska. The scope of the ATV damage to conservation lands in Alaska can be described as astounding.*

The final report, *Shredded Wildlands*, sponsored jointly by the Alaska Conservation Foundation and the Sierra Club, was published by the Sierra Club in 2001. It summarized the general state of ATV management on public lands in Alaska and used photos to document severe environmental degradation that, to the best of Ray's knowledge, continues even today.

ATV damage on the Kenai Peninsula. Ray and Page Spencer, a private pilot and friend, covered hundreds of miles photographing and mapping the extreme environmental impacts of ATV use. (Bane Collection)

> The reality is that the great majority of the environmental damage in the national parks and other conservation units within Alaska took place after the lands were designated as priceless parts of the nation's natural heritage and placed under the care of the National Park Service, National Fish and Wildlife Service and other conservation land managing agencies . . . It has not [been] the law that is lacking but rather those charged with implementing the law. Based on first-hand experience, all-too-many have retreated from their responsibilities in fear of political or bureaucratic retribution for doing what they knew was their job. They rationalized their actions, or lack of action, by calling for more research or seeking "mutual agreements" with local communities and ATV user groups to confine ATV access to designated trails. However, these "agreements" were usually not worth the paper they were printed on.

Shredded Wildlands was Ray's parting shot, not a reprisal so much as an opportunity to once and for all present the uncompromising truth—backed by research and data—about a serious conservation issue in Alaska's national parks. It was also meant to heighten public awareness.

Williams said that *Shredded Wildlands* came at a time when agencies needed to be examining their policies and regulations about all-terrain vehicles. The damage to the thin layer of vegetation protecting the underlying permafrost was expanding as the use of ATVs escalated.

"Ray's work documented a tremendous issue that off-road-vehicles presented in terms of damage to ecosystems. He was knowledgeable, highly respected and presented a calm, rational, fact-based perspective," she said. "*Shredded Wildlands* became a critical document for the conservation community. They relied on it, cited it, and used it for advocacy."

She said Ray's thoughtful presence served him well in the politically charged and often emotional debate about the use of ATVs. "Ray is a gentle person and there is nothing gentle about off-road vehicles when they are off designated trails and being improperly used. Maybe that is why it was so deeply disturbing for him to see the damage they were creating. In working with Ray, I always felt empowered, and hopeful, and confident that we were going to prevail."

Back when Ray and Barbara first arrived on Alaska's Arctic coast, they learned that Iñupiat hunters had a ritual of giving sea mammals a drink of fresh water after they had been taken. It was a way to honor the animal and give thanks to its spirit for giving itself to the harvest. Elders believed that animals could hear what was said about them and would take offense when hunters failed to show respect. Likewise, the Koyukon spoke to trees before felling them. And while Ray was working with the Kuuvanmiut of the Kobuk River, he learned that older Native residents were careful even about how they referred to the landscape. To say a mountain was beautiful was a judgment that another mountain was somehow less so. In the Old Ways, respect for the land and its inhabitants was a walk of humility and gratitude, with all of nature embodying some measure of awareness. Humans were simply members of nature's larger family.

To Ray and Barbara, the Old Way of believing informed their work as school teachers and later in Ray's work for the National Park Service. The Old Ways fed their being. They were not naïve—they had experienced both the wrath and the wonders of what nature could offer. Just as there were times of harvest and plenty, there were also times of storm and tumult.

When they lived in Huslia, the Kobuk River Iñupiat would forage for berries and sometimes run across small pockets of food that mice had collected in caches on the tundra. The caches contained edible roots, which the Iñupiat would gather as part of the day's harvest. But before leaving the cache, the gatherer would leave a small piece of dried fish to replace what had been taken. What the Banes left in Alaska by their teaching and through their conservation work was but a small gift in contrast to the wealth of adventures and traditional wisdom they felt blessed over the years to receive. For their resplendent and rigorous journey, they will always be grateful.

epilogue

Since President Jimmy Carter signed ANILCA in 1980, some of the controversy has died down, while other battles continue to be fought, in what has been dubbed Alaska's "One Hundred Year War."

Many staunch opponents to ANILCA have softened their views. At one time it appeared that President Carter would never be welcome in Alaska. But in a visit to Anchorage in 2000, President Carter spoke to a crowd of supporters who hailed him as a visionary. Ray and Barbara were invited and attended the reception for the President and former Secretary of the Interior, Cecil Andrews.

"'A lot of predictions were made that Alaska would go to hell if this much land was taken away from gas and oil development," Carter said in his speech. "But Alaskans have done well. Tourists come here to find a solitude, a beauty, sites that are not available to a Georgian or someone from Ohio or Maine."

Former Governor Jay Hammond—who had denounced Carter's declaration of monuments as a de facto repeal of statehood—sat with the former President and agreed that most Alaskans now favored the act for which Carter was so reviled. He went so far as to claim that national conservation lands were not "locked up" but "locked open," as places that would always be available for the public to enjoy.

In 2013, more than 2.5 million tourists visited the parks, refuges, and monuments created by ANILCA, spending $1.1 billion and supporting 17,000 jobs in the state. The coastal town of Seward, near Kenai Fjords National Park, eventually rescinded its resolution opposing President

Carter's action. In 1984 it went further and passed new resolutions welcoming Kenai Fjords and the park service.

The new breed of national parks born under ANILCA were unlike any in the nation. Whereas parks in other areas of the country were each enacted by individual pieces of legislation, with their own set of rules to address each park's individual needs, the sum of all of Alaska's parks were enacted under ANILCA by a single act. That meant that every rule implemented in one park in Alaska would set precedents for every other park in the state. Add to that subsistence hunting, trapping, and fishing—activities unheard of in other national parks—and the management of Alaska's public lands is a complicated business to say the least.

Ray and Barbara's ambassadorship for the park service, even amid threats from their community, helped educate the public about what the designation of monuments and the parks meant to the frontier way of life. Untangling the reality from the rhetoric became the mission of Ray's diplomacy. Education was key in Alaskan's acceptance of the parks over the years.

"The economy of Alaska did not collapse, as was the dire discussion at the time," said Jim Stratton, who heads Alaska's regional National Parks Conservation Association. "People realize that the parks are good economic engines and that not much has changed out there."

Not everyone was convinced however. Alaska's Congressional delegation did not attend Carter's reception in Anchorage, and twenty years after its passage Representative Don Young continued to claim that the act was "one of the darkest days in Alaska history, a travesty of justice."

Certain hot-button topics continue to ignite heated debate. The fundamental conflict, says Stratton, is that the state of Alaska interprets ANILCA differently than the federal government.

"For the state, ANILCA provides loopholes for the usual park rules," Stratton explained. "But except for the few specific 'Alaskan-ized' exceptions like subsistence and access for traditional activities, ANILCA is very clear that the parks in Alaska are still to be managed under the national park's Organic Act."

The DCP that Ray blueprinted at Katmai National Park did not disappear when he left to work in Anchorage. Ray's efforts to move Brooks Camp to the south side of the Naknek River as exclusive domain of the bears and to protect its archeological sites were eventually adopted and formalized by

The sound of wolves was a song that kept Ray and Barbara attuned to the immeasurable value of wild places. (Courtesy Roy Corral)

a park service DCP in 1996. However, no funding was ever made available to complete the project. Brooks Camp still hosts tens of thousands of bear-viewing visitors each year, with human pressure continuing to alter natural patterns of bear behavior.

In 1989, during surveys resulting from the *Exxon Valdez* oil spill, archeologists discovered ancient human remains eroding along Katmai's shoreline. In 1990, during efforts to clean up leaking fuel storage tanks that threatened to contaminate Brooks River, Naknek Lake, and Brooks Lake, the NPS discovered more archeological sites including graves. Concerned about the remains of their ancestors, a group of Native Alaskans from South Naknek formed the Council of Katmai Descendants.

The Native American Graves Protection and Repatriation Act (NAGPRA) became the protector of Brooks Camp's archeological sites by giving descendants the power to protect the remains of their ancestors. The Council of Katmai Descendants is recognized by the NPS as the official Alaska Native representatives in cultural matters related to Katmai and Brooks Camp.

Today, in 2015, Ray and Barbara believe that the need for people to be involved in the care and protection of wilderness and parklands is as pressing as ever. Most recently, Ray has written letters and testimony in support of new National Park Service rules curtailing hunting methods that are currently allowed by Alaska's Department of Fish and Game for purposes of predator control. The park service maintains that the hunting practice of crawling into dens to shoot bears and cubs, targeting wolves with pups, and setting up bear baiting stations is outside the intended purpose of the preserves. The Alaska Board of Game argues that these methods are an effective and "traditional" means of predator control, a concept that presumably allows for higher populations of moose and caribou.

The divisive issue has resurrected a vernacular reminiscent of ANICLA's early days; phrases like "federal overreach" on the one hand, and the assertion that national parks and preserves are meant to be managed as ecosystems, not game farms, on the other.

Ray reverts to the fundamental stance that national conservation lands exist for the benefit of the nation as a whole and for future generations to come—which means a constituency beyond the citizens of Alaska, and in this instance, the interests of a sub-group of hunters.

At age 79, Ray Bane's blue eyes still flash with passion about the importance of preserving wilderness. He has volumes of journals, stacks of newspaper articles, and hundreds of photos that chronicle his and Barbara's journey from idealistic young schoolteachers to voices for wilderness.

"I'm a believer," Ray has said time and again. And what he believes is the importance of keeping entire wilderness ecosystems intact—the real deal, where life cycles play out, free of encroachment by modern industrial society. He likens it to protecting the Liberty Bell. "Whether or not I ever visit the Liberty Bell, I've inherited it and it's my responsibility to help preserve it as a legacy of my Nation."

When Ray and Barbara look back over the years, they spend a lot of time reminiscing. They talk about their old friends: the Native elders, Dick Nelson, Jack Hession, Zorro Bradley, and the many people who have enriched their lives.

"Memories are money in the bank at this age," Ray says, "and it's been earning interest in our lifetimes."

Then he reflects "At the end of your life you can respond to it in one of two ways. You can say either 'I wish I had . . .' or 'I'm glad I did . . .'"

"Without a doubt," he says, "Barbara and I are so very glad we did."

—·❖·—

afterword

by Ray Bane

Barbara and I have been blessed with the opportunity to experience Alaska at a truly pivotal time in its history. We saw and participated in the end of an era where dog teams and skin-covered boats continued to be the primary means of travel. We were privileged to live in tiny Native villages largely cut off from the modern world, where ancient customs played an important role in daily life. We were unconditionally welcomed and made to feel part of the communities where we lived and worked. We danced to the heart-thumping beat of skin drums and laughed ourselves into tears at the unabashed humor of our Native friends. We sat beside elders as they slipped from this realm and left warm memories in their wake. We joined other friends to celebrate their lives at memorial potlatches.

Small cabins, tents, and snow block huts lit by the flickering light of lanterns and candles became cultural theaters where we were entertained and educated by Native storytellers sharing tales of their ancestors and of times when the white man was barely more than a rumor. Individuals such as Joe Sun and Ekak took us with them on memory journeys when people traveled by foot, dog team, and hand-made canoes through pure wild lands that both tested and rewarded skill and determination.

How does one thank the land for all that it gave us? From Native elders we were taught that everything in nature has a spiritual essence and deserves respect. Killing or wantonly destroying life for "sport" or pleasure was literally crazy to elders raised in the old ways. Koyukon seniors spoke to trees before cutting them down for firewood or house logs. Mistreatment of nature was considered a spiritual affront that could result in bad luck for the guilty party.

Barbara and I backpacked, floated, dog mushed, and flew light aircraft across some of Alaska's and the world's last great wilderness areas. We poked into narrow canyons to see what lay hidden around the next bend. We eagerly ascended one ridgeline after another and were rewarded by vistas of lands as clean and unscarred as when the first humans tentatively entered the New World.

Alaska was indeed still new when we arrived in 1960. With the isolated exceptions of early mining operations and ghost towns slowly moldering back into the ground, it was still possible to travel hundreds of miles without seeing any obvious sign of human alteration.

With the events surrounding the discovery of oil and development of Prudhoe Bay and the North Slope it became clear that the great wildness of Alaska could not, by itself, serve as an effective buffer against the incursions of modern technology and the consumptive pressures of a fast-growing population. Something had to be done to preserve the last true vestiges of the North American wilderness.

What too many of us failed to realize was that ANILCA did not win the war to preserve the nation's last intact examples of primeval wilderness lands. It was a major accomplishment, but the battle continues. Once the land base was established it had to be resolutely protected and proactively managed to achieve the ideals set forth in the legislation and in the philosophical foundations of the agencies charged with the care of this priceless natural heritage.

We cast our lot with the National Park Service. Our early experiences working with NPS employees like John Kauffmann, Stell Newman, Bill Brown and others who had come to Alaska to pave the way for new national parks, convinced us that this was indeed the agency that could best serve as the caretaker and champion these lands. We did not realize that these NPS pioneers in Alaska were themselves exceptional and among the very best the agency had to offer.

Ultimately, it is not the government agencies that hold the fate of the nation's natural legacy in their hands. Those who are the true owners and beneficiaries of this treasure must step forward and demand of their paid

Ray and Barbara at their
cabin in Bettles, 1979.
(George Wuerthner)

public servants that this priceless heritage be given the preservation it deserves for generations to come.

Living with elderly Eskimos and Indians, who had been reared in the ancient traditions of their cultures and with their spiritual insights, made me realize that we truly can live with nature without destroying its essence. We do not have to abuse the land in order to gain our sustenance or to satisfy our desire to explore wild areas. When we do injure it, we are robbing the future of a precious gift. I end with only one regret. I wish we could have done more.

—⋅✥⋅—

acknowledgments

by Kaylene Johnson-Sullivan

Books are made by teams of dedicated people whose love for words and stories draw readers into worlds that we might never have known otherwise. I'm deeply privileged to have helped to tell the story of Ray and Barbara Bane, whose courage, tenacity, and unfailing good humor are an inspiration. This book is only a small slice of their expansive and exuberant lives. Thanks are due to many in the making of this book. To the following brave and true souls, I offer my sincerest gratitude.

Janice Tower, who made a personal introduction to Ray and Barbara Banes possible. Thank you.

James Engelhardt, editor at the University of Alaska Press, for believing in the Bane's story.

Nanette Stevenson for her editorial acumen and superb technical help with photos. Thank you for your help in slowing down and going deeper.

Luke Wallin for his thoughtful and rigorous reading of the text; his depth of wisdom about wild places, writing, and life made this a better book.

Anne Coray for a poet's eye and a conservationist's heart. Your feedback was exceptional.

Jane Wilkens for her perceptive reading, insightful feedback, and her long and generous patience. Let's go hiking.

Dick Griffith who walked and skied six thousand miles across Alaska and the Arctic. Many of your paths intersected and paralleled the Banes' and your insights about the rigors of the trail were invaluable.

Roy Corral, Mitchell Silver, and Bob Waldrop for their generosity with photos.

Marge Mueller for her good work on complicated maps of the Banes' travels.

Steve Orf of FCI Digital for his color work on photos.

Erik Johnson of Northern Vista Enterprises for excellence in website design.

Christy Andrews, Cyndy Fritz, Hannah Johnson, and Melissa Alger for praying me through deadlines over the years. Sweet blessings, all of you.

And to my beloved husband, Bill Sullivan. Thank you for this most splendid journey.

— ✦✦ —

acknowledgments
by Ray Bane

This book has been many years in the making. It began at the time Barbara and I retired from our professional careers. Something always seemed to intervene and I would set the book aside to a more convenient time. Finally, friends ganged up and insisted that the stories we had shared be published. John Hirashima exclaimed, "Ray, you ought to be dead!" and urged us have our adventures recorded for others to read. Janis and Steve Tower, for whom we have the pleasure of caretaking their piece of heaven on Maui, finally refused to take any more excuses. They arranged for Kaylene Johnson to meet us and begin the process. Without Kaylene the story would still be only an idea. She made it a book.

In addition to the above persons, those who have had a profound impact on the life we lived in Alaska include:

Ekak, Iñupiaq elder who taught me so much about the ancient ways of the Iñupiaq and revealed to me the amazing insights into the natural world he and his people shared.

Dick (Richard) Nelson, a friend and colleague who was a companion, partner, and inspiration in our adventures and work in bush Alaska.

John Kauffmann, NPS planner for Gates of the Arctic who believed that there was no substitute for personal experience when it came to understanding the wilds. He embodied the idealism of the movement to establish new national parks in Alaska. I was proud to be his assistant.

Joe Immaq Sun, Kuuvangmiut elder who resided in the Kobuk River village of Shungnak. Joe was my primary teacher in efforts to understand the fullness of the subsistence lifestyle of the Kuuvangmiut. He unselfishly shared the enormous storehouse of aboriginal wisdom that is the heritage of the People of the Big River.

Zorro Bradley, NPS Anthropologist who had the foresight and energy to make subsistence an integral part of the planning and management of the new national parklands in Alaska.

Neil Morris and the entire Morris family in Bettles who stood beside us even when things got tough following the establishment of national monuments in Alaska.

Henry Beatus, a dear friend and hunting partner in the village of Hughes, Alaska. Henry was a big man in a small body.

Barbara Ekalook Bane, my wife, partner, and closest friend who never doubted me and was always by my side sharing it all. She has always been my guiding beacon.

Finally, a "well done" to all the faithful huskies who pulled us across the breadth of northern Alaska. These include our superb leaders, Twilight and Noatak, and team dogs Big Boy, Kateel, Nanook, Inuikuk, and Melozi.

— ❖ —

sources and
recommended reading

"2013 National Park Visitor Spending Effects." 2014. *Economic Contributions to Local Communities, States, and the Nation.* Natural Resource Report NPS/NRSS/EQD/NRR—2014/824.

"25 Years After Exxon Valdez Oil Spill—How has oil transportation changed in Prince William Sound?" Prince William Sound Regional Citizens Advisory Council. Accessed November 25, 2014, http://www.pwsrcac.org/observer/25-years-exxon-valdez/.

Abbey, Edward. 2006. Postcards from Ed: Dispatches and Salvos from an American Iconoclast. Minneapolis: Milkweed Editions.

"Alaska National Interest Lands Conservation Act," *National Parks Conservation Association.* Accessed November 25, 2014, http://www.npca.org/news/media-center/fact-sheets/anilca.html.

Anderson, Douglas, Wanni W., Ray Bane, Richard K. Nelson, and Nita Sheldon Towarak. 1986 . *Kuuvanmiut Subsistence: Traditional Eskimo Life in the Latter Twentieth Century.* Edited version of 1976 commissioned report. National Park Service.

"Antiquities Act Invoked: Withdrawals Yield Negative Reactions." December 1, 1978. Staff report. *Anchorage Times.* p. 1.

Atkin, Emily. "Photos: 25 Years Later, A Heartbreaking Look Back at Exxons's Alaska Oil Spill," *ClimateProgress.* March 24, 2014, accessed November 24, 2014, http://thinkprogress.org/climate/2014/03/24/3418287/exxon-valdez-25-years-later/.

Bane, G. Ray. 2001. "Shredded Wildlands, All-Terrain Vehicle Management in Alaska," Sierra Club and Alaska Conservation Foundation.

Bane, G. Ray. Fall 1990. "Through Native Eyes." *Interpretation.* Washington D.C.: Washington Division of Interpretation. pp. 3–6.

Bane, G. Ray. February 1987. "The Park Ranger: Never in Anger." *Courier.* National Park Service.

Bane, G. Ray. March 1972. "The Song of the Wolf." *Not Man Apart*. Friends of Earth. p 11.

Bane, G. Ray. March 1975. "A Cabin in the Wilderness: The Modern Myth." *Defenders of Wildlife News*. pp. 174–175.

Bane. G. Ray. 1966. "Environmental Exploitation by the Eskimos of Wainwright, Alaska." U.S. Air Force Contract no. 41(609)-3200, Arctic Aeromedical Laboratory, Seattle.

Breiter, Matthias. 2000. *The Bears of Katmai*. Kenora, Ontario: BreiterView Publishing.

Brown, William E. 2007. *History of the Central Brooks Range: Gaunt Beauty, Tenuous Life*. Fairbanks: University of Alaska Press.

Cole, Dermot. "Thirty-five years ago Carter drew wrath of many Alaskans," *Alaska Dispatch News*. November 30, 2013, accessed November 24, 2014, http://www.alaskadispatch.com/article/20131130/thirty-five-years-ago-carter-drew-wrath-many-alaskans.

Daniel, John. Summer 1993. "A Chance to Do it Right: The National Parks of Alaska." *Wilderness*. pp. 11–25.

Davidson, Art. 1990. *In the Wake of the Exxon Valdez: The Devastating Impact of the Alaska Oil Spill*. New York: Random House.

Dumond, D. E. 1981. *Archaeology on the Alaska Peninsula: The Naknek Regions, 1960–1975*. University of Oregon Anthropological Papers no. 21. Eugene: University of Oregon.

Egan, Timothy. August 24, 2000. "Alaska Changes View on Carter After 20 Years." *The New York Times*.

Egan, Timothy. May 19, 1989. "Wildlife Death Toll Climbs As Spill Clings to Alaska." *The New York Times*. p. 1.

"Exxon-Valdez Oil Spill," *ABC News*. Broadcast March 24, 1989, accessed November 25, 2014, http://abcnews.go.com/Archives/video/march-24-1989-exxon-valdez-oil-spill-9699677.

Falkenberg, Barth J. August 4, 1978. "Just Let It Be." *Christian Science Monitor*. pp. 12–14.

"Final Report, Alaska Oil Spill Commission," *Exxon Valdez Oil Spill Trustee Council*. February 1990, accessed November 25, 2014, http://www.evostc.state.ak.us/index.cfm?FA=facts.details.

Frome, Michael. 1991. *Regreening the National Parks*. Tucson: University of Arizona Press.

Gilbert, Barrie. May 27, 1999. cc to Ray Bane of Barrie's letter to NPS Alaska Regional Director Bob Barbee.

Halliday, Jan. 1998. *Native Peoples of Alaska*. Seattle: Sasquatch Books.

Hensley, William Iggiagruk. 2009. *Fifty Miles from Tomorrow: A Memoir of Alaska and the Real People*. New York: Farrar, Straus and Giroux.

Holleman, Marybeth. 2004. *The Heart of the Sound: An Alaskan Paradise Found and Nearly Lost*. University of Utah Press.

Holleman, Marybeth and Gordon Haber. 2014. *Among Wolves: Gordon Haber's Insights into Alaska's Most Misunderstood Animal*. Fairbanks: University of Alaska Press.

Hunt, Joe. Dec. 2, 1990. "Alaska Facing the Future: Ten years later ANILCA wounds are still healing." *Anchorage Times.*

Kauffmann, John M. 2005. *Alaska's Brooks Range: The Ultimate Mountains.* First edition 1992. Seattle: The Mountaineers.

Kizzia, Tom. "The Alaska Experiment." *National Parks Conservation Association* accessed November 25, 2014, http://www.npca.org/news/magazine/all-issues/2014/winter/the-alaska-experiment.html.

Kurtz, S. Rick. 1995. *Lessons to be Learned: The National Park Service Administrative History and Assessment of the Exxon Valdez Oil Spill.* National Park Service, Alaska Regional Office. p. 40.

Lentfer, Hank and Carolyn Servid. 2001. *Arctic Refuge: A Circle of Refuge.* Minneapolis: Milkweed.

McGinniss, Joe. 1980. *Going to Extremes.* New York: Alfred A. Knopf.

McPhee, John. 1976. *Coming into the Country.* New York: Farrar, Straus and Giroux.

Murie, Margaret. 1997. *Two in the Far North.* 1957. Reprint, Portland: Alaska Northwest Books.

Nash, Roderick Frazier. 2001. (4th Ed.) *Wilderness and the American Mind.* 1976. New Haven: Yale University.

Naske, Claus M. and Herman E. Slotnick. 1987. *Alaska: A History of the 49th State.* Norman: University of Oklahoma Press.

O'Neill, Dan. 1994. *The Firecracker Boys: H-Bombs, Iñupiat Eskimos, and the Roots of the Environmental Movement.* New York: St. Martin's Press.

Raffensberger, Lisa. "The Highs and Lows of the Antiquities Act," *National Public Radio.* May 23, 2008, accessed November 25, 2014, http://www.npr.org/templates/story/story.php?storyId=90631198.

Ringsmuth, Katherine. 2013. *At the Heart of Katmai: An Administrative History of the Brooks River Area.* National Park Service.

Sherwonit, Bill. "The History of Kenai Fjords National Park," *The Conservation Land Trust.* Accessed November 25, 2014, http://www.theconservationlandtrust.org/eng/conflicts_02.htm,

Stephens, Stan. "Then & Now: Changes Since the Exxon Valdez Oil Spill," *Prince William Sound Regional Citizens' Advisory Council.* Accessed November 25, 2014, http://nsgd.gso.uri.edu/aku/akuw94001/akuw94001_part2h.pdf.

Stratton, Jim. November 5, 2014. "National Park Service right to curtail predator control on preserve lands." *Alaska Dispatch News.*

"Vandals damage park service plane." October 24, 1979. Staff report. *Anchorage Daily News.* p. 3.

Vinson, Dale. 2007. "Proceedings of the 2007 George Wright Society Conference." pp. 50–55.

Wagner, Federic H. and Ronald Foresta, R. Bruce Gill, Dale R. McCullough, Michael R. Pelton,

William F. Porter, and Hal Salwasser. 1995. *Wildlife Policies in the U.S. National Parks.* Washington D.C.: Island Press.

Wilderness Act of 1964, Pub.L. 88–577. Accessed November 26, 2014, http://www.wilderness.net/nwps/legisact.

Webster, Donald and Wilfried Zibell. *Iñupiat Eskimo Dictionary.* Fairbanks: Summer Institute of Linguistics, Inc. 1970. Accessed November 26, 2014, http://library.alaska.gov/hist/hist_docs/docs/anlm/200078.pdf.

Wyant, William K. Jr. July 23, 1978. "How Much Alaska To Save? Andrus Makes Presentation Pitch." *St. Louis Post-Dispatch.*

Wyant, Willliam K. 1982. *Westward in Eden: The Public Lands and the Conservation Movement.* Berkley: University of California Press.

For more information about the book visit ourperfectwild.com

conservation organizations

Alaska Wilderness League
122 C St NW
Washington, DC 20001
202-544-5205
810 N St #203
Anchorage, AK 99501
907-222-4046
alaskawild.org
info@alaskawild.org

Alaska Conservation Foundation
911 West 8th Ave., Suite 300
Anchorage, AK 99501
907-276-1917
alaskaconservation.org
acfinfo@alaskaconservation.org

Northern Alaska Environmental Center
830 College Rd
Fairbanks, Alaska 99701-1535
907-452-5021
northern.org
info@northern.org

National Parks Conservation Association
777 6th Street, NW, Suite 700
Washington, DC 20001-3723
800-628-7275
npca.org
npca@npca.org

Alaska Center for the Environment
921 W 6th Avenue, Suite 200
Anchorage, AK 99501
907-274-3621
akcenter.org
info@akcenter.org

Trustees for Alaska
1026 W. 4th Ave., Suite 201
Anchorage, AK 99501
(907) 276-4244
trustees.org
ecolaw@trustees.org

Sierra Club
750 W. 2nd Ave, Suite 100
Anchorage, AK 99501
907-258-6807 fax
sierraclub.org
information@sierraclub.org

---·✧·---

acronyms

ANCS—Alaska Native Claims Settlement Act

ANILCA—Alaska National Interest Lands Conservation Act

ATV—All-Terrain-Vehicle

DCP—Development Concept Plan

EIS—Environmental Impact Statement

FAA—Federal Aviation Administration

GMP—General Management Plan

NANA—Northern Alaska Native Association; now an Alaska Native
regional corporation.

NPS—National Park Service

index